D0987321

Praise for *The Changing Realities of Work and Family*

"Amy Marcus-Newhall, Diane Halpern, and Sherylle Tan have compiled the first comprehensive, multidisciplinary volume on work and family. *The Changing Realities of Work and Family* brings together the best researchers in this field and some extraordinary practitioners to cover an impressive array of topics from several vantage points. The editors skillfully combine contributions that point to the common experiences adult workers face in combining employment with caring for families but also carefully remind us of important differences among workers and families that are often overlooked in this field. The book will be an asset to work-family researchers and professionals as well as an excellent primer for the classroom."

Randy Albelda, University of Massachusetts Boston

"In the context of a rapidly changing U.S. work force, this up-to-date volume provides keen insights into how families, communities, and workplaces can reap substantial benefits from greater investments in supportive work/family policies. This multidisciplinary array of studies examines the experiences of a diverse array of families, and notes the powerful effects of work-family interventions on health outcomes, family life, and workplace productivity and equality."

Joya Misra, University of Massachusetts Amherst

"A multi-disciplinary, multi-level, research-based summary of what we know about integrating work and family in today's complicated world. An important new resource for all researchers concerned with the work-family domain."

Lotte Bailyn, Massachusetts Institute of Technology

Claremont Applied Social Psychology Series

This series bridges the gap between social psychological research and applications of that research to social problems. In each volume, leading authorities provide the most recent theoretical views and empirical findings incorporating their own research and applied activities. An introductory chapter frames the content, illustrating common themes and areas of practical applications. Each volume brings together important new social psychological ideas, research results, and useful applications bearing on each social interest. These volumes will serve the needs of not only practitioners and researchers, but also students and lay people interested in this dynamic and expanding area of psychology.

The Changing Realities of Work and Family: A Multidisciplinary Approach, edited by Amy Marcus-Newhall, Diane F. Halpern, and Sherylle J. Tan

The Changing Realities of Work and Family

A Multidisciplinary Approach

Edited by

Amy Marcus-Newhall, Diane F. Halpern, and Sherylle J. Tan

WILEY-BLACKWELL

A John Wiley & Sons, Ltd., Publication

BOWLING GREEN STATE
UNIVERSITY LIBRARIES

This edition first published 2008
© 2008 Blackwell Publishing Ltd

Blackwell Publishing was acquired by John Wiley & Sons in February 2007. Blackwell's
publishing program has been merged with Wiley's global Scientific, Technical, and Medical
business to form Wiley-Blackwell.

Registered Office
John Wiley & Sons Ltd, The Atrium, Southern Gate, Chichester, West Sussex, PO19 8SQ,
United Kingdom

Editorial Offices
350 Main Street, Malden, MA 02148-5020, USA
9600 Garsington Road, Oxford, OX4 2DQ, UK
The Atrium, Southern Gate, Chichester, West Sussex, PO19 8SQ, UK

For details of our global editorial offices, for customer services, and for information about
how to apply for permission to reuse the copyright material in this book please see our
website at www.wiley.com/wiley-blackwell.

The right of Amy Marcus-Newhall, Diane F. Halpern and Sherylle J. Tan to be identified
as the authors of the editorial material in this work has been asserted in accordance with the
Copyright, Designs and Patents Act 1988.

All rights reserved. No part of this publication may be reproduced, stored in a retrieval system,
or transmitted, in any form or by any means, electronic, mechanical, photocopying, recording
or otherwise, except as permitted by the UK Copyright, Designs and Patents Act 1988, without
the prior permission of the publisher.

Wiley also publishes its books in a variety of electronic formats. Some content that appears in
print may not be available in electronic books.

Designations used by companies to distinguish their products are often claimed as trademarks.
All brand names and product names used in this book are trade names, service marks,
trademarks or registered trademarks of their respective owners. The publisher is not associated
with any product or vendor mentioned in this book. This publication is designed to provide
accurate and authoritative information in regard to the subject matter covered. It is sold
on the understanding that the publisher is not engaged in rendering professional services.
If professional advice or other expert assistance is required, the services of a competent
professional should be sought.

Library of Congress Cataloging-in-Publication Data

The changing realities of work and family / edited by Amy Marcus-Newhall, Diane F. Halpern,
and Sherylle J. Tan.
 p. cm. – (Claremont applied social psychology series)
 Includes bibliographical references and index.
 ISBN 978-1-4051-6345-3 (hardcover : alk. paper) – ISBN 978-1-4051-6346-0 (pbk. : alk.
paper) 1. Work and family. I. Marcus-Newhall, Amy. II. Halpern, Diane F. III. Tan,
Sherylle J.

 HD4904.25.C449 2008
 306.3′6–dc22

                                                                                    2008003582

A catalogue record for this book is available from the British Library.

Set in 10.5/13pt Minion by Graphicraft Ltd, Hong Kong
Printed in Singapore by Markono Print Media Pte Ltd

1 2008

Contents

Tables

Figures

Introduction

Amy Marcus-Newhall

The heterosexual two-parent family with 2.2 children and a stay-at-home mom who cares for the children is no longer the typical American family. The demographics of American families have changed. For example, the number of people per household is getting smaller with only 10 percent comprised of 5 or more people in 2005, down from 21 percent only one generation ago in 1970. In 2005, 73.5 million children (67 percent) under 18 lived with two heterosexual married parents, but they were often step-parents given the high proportion of marriages that end in divorce. An additional 17.2 million children lived with a single-parent mother and 3.5 million lived with a single-parent father. Grandparents lived in 8 percent of all households with children (U.S. Bureau of the Census, 2005). In 2003, approximately 20 percent of male gay parents and 33 percent of female lesbian parents had children under the age of 18 (U.S. Bureau of the Census, 2003). These are just a few of the changes in family structures that defy our stereotypes of the "typical" American family.

The workforce also has changed over the past several decades, with more mothers employed outside the home than ever before. The most common family type in the United States is a dual-earner mother and father, with both parents working to provide the necessary income for their family (White & Rogers, 2000). The romanticized sitcom families from the 1950s are in no way a reality of today's typical American family. Today, 71 percent of all mothers are in the labor force (U.S. Bureau of Labor Statistics, 2006).

Although both the nature of families and the composition of the workforce have changed, there have been relatively few adjustments to the way we manage work and family life so that they are aligned in ways that promote strong families and a strong economy. There is no agreed upon "reality" regarding what it means to achieve work-family "balance," rather there are multiple realities, and there are many who object to the idea of "balance" because it necessarily implies that any gain in one sphere of life causes a loss in the other (Halpern & Murphy, 2005). Whether the metaphor is one of work–family conflict, balance, collaboration, or integration, the dynamics at the intersection of work and family evolve such that new issues, concerns, and benefits constantly arise. To better understand the relationship between work and families, it is necessary to cross the boundaries of traditional academic disciplines. As such, this edited volume *The changing realities of work and family* adopts a multidisciplinary approach, bringing together scholars from academic perspectives such as psychology, women's studies, and economics as well as leaders from the legal, business, and political communities.

This volume is arranged in 4 parts, each addressing important and current questions on the topic of the work-family intersection. Part I addresses how families and employers accommodate and adapt to the dual demands of employment and children. Part II discusses cultural factors that have been (mostly) missing from the work-family literature. Part III links work, stress, and health and speaks to the ways working and caring for families affect health. Part IV examines work and family issues in the fields of politics, business, and the legal system. The last chapter highlights the major themes and findings from this volume, offering a critique of the current research and suggesting implications of these findings for research and policy.

References

Halpern, D. F., & Murphy, S. E. (Eds.). (2005). *From work-family balance to work-family interaction: Changing the metaphor.* Mahwah, NJ: Lawrence Erlbaum Associates, Inc. Publishers.

U.S. Bureau of the Census (2003, February). *Married-couple and unmarried-partner households: 2000.* Retrieved September 29, 2006, from http://www.census.gov/prod/2003pubs/censr-5.pdf

U.S. Bureau of the Census (2005). *Americans marrying older, living alone more, see households shrinking, Census Bureau reports.* Retrieved June 30, 2007, from http://www.census.gov/Press-Release/www/releases/archives/families_households/006840.html

U.S. Bureau of Labor Statistics (2006, September). *Women in the labor force: A databook, Report 996.* Retrieved May 4, 2007, from http://www.bls.gov/cps/wlf-databook-2006.pdf

White, L., & Rogers, S. J. (2000). Economic circumstances and family outcomes: A review of the 1990s. *Journal of Marriage and the Family, 62,* 1035–1051.

Part I

Employment and Children: How Do Families and Employers Accommodate the Demands?

Part I

Introduction

Sherylle J. Tan

With the majority of parents in the workforce (U.S. Bureau of Labor Statistics, 2006), working families and employers are being forced to adapt to and accommodate the needs and demands of a workforce that has changed radically over the past several decades. What is the effect of working mothers and fathers on children and how are parents integrating their work and family lives? Despite the fact that working mothers are now the norm, there is still a great deal of negative sentiment against mothers who work, especially those who choose to work at demanding jobs and have the financial security to stay at home but choose not to. Studies have shown that the general public still believes in the negative impact that working mothers create for their children and general family environment (Bridges, Etaugh, & Barnes-Farrell, 2002; Shpancer, Melick, Sayre, & Spivey, 2006). Often times, working parents (mostly working mothers) attempt to hide or minimize their family commitments and obligations to employers and/or co-workers in order to avoid biases that may prevent them from career success (Drago et al., 2006).

Family Accommodations

When parents work, families must determine how their children will be cared for during working hours. Child care has become an increasingly critical issue as a result of the rise in maternal employment and the dual-earner family. Recent research by the National Institute of Child Health and Human Development Study of Early Child Care and Youth Development (Belsky et al., 2007) has stirred up the controversy of child care. Researchers found that children who were in day care for long periods of time (i.e., long days or more than 40 hours per week) exhibited slightly more problem behaviors up through sixth grade. However, these same children also exhibited higher vocabulary scores when they were in high quality day care centers and when parents were effective. When both day care and parenting were higher quality, the children showed positive developmental outcomes, such as social skills, social-emotional functioning, and reading, math, and vocabulary achievement. Despite these positive findings and despite the fact that this study does not indicate causality, the media hyped these findings as a way to further criticize the working mother and fuel the myths that the best option for families is for mothers to stay out of the workforce to care for their children. A more balanced review would conclude that the positive benefits resulted from quality day care, and the slight increase in behavioral problems was found when both day care and parenting were inadequate. It should not be surprising that this "double whammy" of poor care results in poorer child outcomes.

Employer Accommodations

As a result of the changing demographics of the workforce, many employers and organizations have created work–family policies to help support their employees' family responsibilities. Even when family-friendly workplace policies are available, the decision whether to use these policies is often based on employee perceptions of the culture of the workplace. Many employees are afraid to use such policies because their use may be perceived as a lack of commitment to the workplace, even when their actual performance is on par with other employees. Employees may be rightfully concerned that the use of family-friendly policies, such as parental leave and flexible work schedules may negatively impact their career advancement (Eaton, 2003; Rogier & Padgett, 2004). On the other hand, if policies are usable and employees believe that their managers support their use, then using these policies is associated with increased productivity and organizational commitment (Eaton, 2003). Gender plays a factor in decisions about whether or not to use available policies because of the continued gender inequality in the labor market, that is, women continue to earn less than men and are less likely to move into high-level managerial positions (Catalyst, 2002). While women continue to be the primary caregivers in families, family responsibility continues to shape their work lives and their usage of such policies. Furthermore, mothers, more so than fathers, are often judged as less committed to employment despite their actual commitment and competency (Fuegen, Biernat, Haines, & Deaux, 2004).

How We Do It

In Part 1, researchers review and examine the myths of maternal employment, the positive family adaptations that support working mothers, and the biases associated with parenting. First, Tan reviews the history of working mothers and attempts to clarify the myths of maternal employment using research. Unfortunately, there are several myths that people hold on to despite the research. Despite the large body of research on maternal employment, many people still base their ideas about what is best for children on their personal experience and anecdotes from others. This chapter attempts to pull together current research to answer questions and address the concerns people have regarding working mothers and children. Every family is different and has different choices available and different needs, working or not working, mothers are doing their best to accommodate the demands of their family and their children.

Gottfried and Gottfried examine the adaptations and competencies of maternal employment. Their focus, in contrast to Drago and colleagues, is on the accommodations working parents make in their family life. These researchers first describe three phases of research concerning working mothers: 1) detecting negative effects of maternal employment on child development; 2) examining factors that mediate maternal employment and child development; and 3) examining the positive impacts of maternal employment and the adaptation families. Their chapter examines Phase 3, the "upside" of maternal employment and the positive outcomes associated with it. They discuss the adaptations (e.g., flexible work arrangements) that families make to successfully integrate the family and the working parent.

Drago and colleagues look at the accommodations working parents make in their work life. Working parents can be discriminated against in the workplace due to their parental status, especially mothers who often times have the primary care duties and obligations. To prevent discrimination of this sort, some working parents exhibit bias avoidance behaviors so that they can continue to succeed in their career and not be wrongly judged based on their status as a parent. Bias avoidance behaviors are strategies in which employees attempt to hide or minimize their family commitments to keep from being penalized. Drago and colleagues point out that bias avoidance is disproportionately reported among women (namely, mothers). They discuss the linkages between work–family policies at institutions and bias avoidance behaviors among faculty employed at those institutions. The authors conclude that even with the implementation of work–family policies, it is not enough to reduce incidence of bias avoidance behaviors, rather it is in combination with supportive environments and supervisors that bias avoidance can be reduced.

References

Belsky, J., Vandell, D. L., Burchinal, M., Clarke-Stewart, K. A., McCartney, K., & Owen, M. T. (2007). Are there long-term effects of early child care? *Child Development, 78*(2), 681–701.

Bridges, J. S., Etaugh, C., & Barnes-Farrell, J. (2002). Trait judgments of stay-at-home and employed parents: A function of social role and/or shifting standards. *Psychology of Women Quarterly, 26*, 140–150.

Catalyst (2002) *2002 Catalyst Census of Women Corporate Officers and Top Earners in the Fortune 500.* Retrieved March 4, 2007, from http://www.catalystwomen.org/files/fact/COTE%20Factsheet%202002updated.pdf

Drago, R., Colbeck, C. L., Stauffer, K. D., Pirretti, A., Burkum, K., Fazioli, J., et al. (2006). The avoidance bias against caregiving: The case of academic faculty. *American Behavioral Scientist, 49*(9), 1222–1247.

Eaton, S. C. (2003). If you can use them: Flexibility policies, organizational commitment, and perceived performance. *Industrial Relations, 42*(2), 145–167.

Fuegen, K., Biernat, M., Haines, E., & Deaux, K. (2004). Mothers and fathers in the workplace: How gender and parental status influence judgments of job-related competence. *Journal of Social Issues, 60*(4), 737–754.

Rogier, S. A., & Padgett, M. Y. (2004). The impact of utilizing a flexible work schedule on perceived career advancement potential of women. *Human Resource Development Quarterly, 15*, 89–106.

Shpancer, N., Melick, K., Sayre, P., & Spivey, A. (2006). Quality of care attributions to employed versus stay-at-home mothers. *Early Child Development and Care, 176*(2), 183–193.

U.S. Bureau of Labor Statistics (2006, September). Women in the labor force: A databook, Report 996. Retrieved May 4, 2007, from http://www.bls.gov/cps/wlf-databook-2006.pdf

1

The Myths and Realities of Maternal Employment

Sherylle J. Tan

The most dramatic change in families in the past 30 years is the increased rate of maternal employment outside the home. Working mothers have become a reality of modern society and thus there has been increased interest especially among working families about the impact of maternal employment and child care. As with many emotional controversies, stereotypes and myths have been associated with the idea of the "working mother." Common myths include "mothers work to afford extra luxuries," "working mothers are selfish," and "day care is bad for children." These myths need to be examined based on the available research and realities of contemporary society.

Today, the typical American family with young children has a working mother and children in child care (Boushey & Wright, 2004). In 2004, about 70 percent of children under the age of 18 had mothers in the workforce (U.S. Bureau of Labor Statistics, 2005). Two decades earlier, this statistic was only slightly lower at 68 percent (Hayghe, 1984). It was in the 1960s and 1970s when the number of mothers employed outside the home was rising rapidly that "work and family" first emerged as a distinct domain of research (Perry-Jenkins, Repetti, & Crouter, 2000). Since then, an increasing amount of research has been conducted, much of it concerning the effect on children of having an employed mother.

Mothers work for many reasons, but the reality is that the majority do work and with mothers working outside of the home, child care is a necessity. Many families, especially low-income families, do not have a choice because mothers are working for necessities, such as food and shelter. The large body of research on maternal employment points to some unambiguous findings: Maternal employment is not bad for our children. In fact, there are many positive consequences of maternal employment for children, other family members, and mothers. For example, research shows that having a working mother leads to increased academic achievement (Makri-Botsari & Makri, 2003), enhanced cognitive outcomes (Vandell & Ramanan, 1992), and fewer behavior problems (Youngblut et al., 2001) in children. Furthermore, early maternal employment benefits single mothers and lower income families by increasing family income (Harvey, 1999; Vandell & Ramanan, 1992) and improving the mother's mental health (Makri-Botsari & Makri, 2003).

Yet despite these research findings, many of the myths and stereotypes still exist. One thing is clear, women, and especially mothers, are in the workforce and are an integral part of the American economy. Today's families continue to struggle with questions and guilt due to maternal employment. This chapter seeks to clarify the research and to disentangle the myths and realities.

Women Have Always Worked!

The idea of working mothers is nothing new. Throughout history, mothers have always worked in some capacity and women have always worked. Women, as well as men have always been family breadwinners (Coontz, 1997). Ideas and opinions of what kind of work women should do, acceptance of women's work outside the home, the meaning of work to women, and the percentages of mothers who have worked fluctuated throughout American history (Melton, 1999). Mothers working and raising children was at one time a historical norm (Coontz, 1997).

> Women have always worked – in their home and the home of others, in fields, factories, shops, stores, and offices. The kind of work done has varied for women of different classes, races, ethnic groups, and geographical locations. And the nature of women's work has changed over time with urbanization and industrialization. What remains the same is that the ways in which women have worked involve a constant tension between two areas of women's lives: the home and the marketplace. (Kessler-Harris, 1981, p. 10)

Prior to the industrial revolution, work relied heavily on household production and most work was private. Women, including mothers, worked alongside their husbands on the farm and in family businesses, and all family members were involved in labor for the common good (Coontz, 1997). During this agrarian pre-industrial era, women's work was necessary for the family to survive, and work was recognized as a family industry which focused on a cooperative lifestyle (Hayden, 1982). All family members were integral to production of goods; everyone was involved in labor and work. Responsibilities were not gender segregated in to specialized jobs (Coontz, 1997). Historians found that "not only did women work, but they were *recognized* as workers, and the values of that labor – both to their households and their communities – was openly and repeatedly acknowledged" (Boydston, 1990, p. 5). There were numerous economic values to wives and certainly women's labor was gender-prescribed. However, the gender division of work did not mean that women were less productive (Boydston, 1990). All family members needed to be productive for family survival.

During this time, childrearing after infancy was not viewed as uniquely a woman's task, rather both mothers and fathers shared responsibility in training, educating, and disciplining children. Both mothers and fathers were equally involved in the childrearing process as both were involved in household production of goods. It was not until after 1830 with the birth of the Industrial Revolution that motherhood rose to new heights of importance and where children became the primary focus of womanly activity. It was this romanticism of motherhood that led to the de-emphasis on women's identity as producers within economy and thus the ideology of domesticity grew (Baxandall & Gordon, 1995). Known by historians as "the ideology of republican motherhood," childrearing became considered the primary emphasis of women's identities almost to the point of exclusion of other domestic work (Boydston, 1990). Thus, women's domestic work became less recognized and less valued and the idea that a woman's place was in the home was born.

The Industrial Revolution also brought about changes within society and changes to how work was perceived (Kessler-Harris, 1981). The shift from the production of goods in the home to the reliance on consumer goods led to the need for families to earn money outside of the home (Coontz, 1997). These changes influenced the development of the republican motherhood; most notably for families there was an evolution of work in which fathers were needed to work outside of the home, due to patriarchical dominance. Thus, the cooperative lifestyle that had been the norm in pre-industrial society began to disintegrate and with it the devaluation of women's domestic work emerged. The norm had changed to a new division of labor, fathers worked outside the home in factories and offices, while a mother's place was in the home to raise the children. The work that women did at home had been transformed from production of goods to household maintenance. The changes in societal norms of work developed into two distinct categories of work: 1) one parent needed to maintain the household: and 2) the other parent needed to work outside the home for pay. Women were no longer considered workers because their duty was to maintain the household and this was separate from work done for pay (Kessler-Harris, 1981).

The mother's duty to the home was important and became the social norm. In the 1950s, women were faced with multiple opportunities which included continuing their education, being married, and having children (Wattenberg, 2000a). For the first time women were afforded these choices and often were torn by the need to choose. Women who entered the workforce often were unmarried in keeping with societal norms, and they were expected to leave the workforce upon marriage. In the 1960s and 1970s, women became a larger part of the labor workforce. The increasing number of employed women coincided with the falling wages in the early 1970s, which created a need for women, most especially married women and mothers, to work (Coontz, 1997). Employed women now included not only poor and working class women who always have worked, but also middle-class, educated women. Mothers entered the labor force to "help the family" build a nest egg, often to send their children to college, and to help with the rising costs of household expenses. This new rationale that mothers entered the workforce only for the good of the family was consistent with cultural norms (Wattenberg, 2000b). A mother's income was no longer a bonus or supplement, but rather became a necessity for the family. It was during this time that the domain of work and family emerged as an area of research with an initial focus on working mothers and dual-career families (Perry-Jenkins et al., 2000). More recently, the majority of couples are dual-earners who are moving toward equally shared breadwinning (Nock, 2001). This movement, although initially controversial in current time, is actually a return to a cooperative lifestyle that was the norm in the past in which both husband and wife worked to support their family (Coontz, 1997).

Myths of Maternal Employment

As more women entered the workforce, many of them mothers, questions about the impact of maternal employment were posed. The controversy over maternal employment was fueled by the idea that mothers in the workforce somehow disturbed the development of children and their attachment to their mother. The examination of issues regarding work and family, especially at the consequences of having a working mother involves many disciplines and theoretical perspectives. As researchers attempt to uncover the impact of maternal employment, political and social forces have chosen sides in the "mommy wars," a term coined in the 1980s by *Child* magazine and popularized by the media, referring to the so-called "war" or tension that exists between stay-at-home and working mothers. A polarization of the two camps has created maternal guilt for many working mothers and repeated messages that a mother's place is best spent in the home. Despite the tension and continued debate between working and stay-at-home mothers, there is empirical support to show that one choice is not better than the other and that the myths are just that, myths.

> Myth 1: Mothers are only in the labor force to earn some extra spending money: Married women who have husbands to support them should stay home and leave the good paying jobs for men.

The reality is that many American families are unable to support themselves on a single income. Many families have no choice about maternal employment because they need mothers to work in order to maintain a basic standard of living. In fact, the proportion of married-couple families with the wife in the paid labor force rose from approximately 40 percent in 1972 to 61 percent in 2004 (U.S. Census Bureau, 2005). In that same year, the median income for married-couple families with both husband and wife in the labor force was $63,813 compared to $44,923 for those without the wife in the paid labor force. The additional income is often essential. According to Amelia Warren Tyagi (2004), often times a mother's choice to work "comes down to dollars and cents, and the calculation is brutal. In one column sits that big-eyed slobbery youngster, and a mother's heart beating to be there so she can give him everything."

Warren and Tyagi (2003) discuss the "two-income trap" and the myth that families are spending too much money on frivolous luxuries, which require a two-income family. They find that it is not over-consumption that requires families to have a two-income household rather it is the necessities of life that cost disproportionately more than they did only a few decades ago. The rising costs of health insurance and home ownership have made these a "luxury" for many families. For a majority of families, the number one predictor of bankruptcy is having children. Having children is costly; families want to have a "good" home for their children and for it to be a "good" home, the home must be in a "good" neighborhood. A good neighborhood is often defined by the school district that their children will attend and the costs of homes are often dictated by these same factors. The rising cost of homes has been an issue for families of all compositions. Since the mid-1970s, the amount earmarked for the mortgage has increased 69 percent (adjusted for inflation; Tyagi, 2004). Home prices have risen more than three times as fast for couples with young children (Warren & Tyagi, 2003). Yet, at the same time, the average father's income has increased by less than 1 percent, which makes it near impossible for the average family to make it on one income (Tyagi, 2004).

Nearly half of working mothers work to support their family and/or themselves, in other words they are the single head of the household. More specifically, in 2004, 27 percent of women in the labor force were single, 13 percent divorced, 3 percent widowed, and 4 percent separated (U.S. Bureau of Labor Statistics, 2005). Nearly 41 percent of all family households with children under 18 years maintained by women with no spouse present lived in poverty (U.S. Census Bureau, 2005). Many women are clearly not working to simply afford luxuries and to have extra spending money; they are working to pay the rent, to put food on the table, to keep their families healthy, and to maintain a basic standard of living for their families. They are working to keep their families out of poverty and to prevent many of the negative consequences associated with poverty.

In addition to the financial reasons for mothers' work, the workforce needs women. In reality, the economy would collapse without working women. With women composing about half of the workforce (Bond et al., 2003), women have become an integral part of the American economy, with many American businesses and industries dependent upon the work of women. Even if all the employed married women gave their jobs to unemployed men, there would still be 1.2 million unfilled jobs; women are an important part of the workforce and are needed (U.S. Department of Labor, 1993).

Myth 2: Only selfish mothers work.

Women work primarily to help support their family financially, and secondarily, for their own personal self-actualization (Scarr, Phillips, & McCartney, 1989). Finances aside, there are benefits of maternal employment, not only for the mother, but also for the entire family, such as enhanced maternal self-esteem, psychological well-being, and quality of attention to children's needs (Scarr et al.). However, it is important to note that the impact of maternal employment may differ for families based on socioeconomic status so blanket generalizations need to be made cautiously.

Work is fulfilling and enjoyable for many women and there is research that shows that middle class employed mothers exhibit lower levels of depression than their stay-at-home counterparts. Considerable research has documented that employed mothers have significantly better mental health than nonemployed mothers (Aneshenselm 1986; Kessler & McRae, 1982) and employment can have a positive effect on mothers' emotional well-being (Repetti, Mathews, & Waldron, 1989). Thus, employment can serve as a buffer for maternal depression and stress, which is often prevalent in lower socioeconomic families (Hetherington, 1979; Stewart & Salt, 1981). There is an important caveat to this buffer, the relationship between employment and positive maternal well-being occurs when mothers desire employment (Gove & Zeiss, 1987), have quality employment (Baruch & Barnett, 1987), and stable childcare arrangements (Goldberg & Easterbrooks, 1988). Thus, it is not maternal employment per se that positively impacts children's outcomes and the mother's well being, rather it is the working conditions, complexity of the job, and other elements of employment that impact the mother and the family (Parcel & Menaghan, 1997). It is important to point out that if the mother is not satisfied with her job or childcare arrangements, employment can be a stressor. It can also be especially stressful when there is no father or other adult support (Hoffman, 1989).

In addition to the psychological benefits for the mother and financial benefits to the family, there are benefits for the children. Maternal mood and depression affect children and research clearly shows that maternal depression has negative consequences for the developmental outcomes of children (Downey & Coyne, 1990; Yarrow, 1979). The improvement in a mother's sense of psychological well-being indirectly impacts the mother's ability to parent in warm, supportive, and emotionally positive ways (McLoyd, 1990). Raver (2003) found that for low income families, maternal employment is predictive of decreases in symptoms of depression over time and decreases in mothers' use of angry and coercive parenting styles. These findings with low income families are qualified by the characteristics and quality of mothers' jobs. Thus, employed mothers exhibit higher-levels of interaction and verbal stimulation with children when they are satisfied with their employment status (Hoffman, 1986). Mothers who have jobs that require complex interactions with people are more likely to exhibit positive parenting styles that are warm and responsive (Greenberger & Goldberg, 1989; Greenberger, O'Neil, & Nagel, 1994). Employed mothers who have positive job experiences and work environments are observed to exhibit positive interactions with their young children (Costigan, Cox, &

Cauce, 2003). Positive employment experiences lead to positive parenting. Mothers who are satisfied with their jobs are likely to be less depressed and have positive emotional well-being which leads to positive interactions and parenting with their children.

It is clear that there is empirical research that demonstrates that the idea that mothers who chose to work often do so for reasons other than selfishness. A mother's choice to work is not only beneficial to the mother's well-being, but also can have positive influences and effects on the family, especially children.

Myth 3: Working mothers neglect their children leading these children into juvenile delinquency and other antisocial behaviors.

Concerns of maternal employment have led to pervasive beliefs of delinquency due to maternal neglect and low supervision because working mothers are too busy to care for their children (Vander Ven, Cullen, Carrozza, & Wright, 2001). It is believed that there is an increase in juvenile delinquency and that this increase has occurred in conjunction with mothers entering the workforce. Some believe that maternal employment is the cause for children to become criminals and engage in criminal behaviors (Greenberg, Goldberg, Crawford, & Granger, 1988).

The media has publicized juvenile crime leading the public to believe that it has become more frequent and this correlates with the increase in working mothers. However, 2001 rates for juvenile arrest for property crime offenses were at their lowest since the 1960s and overall there has been a decrease in juvenile arrests (Snyder, 2003). Further, numerous studies have been unable to document negative effects of having a working mother (Parcel & Menaghan, 1994). Contemporary research has found very little connection with delinquency, especially among children of regularly employed mothers (Farnworth, 1984). Aughinbaugh and Gittleman (2003) examined the impact of early maternal employment on risky behaviors in adolescents using data from a national sample of mothers and adolescents. Risky behaviors, such as smoking cigarettes, drinking alcohol, using marijuana and other drugs, engaging in sex, and criminal activities, were not found to be related with mother's employment in their early childhood. There was no positive association with the greater hours a mother worked in early childhood and engagement in risky behaviors among adolescents. Furthermore, these findings did not demonstrate that adolescent involvement in risky behaviors was related to maternal employment during adolescence. Rather, maternal employment may serve positively by affording adolescents with some necessary independence and an employed role model.

However, there are work factors that may influence mothers' parenting, and how they interact with their children. Although there is no empirical evidence to suggest that maternal employment during adolescence increases risky behaviors (Aughinbaugh & Gittleman, 2003; Vander Ven & Cullen, 2004), there is some research that has found negative correlational relationships when mothers work in coercive and alienating environments (e.g., Vander Ven & Cullen, 2004). It is not so much the mother's employment that causes their children to commit crimes rather it is the type of employment that mothers engage in (i.e., menial, coercive, unsatisfying, and low-paying maternal employment) which may correlate with some aspect of the way mothers who work at menial jobs act as parents. When mothers are employed in jobs that are menial and unsatisfying, employment is often unstable. Erratic and coercive employment and unpleasant experiences at work may result in erratic and coercive parenting behaviors (Colvin, 2000). Erratic work experiences disrupt family interactions leading to unstable and inconsistent parenting behaviors and supervision (Colvin & Pauly, 1983). Thus, it is not work per se that causes poor parenting, but a combination of factors that accompany low wage menial work that has negative effects on children.

Furthermore, there are cases in which maternal employment actually serves as a buffer to risky behaviors and delinquency by raising the living conditions of children above poverty (Vander Ven et al., 2001). Research has substantiated the negative consequences of poverty including its link to delinquency. As maternal employment helps to move families out of poverty by increasing family incomes, maternal employment promotes positive advantages for children. Maternal employment does NOT cause the delinquency of children, any more than it causes other types of behavioral problems in children (Vander Ven et al., 2001). These findings hold true whether maternal employment is in children's preschool years or in adolescence. This myth of maternal employment is a socially-constructed problem that fails to consider the broader context in which some mothers work, rather than a problem that is supported by empirical data and research.

Myth 4: Child care is bad for children.

One of the most important questions, the one that instigated the so-called "mommy wars," is the issue of child care. As women entered the workforce, children were placed in care outside of the home. Many people questioned the effect of child care on children's cognitive, social, and emotional development, especially during the early years. The early years of the child's life are especially important. This is the time when foundations for cognitive, social, and emotional development are established in the brain (Shonkoff & Phillips, 2000).

Researchers and parents alike questioned the impact of child care on early development. Is child care bad for our children? These questions along with the rising number of young children with mothers in the workforce have sparked the interest of policymakers and the public in determining the implications of child care to children's early development and readiness for school.

Some feared the detrimental effects of separating mothers from their children (Friedman, Randolph, & Kochanoff, 2001). The concern was that the substantial reduction of time with the mother at an early age could affect the child's attachment and relationship with the mother by disrupting the bonding process with the mother. In fact, early applied research on child care found that participation in child care was not detrimental to children's development or attachment to the mother and has not documented the negative consequences of child care (Silverstein, 1991). Later findings with a large national study of children have maintained that child care is unrelated to the attachment of children to their mothers (NICHD, 1997). However, there have been inconsistent findings regarding the relation of child care to children's development and behavior problems. Some studies report negative cognitive and social outcomes when children are in child care for long periods during their first year of life (e.g., Belsky, 1988; Belsky & Eggbeen, 1991; Brooks-Gunn, Han, & Waldfogel, 2002). However, the majority of psychologists continue to maintain that those findings are inconclusive, that they pertain to a small number of children (i.e., most are doing fine) and that further research is warranted.

The fact remains that there are many children in child care today. Child care has become the norm in modern American society and the norm for working families. With the previous research findings in mind and the realities of working families and society, concerns and research shifted from questions about whether mothers should work and is child care bad to a more important question, "Does quality of child care matter?"

Not all types of child care are created equal. The quality of child care is particularly salient in the development of children, and especially for children from low income families or families with poor quality home environments (e.g., NICHD Early Child Care Research Network, 2002; Peisner-Feinberg & Burchinal, 1997; Votruba-Drzal, Coley, & Chase-

Lansdale, 2004). Poverty in early childhood has long-lasting negative consequences for cognitive development and academic outcomes (Brooks-Gunn, 2003). Income is associated with preschool children's cognitive development, achievement, and behavior. Furthermore, the effects of low income on achievement do not diminish during the elementary school year but rather increase and predict rates of school completion. On average, children from disadvantaged families performed poorly on achievement tests even if their family's situation improved later on in childhood or adolescence (Furstenberg, Brooks-Gunn, & Morgan, 1987). However, quality child care coupled with early childhood education can make a positive difference in the later success of children from low income families. High quality child care can help diminish socioeconomic disparities in the preschool years, providing children from poor families a more equal footing with their more affluent peers upon entering school.

The quality of the child care center has been found to be positively related with preschool children's developmental outcomes. Quality of child care not only affects the developmental outcome of children from low income and at-risk backgrounds, but has positive effects for children of all backgrounds (Peisner-Feinberg & Burchinal, 1997). High quality child care has been found to be related to fewer reports of problem behaviors, higher cognitive performance, enhanced language ability, and better school readiness (Peisner-Feinberg & Burchinal, 1997). Furthermore, long hours in child care were not detrimental to the development of low income children, except when the quality of child care was low (Votruba-Drzal et al. 2004). Actually, more extensive, high-quality child care fostered children's social-emotional development.

High quality child care coupled with early childhood education programs can provide young children with the skills and enrichment that can increase their chances of success in school. Research has shown that participation in preschool is associated with higher rates of school completion and lower rates of juvenile arrest (Reynolds, Temple, Robertson, & Mann, 2001). Children who participate in these settings perform better on tests of cognitive and social skills and disadvantaged children receive greater benefits than other children (Peisner-Feinberg & Burchinal, 1997).

Conclusions

The accumulation of research on maternal employment has not supported the hypothesis that maternal employment is bad. Findings are consistently

positive – except when care is poor, just as poor home care would be expected
to have negative effects on child outcomes. The increase in the number
of mothers in the workforce is not new, instead it is a return to work
and family arrangements from the past (Coontz, 1997). The reality is that
there are positive effects of maternal employment and regardless of the
reason that mothers work; working mothers are here to stay (Scarr et al.,
1989).

The benefits of maternal employment are often tied with other aspects
of the environment, such as working mothers' wages, job quality, job satisfaction, and maternal depression. Children are not solely influenced by
maternal employment but by many other factors that interact with their
environment (Bronfrenbrenner, 1979). Society as a whole needs to shift from
focusing on the negative impacts of maternal employment and attacking
working mothers to looking at contextual factors, such as the implications
of family income, poverty, job stress, and job quality, that impact families
and children's developmental outcomes (Gottfried, 2005; Hoffman &
Youngblade, 1998). In fact, a positive consequence of maternal employment
is the increase in family income for single mothers and lower income families (Harvey, 1999; Vandell & Ramanan, 1992). In this sense, children benefit
directly from steady maternal employment through the gains in family income
(Fuller et al., 2002).

Public policies need to coincide with the needs and realities of contemporary families and should be backed by strong empirical evidence. The
lack of work–family and child-care policies in the US is most likely related
to the negative perception of working mothers. Many myths have fueled
these negative ideas. As this chapter has attempted to clear up myths with
empirical research, the public continues to maintain a mismatch between
reality and myth/perception. On the one hand it is believed that it is okay
for poor, single mothers to work because they have no choice whereas on
the other hand, married mothers should remain in the home. Employers,
public policy makers, and society need to examine the true needs of families and children to put an end to the so-called "mommy wars" and keep
the myths of maternal employment in check.

References

Aneshenselm, C. S. (1986). Marital and employment role-strain, social support,
    and depression among adult women. In S. E. Hobfoll (Ed.), *Stress, social
    support, and women* (pp. 99–114). New York: Hemisphere.

Aughinbaugh, A., & Gittleman, M. (2003). Maternal employment and adolescent risky behavior. *Bureau of Labor Statistics Working Papers, Working Paper 366*. Retrieved November 5, 2004, from http://www.bls.gov/ore/abstract/ec/ ec030030.htm

Baruch, G. K., & Barnett, R. C. (1987). Role quality, multiple role involvement, and psychological well-being in midlife women. *Journal of Personality and Social Psychology, 51*, 578–585.

Baxandall, R., & Gordon, L. (Eds.) (1995). *America's working women: A documentary history 1600 to the present*. New York: W. W. Norton & Company, Inc.

Belsky, J. (1988). The "effects" of infant day care reconsidered. *Early Childhood Research Quarterly, 3*, 235–272.

Belsky, J., & Eggbeen, D. (1991). Early and extensive maternal employment and young children's socioemotional development: Children of the National Longitudinal Survey of Youth. *Journal of Marriage and Family, 53*, 1083–1110.

Boushey, H., & Wright, J. (2004). *Working moms and child care*. Washington, DC: Center for Economic and Policy Research.

Boydston, J. (1990). *Home and work: Housework, wages, and the ideology of labor in the Early Republic*. New York: Oxford University Press.

Bronfrenbrenner, U. (1979). *The ecology of human development*. Cambridge, MA: Harvard University Press.

Brooks-Gunn, J. (2003). Do you believe in Magic?: What we can expect from early childhood intervention programs. *Social Policy Report, 17*(1), 1–14.

Brooks-Gunn, J., Han, W. J., & Waldfogel, J. (2002). Maternal employment and child cognitive outcomes in the first three years of life: The NICHD Study of Early Child Care. *Child Development, 73*(4), 1052–1072.

Colvin, M. (2000). *Crime and coercion: An integrated theory of chronic criminality*. New York: St. Martin's Press.

Colvin, M., & Pauly, J. (1983). A critique of criminology: Toward an integrated structural Marxist theory of delinquency production. *American Journal of Sociology, 89*, 513–551.

Coontz, S. (1997). *The way we really are: Coming to terms with America's changing families*. New York: Basic Books.

Costigan, C. L., Cox, M. J., & Cauce, A. M. (2003). Work-parenting linkages among dual-earner couples at the transition to parenthood. *Journal of Family Psychology, 17*, 397–408.

Downey, G., & Coyne, J. C. (1990). Children of depressed parents: An Integrative review. *Psychological Bulletin, 108*(1), 50–76.

Farnworth, M. (1984). Family structure, family attributes, and delinquency in a sample of low-income, minority males and females. *Journal of Youth and Adolescence, 13*, 349–364.

Friedman, S. L., Randolph, S., & Kochanoff, A. (2001). Childcare research at the dawn of a new millennium: Taking stock of what we know. In G. Bremner

& A. Fogel (Eds.), *Blackwell handbook of infant development: Handbooks of developmental psychology* (pp. 660–692). Malden, MA: Blackwell.

Goldberg, W. A., & Easterbrooks, M. A. (1988). Maternal employment when children are young. In A. Gottfried & A. Gottfried (Eds.), *Maternal employment and children's development: Longitudinal research* (pp. 121–154). NY: Plenum.

Gottfried, A. E. (2005). Maternal and dual-earner employment and children's development: Redefining the research agenda. In D. F. Halpern & S. E. Murphy (Eds.), *From work-family balance to work-family interaction: Changing the metaphor* (pp. 197–217). Mahwah, NJ: Lawrence Erlbaum.

Gove, W. R., & Zeiss, C. (1987). Multiple roles and happiness. In F. Crosby (Ed.), *Spouse, parent, worker: On gender and multiple roles* (pp. 125–137). New Haven, CT: Yale University Press.

Greenberger, E., & Goldberg, W. A. (1989). Work, parenting, and the socialization of children. *Developmental Psychology, 25*(1), 22–35.

Greenberger, E., Goldberg, W. A., Crawford, T., & Granger, J. (1988). Beliefs about the consequences of maternal employment for children. *Psychology of Women Quarterly, 12,* 35–59.

Greenberger, E., O'Neil, R., & Nagel, S. K. (1994). Linking workplace and homeplace: Relations between the nature of adults' work and their parenting behaviors. *Developmental Psychology, 30*(6), 990–1002.

Hayden, D. (1982). *The Grant domestic revolution: A history of feminist designs for American homes, neighborhoods, and cities.* Cambridge: The MIT Press.

Hayghe, H. (1984). Working mothers reach record number in 1984. *Monthly Labor Review, 107*(12), 31–33.

Hetherington, E. M. (1979). A child's perspective. *American Psychologist, 34,* 851–858.

Hoffman, L. (1986). Work, family, and the child. In M. S. Pallak & R. O. Perloff (Eds.), *Psychology and work: Productivity, change, and employment* (pp. 173–220). Washington, DC: American Psychological Association.

Hoffman, L. (1989). Effects of maternal employment in the two-parent family. *American Psychologist, 44*(2), 283–292.

Hoffman, L. W., & Youngblade, L. M. (1998). Maternal employment, morale, and parenting: Social class comparisons. *Journal of Applied Developmental Psychology, 19,* 389–414.

Kessler, R. C., & McRae, J. A., Jr. (1982). The effect of wives' employment on the mental health of married men and women. *American Sociological Review, 47,* 216–227.

Kessler-Harris, A. (1981). *Women have always worked: A historical overview.* Old Westbury, NY: The Feminist Press.

Makri-Botsari, E., & Makri, E. (2003). Maternal employment: Effects on her mental health and children's functional status. *Psychological Studies, 48,* 36–46.

McLoyd, V. C. (1990). The impact of economic hardship on Black families and children: Psychological distress, parenting, and socioemotional development. *Child Development, 61,* 311–346.

Melton, B. (1999). In and out of the kitchen: Women's work and networks in nineteenth-century American fiction. In K. Wells (Ed.), *Domestic goddesses*. Retrieved May 2, 2006, from http://www.womenwriters.net/domesticgoddess/melton.html

National Institute of Child Health & Human Development (1997). The effects of infant child care on infant–mother attachment security: Results of the NICHD Study of Early Child Care. *Child Development, 68*(5), 860–879.

NICHD Early Child Care Research Network. (2002). Early child care and children's development prior to school entry: Results from the NICHD study of early child care. *American Educational Research Journal, 39*(1), 133–164.

Nock, S. L. (2001). The marriages of equally dependent spouses. *Journal of Family Issues, 22*, 755–775.

Parcel, T. L., & Menaghan, E. G. (1994). Early parental work, family social capital, and early childhood outcomes. *American Journal of Sociology, 99*, 972–1009.

Parcel, T. L., & Menaghan, E. G. (1997). Effects of low-wage employment on family well-being. *Future of Children, 7*(1), 116–121.

Perry-Jenkins, M., Repetti, R. L., & Crouter, A. C. (2000). Work and families in the 1990s. *Journal of Marriage and Family, 62*, 981–998.

Raver, C. C. (2003). Does work pay psychologically as well as economically? The role of employment in predicting depressive symptoms and parenting among low-income families. *Child Development, 74*(6), 1720–1736.

Repetti, R. L., Matthews, K. A., & Waldron, I. (1989). Employment and women's health: Effects of paid employment on women's mental and physical health. *American Psychologist, 44*(11), 1394–1401.

Reynolds, A. J., Temple, J. A., Robertson, D. L., & Mann, E. A. (2001). Long-term effects of an early childhood intervention on educational achievement and juvenile arrest. *JAMA, 285*(18), 2339–2346.

Scarr, S., Phillips, D., & McCartney, K. (1989). Working mothers and their families. *American Psychologist, 44*(11), 1402–1409.

Shonkoff, J. P., & Phillips, D. A. (Eds.) (2000). *From neurons to neighborhoods: The science of early childhood development*. Washington, DC: National Academy Press.

Silverstein, L. (1991). Transforming the debate about child care and maternal employment. *American Psychologist, 46*(10), 1025–1032.

Snyder, H. N. (2003, December). Juvenile Arrests 2001. *Juvenile Justice Bulletin*. Retrieved November 23, 2006, from http://www.ncjrs.gov/pdffiles1/ojjdp/201370.pdf

Stewart, A. J., & Salt, P. (1981). Life stress, life-styles, depression, and illness in adult women. *Journal of Personality and Social Psychology, 40*(6), 1063–1069.

Tyagi, A. W. (2004, March 22). Why women need to work [Electronic version]. *Time Magazine, 56*. Retrieved March 23, 2006, from http://www.time.com/time/archive/printout/0,23657,993642,00.html

U.S. Bureau of Labor Statistics (2005, May). Women in the labor force: A databook, Report 985. Retrieved April 24, 2006, from http://www.bls.gov/cps/wlf-databook2005.htm

U.S. Census Bureau (2005, June). Current population survey, 2005 Annual social and economic supplement. Retrieved April 24, 2006, from http://pubdb3.census.gov/macro/032005/pov/new03_100_01.htm

U.S. Department of Labor, Women's Bureau (1994). *1993 Handbook on women workers: Trends and issues.* Washington, DC: U.S. Government Printing Office.

Vandell, D. L., & Ramanan, J. (1992). Effects of early and recent maternal employment on children from low-income families. *Child Development, 63,* 938–949.

Vander Ven, T., & Cullen, F. T. (2004). The impact of maternal employment on serious youth crime: Does the quality of working conditions matter? *Crime and Delinquency, 50*(2), 272–291.

Vander Ven, T. M., Cullen, F. T., Carrozza, M. A., & Wright, J. P. (2001). Home alone: The impact of maternal employment on delinquency. *Social Problems, 48*(2), 236–257.

Votruba-Drzal, E., Coley, R. L., & Chase-Lansdale, P. L. (2004). Child care and low-income children's development: Direct and moderated effects. *Child Development, 75*(1), 296–312.

Warren, E., & Tyagi, A. (2003). *The two-income trap: Why middle-class mothers and fathers are going broke.* New York: Basic Books.

Wattenberg, B. (Host). (2000a). Interview with Alice Kessler-Harris (online transcript). In J. C. Sorenson, J. Mernit, & V. Cannato (Producers), *The first measured century*, Virginia: PBS. Retrieved August 9, 2006, from http://www.pbs.oef/fmc/interviews/kesslerharris.htm

Wattenberg, B. (Host). (2000b). Interview with William Chafe (online transcript). In J. C. Sorenson, J. Mernit, & V. Cannato (Producers), *The first measured century*, Virginia: PBS. Retrieved August 9, 2006, from http://www.pbs.oef/fmc/interviews/kesslerharris.htm

Yarrow, L. J. (1979). Emotional development. *American Psychologist, 34*(10), 951–957.

Youngblut, J. M., Brooten, D., Singer, L. T., Standing, T., Lee, H., & Rodgers, W. L. (2001). Effects of maternal employment and prematurity on child outcomes in single parent families. *Nursing Research, 50,* 346–355.

2

The Upside of Maternal and Dual-Earner Employment: A Focus on Positive Family Adaptations, Home Environments, and Child Development in the Fullerton Longitudinal Study

Adele Eskeles Gottfried and Allen W. Gottfried

Over the course of the twentieth century, and into the twenty-first, the impact of maternal employment on families and children's development has been a pervasive topic of research interest and public policy. The demographic trend of increasing maternal employment across this time period, including mothers with young children, corresponds to this interest (Barnett, 2005; Bianchi, 2000; Gottfried, Gottfried, & Bathurst, 2002). Mothers' provision of financial support, as well as enhancing their personal satisfaction, are the predominant factors supporting this demographic trend. Despite the fact that the majority of mothers are employed, pervasive findings across the research literature indicating that children of employed mothers develop equivalently well as those of stay-at-home mothers, and evidence of positive aspects of the role of maternal employment for children, maternal employment continues to be portrayed negatively. Indeed, researchers continue to frame research questions to ferret out negativity. Apparently, the traditional family consisting of a male earner and stay-at-home mother continues to be the standard by which maternal employment is judged (Gottfried & Gottfried, 2006).

In our prior work, three sequential phases of research on maternal employment were delineated (Gottfried et al., 2002; Gottfried & Gottfried,

2006). In the earliest phase, – Phase one – research concentrated on attempting to detect the negative impact of maternal employment on children's development. In this regard, research questions were framed in order to discover such effects. However, research findings did not support a negative impact of maternal employment on children's development. When comparing the development of children of employed and non-employed mothers, the overwhelming pervasive findings have been an absence of significant difference in their development (Gottfried & Gottfried, 1988a, 1994; Gottfried, Gottfried, & Bathurst, 1995, 2002). As a result, research moved on to Phase 2 which is the predominant phase today (Gottfried et al., 2002; Gottfried & Gottfried, 2006). Phase 2 research focuses on elucidating factors that mediate between maternal employment on the one hand and children's development on the other. Examples of mediating factors are home environment, family relationships, maternal attitudes towards employment and parenting, and spillover between work and family. Whereas much has been found about the role of environment and family context in mediating the relationship between maternal employment and children's development, even within Phase 2 researchers continue to frame research issues oriented toward discovering a negative impact of maternal employment for children (see reviews in Gottfried, 2005; Gottfried et al., 2002; Gottfried & Gottfried, 2006).

The present chapter focuses on what we have designated as Phase 3 (Gottfried, 2005; Gottfried et al., 2002; Gottfried & Gottfried, 2006). Phase 3 focuses on: (a) the positive impact of maternal employment on children's development, home environment, and families; and (b) family adaptations that support families and children when mothers are employed. Consistent with this emphasis, this chapter presents what we term the upside of maternal employment, that is, the positive aspects of maternal employment for children's development and for family functioning using a Phase 3 perspective.

In presenting evidence supporting the upside of maternal employment, we will highlight the findings of our research from the Fullerton Longitudinal Study (FLS). These findings provide evidence for the positive, adaptational, and longitudinal impact of maternal employment on children from ages 1- through age 24-years. Additionally, results of the FLS have been supported by others' research, and pertinent literature will be cited to indicate the generalizability of these findings beyond the FLS itself. It should be noted that the present chapter focuses specifically on documenting positive child developmental outcomes and family adaptations. We highlight the pervasive positive findings of the literature because, in our view, positive findings have been ignored due to an inordinate amount of attention paid to negative findings that have not been supported by the literature at large.

The Fullerton Longitudinal Study

The Fullerton Longitudinal Study (FLS) is a cross-time investigation from infancy through early adulthood. It was initiated in 1979 with 130 healthy 1-year-old infants and their families with no less than 80 percent of the participants returning for any assessment. At the outset of the investigation, the participants resided within an hour of the research site. Because geographic mobility is common in the course of development and family life, the study population eventually resided throughout the United States and even abroad (Gottfried, Gottfried, & Guerin, 2006). This is important to note because the developmental trends obtained in the FLS are not confounded with specific geographic proximity. The sample represents a wide range of the middle-class as measured by the Hollingshead Four Factor Index of Social Status (Gottfried, 1985; Gottfried, Gottfried, Bathurst, Guerin, & Parramore, 2003; Hollingshead, 1975) ranging from semi-skilled workers through professionals. Developmental assessments were conducted every six months from ages 1 through 3.5 years, and annually from ages 5 through 17. At age 24 the study participants were surveyed as to their educational progress and work status, and they are currently being surveyed at age 29 years. For additional details concerning the FLS sample characteristics, design, methods, and measures see Gottfried, Bathurst, and Gottfried (1994); Gottfried, Gottfried, and Bathurst (1988), Gottfried, Gottfried, Bathurst, and Guerin (1994), Gottfried and Gottfried (1984), and Guerin, Gottfried, Oliver, and Thomas (2003).

Throughout the course of this investigation, numerous developmental assessments were conducted including intellectual, cognitive, affective, social, academic, motivational, and behavioral adjustment domains as well as assessment of the proximal home environment and involvement of mothers and fathers with their children in families in which the mothers were employed and not employed.

The research concerning maternal and dual-earner employment extends from infancy through age 24 thus far. Having a longitudinal study of children from infancy through early adulthood affords us the unique opportunity to determine the short- and long-term effects of maternal and dual-earner employment on children's development over this extensive time period providing a comprehensive long-term perspective on the issues. The variables included fall into several categories including: maternal and paternal employment status, work schedules and intensity, demographic family factors, child developmental outcomes, child academic performance, children's adult educational attainment, family environment, parental involvement, maternal employment attitudes, parenting satisfaction, and role balance between parents (Gottfried et al., 1988, 1994, 1995, 2002). The reader is referred to our prior publications for the specific measures utilized. Throughout the research, measures used were either previously standardized, or psychometrically analyzed for inclusion in the research.

At the initiation of the study 36 percent of the mothers were employed. By the time the children reached age 17 years, 83 percent of the mothers were employed. Because the overwhelming majority of mothers were employed by the end of adolescence, data analyses over the course of the study involving comparisons between employed and non-employed mothers are based on an increasingly larger employed group and an increasingly smaller non-employed group. Furthermore, by the 12-year assessment, there had been only one mother who had never been employed. These trends themselves represent an important ecology in which the children are raised. Further, the rates of maternal employment within the FLS are consistent with national data (Gottfried et al., 1994), and hence are representative of such trends.

With regard to collection of data, variables were measured in a variety of ways. Children's development was assessed in the university lab using standardized instruments. Parents completed self-report inventories and surveys. Home environment was assessed both directly in the home in infancy, preschool, and elementary school, as well as through parental completion of surveys throughout the study. Children's academic achievement was assessed through the administration of standardized measures, their teachers' completion of standardized behavior checklists, as well as school records in the high school years, providing cross-informant and cross-context methodology. Extensive, multivariate analyses, controlling for factors including family socioeconomic status (SES), marital status, number of children, and gender were conducted. The results reported below are based on these analyses. Over two decades of careful research and analyses of our data resulted in patterns of positive child and environmental outcomes and family adaptations. Not only were these favorable outcomes consistently obtained in the FLS, but they have been supported by the vast literature in this field. Hence, after careful reflection, it became apparent to us that the message of the upside of maternal employment needs to be clearly advanced to the scientific audience, as well as the public.

The Upside of Maternal Employment

Impact on Children's Development

Maternal Employment is not Detrimental to Children's Development
The major finding of the Fullerton Longitudinal Study is that when children of employed and non-employed mothers were compared regarding their developmental outcomes, maternal employment was not significant. It should be emphasized that analyses were conducted controlling for demographic factors including SES, family size, marital status, and child gender, and results were predominantly and overwhelmingly non-significant for maternal employment both before and after the inclusion of such controls (Gottfried et al., 1988, 1994). These analyses extended into the early adulthood years in which there was no significant relationship obtained between maternal employment and the number of years of education attained at age 24. This major conclusion, that of lack of significant differences between the children of employed and non-employed mothers, occurred in both contemporaneous analyses from infancy through age 17-years, and also prospectively from infancy through early adulthood. In prospective analyses, earlier maternal employment was entered into regressions to predict subsequent development over time. Predictions from infancy, the preschool years, school age years, and early adolescence likewise showed no long-term significance. Hence, early maternal employment bore no immediate or subsequent relationships to children's development. There were no "sleeper" effects, meaning that there were no subsequent adverse outcomes obtained given earlier nonsignificance of maternal employment. There were just no adverse outcomes either contemporaneously or in later years. Children with employed and non-employed mothers developed equivalently across the years in the FLS.

These results of the FLS with regard to finding no detriment of maternal employment to children are supported by a pervasive plethora of research literature documenting the same finding. Whereas it is beyond the scope of this chapter to review these studies, there have been reviews by ourselves and others to which the interested reader is referred (Etaugh, 1974; Goldberg, Prause, Lucas-Thompson, & Himsel, 2008; Gottfried & Gottfried, 1988b; Gottfried et al., 1994, 2002; Gottfried, Gottfried, Bathurst,

& Killian, 1999; Hoffman, 1989; Lerner, 1994; Zaslow, Rabinovich, & Suwalsky, 1991). Hence, this conclusion has been obtained across many samples, demographics, over time, and across occupational and socioeconomic status. The public myth of adverse outcomes to children created by maternal employment is not only untrue, but it is also of questionable ethics to continue to promulgate this view given the overwhelming evidence to the contrary.

Impact on Home Environment

Proximal Environment
In the FLS, a major research issue investigated concerns the relationships between maternal employment status and the home environments to which children are exposed. Detailed measures of the proximal home environment have been studied. Proximal home environment encompasses the cognitive, social-emotional, and physical stimulation available to children in the home, as well as family interpersonal relationships (Gottfried & Gottfried, 1984). Maternal employment status is itself a distal variable which categorizes mothers on the basis of employment or nonemployment, but itself does not provide direct information about the quality of environment to which children are exposed (Gottfried et al., 1988). Both contemporaneously and across time, we found that the quality of home environments provided to children by employed and non-employed mothers, from infancy through early adolescence, were not significantly different and hence were equivalent (Gottfried et al., 1988; 1994, 1995, 2002). The home environment measures comprised major widely accepted indices of established psychometric criteria , including the HOME Inventory (Caldwell & Bradley, 1984) and Purdue Inventories (Wachs, 1976) involving direct observations of the homes, the Family Environment Scale (Moos & Moos, 1986) involving surveys completed by parents, as well as the Home Environment Survey (Gottfried et al., 1988, 1994).

Whereas overall there was equivalence in the quality of proximal home environment provided for the children of employed and non-employed mothers, the data revealed some areas of difference in that employed mothers encouraged self-help and independence skills more, such as in toilet training and dressing oneself. Further, the homes of employed mothers had significantly more adults in the home and more adults caring for the child. Presumably, these are family adaptations that allow the parents to be employed (Gottfried et al., 1988).

Another environmental domain showing differences between employed and non-employed mothers concerned their educational attitudes. At ages 5 and 7, employed mothers had significantly higher educational aspirations for their children compared to non-employed mothers, and both they and their children watched significantly less TV. Mothers' more positive educational attitudes proved to be a longitudinal trend beginning at age 3.5 years through age 7. At age 7, the children of employed mothers had more out of school lessons, and were exposed to a significantly greater diversity of experience (Gottfried et al., 1988). Consistent with this finding for educational attitudes, mothers employed when their children were age 5 years were more involved in discussing school activities, caring for, and doing things with their child subsequently at age 7. Hence, the employed mothers in the FLS had a stronger educational orientation including higher aspirations and engagement in educationally oriented activities early in the schooling of their children, and this pattern held true over time. All of these findings were independent of socioeconomic status, marital status, number of children in the home, and child gender. Further at age 5, maternal educational attitudes were positively related to children's intellectual functioning, reading and math achievement, and social adjustment in subsequent years. Results occurred above and beyond the influence of SES (Gottfried, 1991; Gottfried et al., 1988).

Whereas little significance emerged in the home environments provided to children of employed and non-employed mothers, children's development has been found to be pervasively related to quality of home environment across the literature (e.g., Bradley, 2002; Gottfried, 1984; Gottfried & Gottfried, 1984; Gottfried et al., 1988, 1994). Based on the patterns of evidence in the maternal employment and home environment literature, we advanced the conclusions that: (a) maternal employment per se is not related to children's development; (b) any significant relationship obtained between maternal employment status and children's development would be due to its relationship to the proximal home environment provided for the child (Gottfried et al., 1988); and (c) employed and non-employed mothers are equivalently efficacious with regard to their parenting. These findings and conclusions are consistent with the preponderance of research in this area (Gottfried, 2005; Gottfried et al., 1995, 1999, 2002; Gottfried & Gottfried, 2006).

Maternal Employment and Parenting Attitudes
Another domain of research regards mothers' attitudes towards the dual roles of employment and parenting, and parenting satisfaction itself. Across

a wide array of studies, the literature converges on the following. Employed mothers' attitudes towards their dual roles of employment and parenting are positively related to their children's development and to the quality of their home environments. For example, in the FLS, when children were 5-years of age, mothers' attitudes towards employment and the dual roles of career and family were positively related to children's interest and participation in school and educational stimulation in the home. When children were 7-years of age, the children of mothers who were more confident and less stressed with regard to their dual roles, had higher academic achievement. More positive attitudes also were related to fewer child behavior problems at ages 5 and 7 years. Mothers with more favorable employment related attitudes were more involved with their children (Gottfried et al., 1988).

Analyses on maternal attitudes towards the dual roles of employment and parenting conducted in the FLS through age 17 years have indicated a host of favorable outcomes through the adolescent years when maternal attitudes were more positive. These findings include fewer child behavior problems, greater family cohesion, less family conflict, more positive parenting satisfaction, more emotional and practical parenting support, and more effectiveness in setting limits (Gottfried et al., 2002). Overall, mothers' positive attitudes towards their dual roles of employment and parenting are important in family adaptations to parenting. The reader is referred to Gottfried et al. (2002) for an extensive review of literature indicating the role of parenting attitudes and role satisfaction in children's development and home environment.

Family Role Adaptations

Increased Father Involvement

Arguably, the most significant family adaptation that has occurred in mother-employed homes is the increase in fathers' involvement with their children. This is a pervasive finding across the literature that has been extensively documented and reviewed (Gottfried et al., 1988, 1994, 1995, 1999, 2002; Gottfried & Gottfried, 2006). The most salient findings are the following:

- Father involvement with their children is significantly greater when mothers are employed, and increases as the number of mothers' employment hours increase. These findings have been obtained across age from infancy through adolescence, cross-culturally, and cross-nationally.

- Long-term patterns of increased fathers' involvement were established during the children's preschool years, and were maintained throughout their children's adolescence. Interestingly, when children were ages 8 and 12 years, fathers spent significantly more weekday, but not weekend, time with children when mothers were employed. This indicates family adaptation inasmuch as fathers were more available during the hours that mothers were likely to be working. The overall pattern of findings in the FLS reveals that patterns of father involvement are formed early and persist over time. The types of activities in which the fathers were engaged include caretaking responsibilities, cognitive stimulation, and play.
- Father involvement itself has been found to be positively related to child outcomes across the literature. For example, in the FLS, greater father involvement has been found to be related to more mature social adjustment at age 6, higher IQ (ages 6 and 7), and higher academic achievement (ages 6 and 7) (Gottfried, 1991). Tamis-LeMonda and Cabrera (1999) have supported these conclusions by reporting that higher involvement of fathers with their children is associated with a host of favorable affective and cognitive outcomes. Conclusions by Parke (2002) and Radin (1994) likewise support these findings.
- These findings for increased father involvement demonstrate that there is a balance of parental roles that exists in dual-earner households. Rather than being interpreted as simply a compensation for maternal employment which others have suggested (Gottfried & Gottfried, 1994), we proposed that increased father involvement is a selective choice made by the parents which is a positive family adaptation in dual-earner families. Certainly, no one would object to children having increased exposure to fathers.

Mothers' Time Involvement

It has been proposed that employed mothers reorient their time allocation in order to meet their dual demands of employment and parenting. For example, employed mothers spend less time in volunteer work, get less sleep, and have less free and leisure time to try to balance paid work and child involvement. In a study of time use trends from 1965 to 1998, Bianchi (2000) concluded that the time spent with children by employed mothers was not dramatically less than that of non-employed mothers (ranging from 82 to 92 percent of time that non-employed mothers spent with their children). Bianchi (2000) further found that fathers' time with children increased over the years spanning 1965 to 1998 which counteracts any decrease in mothers' time due to employment. This supports the prior conclusion. Based on this research, Bianchi (2000) concluded that there are so few child-related negative outcomes of maternal employment due to reallocation of maternal time and priorities, delegation of family work to others, increased preschool enrollment for children of employed and non-employed mothers, and redefinition of parenting roles. Results of the FLS were similar to those of Bianchi in that there have been no significant differences obtained in maternal involvement comparing employed and non-employed mothers. These findings further support the view that families create adaptations to support children's needs and development. Some of these adaptations may involve reallocation of one's own commitments.

Group Differences

Gender
The most pervasive gender finding has been for daughters of employed mothers to have more egalitarian gender-role concepts, and higher aspirations and achievement (Etaugh, 1974; Goldberg et al., 2008; Hoffman, 1989; Hoffman & Youngblade, 1999; Nelson & Keith, 1990; Wolfer & Moen 1996; Wright & Young, 1998). Zick and Allen (1996) found that adolescent daughters, but not sons, were more likely to be employed when their mothers were employed.

Regarding impact of maternal employment on boys, despite early predictions that middle-class boys would be adversely impacted by their mothers' employment, this finding has not been substantiated in up-to-date and well-designed studies. Rather, boys have not been shown to be adversely affected, and in some studies boys show greater egalitarian attitudes toward gender roles and fewer sex-role stereotypes (Gottfried et al., 2002; Lerner & Abrams, 1994).

Positive Effect on Lower SES and Welfare to Work Families
Evidence continues to accrue showing that maternal employment is associated with favorable outcomes for children of lower socioeconomic status, regardless of whether employment is freely chosen or not as is the case with welfare reform (Gottfried, 2005). Cognitive and academic achievements, as well as social development, are more positive when mothers of lower socioeconomic status are employed. Research indicating this positive outcome has been available over many decades (Cherry & Eaton, 1977; Gottfried

et al., 1995; Heyns, 1982; Hoffman & Youngblade, 1999; Rieber & Womack, 1968; Zaslow & Emig, 1997).

More recent evidence concerns the impact of welfare reform, or involuntary employment, on children's outcomes. At its inception it was suggested that when mothers must work involuntarily, there could be new stressors added to family life (Wilson, Ellwood, & Brooks-Gunn, 1995; Zaslow & Emig, 1997). However, there is recent evidence reporting positive findings for both mothers' parenting and children's outcomes (Dunifon, Kalil, & Danziger, 2003; Fuller et al., 2002; Gennetian & Miller, 2002; Gennetian & Morris, 2003). Researchers have suggested reasons for these outcomes including increased income and resources, and higher maternal self-esteem. Therefore, the role of socioeconomic status is of exceptional importance in interpreting results of maternal employment research. Indeed, McLoyd and her colleagues have found that unemployment is itself stressful and detrimental in families of low socioeconomic families (McLoyd, Jayaratne, Ceballo, & Borquez, 1994). Unemployment is associated with a host of adverse outcomes, as is poverty itself.

Regarding families of middle socioeconomic status, expectations of adverse impact of maternal employment on children continue despite the absence of such evidence. We have suggested that this is the case because maternal employment violates the traditional societal norm of the single-male-earner family with mother as primarily involved in home and family activities (Gottfried et al., 1999). The single-male earner family may continue to be interpreted as the standard to which all other families are compared. However, this expectation is an anachronism because it does not match the demographic data as maternal employment is a majority phenomenon. It is probable that this myth continues to be perpetuated because mothers' employment is justified as a necessity in less-advantaged families, whereas in homes with more economic resources mothers' employment is considered a non-necessity, and therefore viewed negatively.

Ethnicity
Differences in maternal employment perceptions exist in varying ethnic groups. For example, McLoyd (1993) proposed that maternal employment is more central to the economic well-being of African-American families than is the employment of European-American families and therefore may be more positively accepted. In African-American families work is viewed as compatible with maternal and marital roles (Bridges & Etaugh, 1994; McLoyd, 1993). Wolfer and Moen (1996) found that daughters of African-American mothers were more likely to stay in school longer the more years

their mothers worked during childhood and preadolescence. For daughters of European-American mothers, duration of staying in school was not related to maternal employment. For African-American mothers, maternal employment role modeling appears to have an impact on daughters' schooling. Such findings indicate that the upside of maternal employment is likely to be interpreted differently depending on the experiences related to one's ethnic background.

Work-Related Variables

Parental Occupation
In the FLS, an outcome has been that maternal and paternal occupational status are positively related to aspects of intellectual performance, IQ, academic achievement, and home stimulation and family climate (Gottfried et al., 1988, 1994). Mothers of higher occupational status had more positive educational attitudes and higher aspirations for their children, and favorable perceptions of their dual responsibilities between employment and parenting (Gottfried et al., 1988, 1994). Castellino, Lerner, Lerner, and von Eye (1998) found that young adolescents had higher career aspirations when their mothers had higher occupational statuses and higher education. Gottfried (2000) found that adolescents were more satisfied with their own employment when their mothers were employed and had higher occupational status and education, and when fathers had greater job flexibility. These results suggest that parental occupational status may ultimately affect children's career paths. Parcel and Menaghan (1994) suggested that the quality of home environment is positively related to the complexity of maternal occupations. This provides further support for an important role of parental occupation in development.

Employment Schedules
There is continued research on employment schedules and their impact on children and the family. Overall, the predominance of research documents that compared to non-employment, mothers' part-time and full-time employment schedules do not result in significant differences in child development or family environment (Goldberg et al., 2008; Gottfried & Gottfried, 1988b; Gottfried et al., 1995) Inasmuch as there is no one standard or criterion defining part- and full-time employment across the literature (Gottfried et al., 1995), we continue to recommend that future studies use work hours as a continuous criterion rather than using arbitrary

cutoffs designating part-time vs. full-time employment. Thus far, there has not been a specific number of maternal work hours identified as optimal for children's development or family environment (Gottfried et al., 1999). A recent study on the relationship of nonstandard work schedules to young children's cognitive development concluded that the work schedule is affected by type of child care options and home environment (Han, 2005). Additionally, demographic factors such as SES must be controlled in studies of employment schedules and hours because mothers who work more hours than others may have a greater economic need to do so, a factor which by itself could result in significant child development or family environment differences when not controlled regardless of employment hours or schedule. It is perhaps due to family adaptations documented previously that there is generally an absence of relationship between mothers' employment schedules and number of work hours to children's development.

Work and Family Adaptations
Many work and family adaptations have been advanced in the literature, which include a balance of roles between parents, increased father participation, increased child participation in family responsibilities, non-parental child care, alternating work schedules of parents, work restructuring and family-responsive work policies (Gottfried, 2005; Hughes & Galinsky, 1988; Murphy & Zagorski, 2005). Work restructuring may include flextime, shift work, job sharing, part-time employment, a compressed work week, work at home, personal days for family responsibilities, time bank, relocation assistance, and benefits. Nontraditional work schedules have likewise emerged as family adaptations (Gottfried et al., 1999; Gottfried, 2005).

Conclusions

We intended to portray a decidedly "Upside" to maternal employment. What we sought to document are the plethora of positive outcomes of maternal employment for children and families, as well as the adaptations that families undertake to make parental employment a success. In fact, our previous and present conclusions concerning the absence of adverse impact of maternal employment on children's development (Gottfried et al., 1988, 1994, 1995, 2002; Gottfried & Gottfried, 2006) continue to be supported as shown by the results of a recent meta-analysis of maternal employment and children's achievement (Goldberg et al., 2008). We believe that the message should be clear that maternal employment needs to be reframed as positive and adaptive in children's and family life. Hence, in view of these consistently positive and adaptive findings, we raise the question of what would be the alternative to, or the other side of, maternal employment? The stress of loss of employment, or absence of sufficient family resources, has been amply documented not only in the child development literature, but also in the literature of the impact of poverty and low socioeconomic status on families (Hoff, Laursen, & Tardif, 2002).

We conclude that to perpetuate adverse myths of the impact of maternal employment on children and families is a disservice to the public, and may be unethical in view of the vast amount of scientific data to the contrary. The myth of superiority of maternal non-employment is erroneously influenced by flawed and uninformed perceptions that maternal employment is itself detrimental to children and family life and this conclusion is harmful and unfounded.

Unfortunately, adverse myths of the role of maternal employment on children's development continue to be perpetuated by media that inflame this issue with negatively biased treatment of the issue. Newspapers, magazines, and TV portrayals of maternal employment emphasize the adversity of maternal employment and guilt of mothers, such as an article entitled "The Case for Staying Home: Caught between the Pressures of the Workplace and the Demands of being a Mom, More Women are Sticking with the Kids" (Wallis, 2004). Such messages may encourage sales, but are likely to be detrimental to the readers in light of research findings.

We continue to strongly assert that this message of the "Upside" of maternal employment must be disseminated directly to the public and to professionals working with the public. Our research has already contributed to law as it provided a foundation for a California Supreme Court ruling, *Burchard v. Garay* (1986), in which it was ruled that parental employment in and of itself is not to be used in child custody determination. At this point in time, it now becomes an ethical issue for investigators and professionals to keep up to date with the many positive findings regarding maternal employment. Moreover, researchers need to conduct research framing issues around the competencies of children, parents, and families in which mothers are employed. Granting agencies need to fund research to investigate positive family adaptations which can then be transformed into positive recommendations and practices for families. This is the legacy we hope to provide for future children, families, researchers, professionals, and the public.

References

Barnett, R. C. (2005). Dual-earner couples: Good/bad for her and/or him? In D. F. Halpern & S. E. Murphy (Eds.), *From work-family balance to work-family interaction: Changing the metaphor* (pp. 151–171). Mahwah, NJ: Lawrence Erlbaum Publishers.

Bianchi, S. (2000). Maternal employment and time with children: Dramatic change or surprising continuity? *Demography, 37*, 401–414.

Bradley, R. H. (2002). Environment and parenting. In M. H. Bornstein (Ed.), *Handbook of parenting* (Vol. 2, 2nd ed., pp. 281–314). Mahwah, NJ: Lawrence Erlbaum Associates.

Bridges, J. S., & Etaugh, C. (1994). Black and white college women's perceptions of early maternal employment. *Psychology of Women Quarterly, 18*(3), 427–431.

Burchard v. Garay 42 Cal. 3d; *Cal.Rptr.*, P.2d, (Sept. 1986).

Caldwell, B., & Bradley, R. (1984). *Home observation for measurement of the environment*. Little Rock: University of Arkansas.

Castellino, D. R., Lerner, J. V., Lerner, R. M., & von Eye, A. (1998). Maternal employment and education: Predictors of young adolescent career trajectories. *Applied Developmental Science, 2*(3), 114–126.

Cherry, F. F., & Eaton, E. L. (1977). Physical and cognitive development in children of low-income mothers working in the child's early years. *Child Development, 48*(1), 158–166.

Dunifon R., Kalil, A., & Danziger, S. K. (2003). Maternal work behavior under welfare reform: How does the transition from welfare to work affect child development? *Children and Youth Services Review, 25*, 55–82.

Etaugh, C. (1974). Effects of maternal employment on children: A review of recent research. *Merrill-Palmer Quarterly, 20*(2), 71–98.

Fuller, B., Caspary, G., Kagan, S. L., Gauthier, C., Huang, D. S., Carroll, J., & McCarthy, J. (2002). Does maternal employment influence poor children's social development. *Early Childhood Research Quarterly, 17*, 470–497.

Gennetian, L. A., & Miller, C. (2002). Children and welfare reform: A view from an experimental welfare program in Minnesota. *Child Development, 73*, 601–620.

Gennetian, L. A., & Morris, P. A. (2003). The effects of time limits and make-work-pay strategies on the well-being of children: Experimental evidence from two welfare reform programs. *Children and Youth Services Review, 25*, 17–54.

Goldberg, W. A. Prause, J., Lucas-Thompson, R., & Himsel, A. (2008). Maternal employment and children's achievement in context: A meta-analysis of four decades of research. *Psychological Bulletin, 134*, 77–108.

Gottfried, A. E. (1991). Maternal employment in the family setting: Developmental and environmental outcomes. In J. Lerner & N. Galambos (Eds.), *The employment of mothers during the child rearing years* (pp. 63–84). New York: Garland.

Gottfried, A. E. (2000, February). *Developmental aspects of adolescent employment in the family setting.* Presented at the Annual Faculty Creative Activities Fair, California State University, Northridge.

Gottfried, A. E. (2005). Maternal and dual-earner employment and children's development: Redefining the research agenda. In D. F. Halpern, & S. E. Murphy (Eds.), *From work-family balance to work-family interaction: Changing the metaphor* (pp. 197–217). Mahwah, NJ: Lawrence Erlbaum Publishers.

Gottfried, A. E., Bathurst, K., & Gottfried, A. W. (1994). Role of maternal and dual-earner employment in children's development: A longitudinal study from infancy through early adolescence. In A. E. Gottfried & A. W. Gottfried (Eds.), *Redefining families: Implications for children's development* (pp. 55–97). New York: Plenum Publishing.

Gottfried, A. E., & Gottfried, A. W. (1988a). *Maternal employment and children's development: Longitudinal research.* New York: Plenum.

Gottfried, A. E., & Gottfried, A. W. (1988b). Maternal employment and children's development: An integration of longitudinal findings with implications for social policy. In A. E. Gottfried & A. W. Gottfried (Eds.), *Maternal employment and children's development: Longitudinal research* (pp. 269–287). New York: Plenum.

Gottfried, A. E., & Gottfried, A. W. (2006). A long-term investigation of the role of maternal and dual-earner employment in children's development: The Fullerton Longitudinal Study. *American Behavioral Scientist, 49,* 1–18.

Gottfried, A. E., Gottfried, A. W., & Bathurst, K. (1988). Maternal employment, family environment, and children's development: Infancy through the school years. In A. E. Gottfried & A. W. Gottfried, (Eds.), *Maternal employment and children's development: Longitudinal research* (pp. 11–58). New York: Plenum.

Gottfried, A. E., Gottfried, A. W., & Bathurst, K. (1995). Maternal and dual-earner employment status and parenting. In M. H. Bornstein (Ed.), *Handbook of Parenting* (Vol. 2, pp. 139–160). Mahwah, NJ: Lawrence Erlbaum Associates.

Gottfried, A. E., Gottfried, A. W., & Bathurst, K. (2002). Maternal and dual-earner employment status and parenting. In M. H. Bornstein (Ed.), *Handbook of parenting* (Vol. 2, 2nd ed., pp. 207–229). Mahwah, NJ: Lawrence Erlbaum Associates.

Gottfried, A. E., Gottfried, A. W., Bathurst, K., & Killian, C. (1999). Maternal and dual-earner employment: Family environment, adaptations, and the developmental impingement perspective. In M. Lamb (Ed.), *Parenting and child development in "nontraditional" families* (pp. 15–37). Mahwah, NJ: Lawrence Erlbaum Associates.

Gottfried, A. W. (Ed.) (1984). *Home environment and early cognitive development: Longitudinal research.* New York: Academic Press.

Gottfried, A. W. (1985). Measures of socioeconomic status in child development research: Data and recommendations. *Merrill-Palmer Quarterly, 32,* 85–92.

Gottfried, A. W., & Gottfried, A. E. (1984). Home environment and cognitive development in young children of middle-socioeconomic-status families. In

A. W. Gottfried (Ed.), *Home environment and early cognitive development: Longitudinal research* (pp. 57–115). New York: Academic Press.

Gottfried, A. W., Gottfried, A. E., Bathurst, K., & Guerin, D. (1994). *Gifted IQ: Early developmental aspects. The Fullerton Longitudinal Study.* New York: Plenum Publishing.

Gottfried, A. W., Gottfried, A. E., Bathurst, K., Guerin, D. W., & Parramore, M. (2003). Socioeconomic status in children's development and family environment: Infancy through adolescence. In M. Bornstein (Ed.), *Socioeconomic status and parenting* (pp. 189–207). Mahwah, NJ: Lawrence Erlbaum Associates.

Gottfried, A. W., Gottfried, A. E., & Guerin, D. W. (2006). The Fullerton Longitudinal Study: A long-term investigation of intellectual and motivational giftedness. *Journal for the Education of the Gifted, 29,* 430–450.

Guerin, D. W., Gottfried, A. W., Oliver, P. H., & Thomas, C. W. (2003). *Temperament: Infancy through adolescence.* New York: Kluwer Academic/ Plenum Publishers.

Han, W-J. (2005). Maternal nonstandard work schedules and child cognitive outcomes. *Child Development, 76,* 137–154.

Heyns, B. (1982). The influence of parents' work on children's school achievement. In S. B. Kamerman & C. D. Hayes (Eds.), *Families that work: Children in a changing world* (pp. 229– 267). Washington DC: National Academy Press.

Hoff, E., Laursen, B., & Tardif, T. (2002). Socioeconomic status and parenting. In M. H. Bornstein (Ed.), *Handbook of Parenting* (Vol.2, 2nd ed., pp. 231–252). Mahwah, NJ: Lawrence Erlbaum Associates.

Hoffman, L. W. (1989). Effects of maternal employment in the two-parent family. *American Psychologist, 44,* 283–292.

Hoffman, L. W., & Youngblade, L. M. (1999). *Mothers at work: Effects on children's well-being.* New York: Cambridge University Press.

Hollingshead, A. B. (1975). *Four factor index of social status.* Unpublished manuscript, Yale University (Department of Sociology).

Hughes, D., & Galinsky, E. (1988). Balancing work and family lives: Research and corporate applications. In A. E. Gottfried & A. W. Gottfried (Eds.), *Maternal employment and children's development: Longitudinal research* (pp. 233–268). New York: Plenum.

Lerner, J. V. (1994). *Working women and their families.* Thousand Oaks, CA: Sage.

Lerner, J. V., & Abrams, L. A. (1994). Developmental correlates of maternal employment influences on children. In C. B. Fisher & R. M. Lerner (Eds.), *Applied developmental psychology* (pp. 174–206). New York: McGraw-Hill.

McLoyd, V. C. (1993). Employment among African-American mothers in dual-earner families: Antecedents and consequences for family life and child development. In J. Frankel (Ed.), *The employed mother and the family context* (pp. 180–226). New York: Springer.

McLoyd, V. C., Jayaratne, T. E., Ceballo, R., & Borquez, J. (1994). Unemployment and work interruption among African American single mothers: Effects on parenting and adolescent socioemotional functioning. *Child Development, 65,* 562–589.

Moos, R. H., & Moos, B. S. (1986). *Family environment scale. The manual.* Palo Alto, CA: Consulting Psychologists Press.

Murphy, S. E., & Zagorski, D. A. (2005). Enhancing work-family and work-life interaction: The role of management. In D. F. Halpern & S. E. Murphy (Eds.), *From work-family balance to work-family interaction: Changing the metaphor* (pp. 27–47). Mahwah, NJ: Lawrence Erlbaum Publishers.

Nelson, C., & Keith, J. (1990). Comparisons of female and male early adolescent sex role attitude and behavior development. *Adolescence, 25,* 183–203.

Parcel, T. L., & Menaghan, E. G. (1994). *Parents' jobs and children's lives.* New York: Aldine de Gruyter.

Parke, R. D. (2002). Fathers and families. In M. H. Bornstein (Ed.), *Handbook of parenting* (Vol. 3, 2nd ed., pp. 27–73). Mahwah, NJ: Lawrence Erlbaum Associates.

Radin, N. (1994). Primary-caregiving fathers intact families. In A. E. Gottfried & A. W. Gottfried (Eds.), *Redefining families: Implications for children's development.* (pp. 11–54). New York: Plenum.

Rieber, M., & Womack, M. (1968). The intelligence of preschool children as related to ethnic and demographic variables. *Exceptional Children, 34,* 609–614.

Tamis-LeMonda, C. S., & Cabrera, N. (1999). *Perspectives on father involvement: Research and policy.* (Social Policy Report, Vol. XIII, No. 2, pp. 1–25). Ann Arbor MI: Society for Research in Child Development.

Wachs, T. D. (1976). *Purdue Home Stimulation Inventories* (Sections I, II, and III). Unpublished manual, Purdue University.

Wallis, C. (March 22, 2004). The case for staying home. *Time, 163*(12), 51–59.

Wilson, J. B., Ellwood, D. T., & Brooks-Gunn, J. (1995). Welfare-to-work through the eyes of children. In P. L. Chase-Lansdale & J. Brooks-Gunn (Eds.), *Escape from poverty: What makes a difference for children* (pp. 63–86). New York: Cambridge University Press.

Wolfer, L. T., & Moen, P. (1996). Staying in school: Maternal employment and the timing of black and white daughters' school exit. *Journal of Family Issues, 17,* 540–560.

Wright, D. W., & Young, R. (1998). The effects of family structure and maternal employment on the development of gender-related attitudes among men and women. *Journal of Family Issues, 19,* 300–314.

Zaslow, M. J., & Emig, C. A. (1997). When low-income mothers go to work: Implications for children. *The future of children: Welfare to work, 7,* 110–114.

Zaslow, B. A., Rabinovich, B. A., & Suwalsky, J. T. D. (1991). From maternal employment to child outcomes: Preexisting group differences and moderating variables. In J. V. Lerner & N. L. Galambos (Eds.), *Employed mothers and their children* (pp. 237–282). New York: Garland.

Zick, C. D., & Allen, C. R. (1996). The impact of parents' marital status on the time adolescents spend in productive activities. *Family Relations: Journal of Applied Family and Child Studies, 45,* 65–71.

3

Work–Family Policies and the Avoidance of Bias Against Caregiving

Robert Drago, Carol Colbeck, Carol Hollenshead, and Beth Sullivan

Many universities have recently introduced or enhanced policies intended to make faculty careers more compatible with family commitments. In 2005, the presidents of nine major universities issued a joint statement highlighting their commitment to "[c]ontinuing to develop academic personnel policies, institutional resources, and a culture that supports family commitments."[1] A different group of ten presidents and chancellors approved an American Council on Education proposal for greater flexibility in academic careers (2005). That same year, Princeton introduced an automatic stoppage of the tenure clock policy for new parents, while Harvard Law School implemented a paid leave policy for faculty who are either sole or co-equal caregivers to new children.[2]

Part of the context for these initiatives is the recent discovery of "bias avoidance" behaviors among academic faculty (Drago & Colbeck, 2003). Bias avoidance behaviors are strategies that involve minimizing or hiding family commitments in order to achieve career success. Underlying such strategies is the notion that there exist biases against caregiving in the academy, such that faculty who admit to family responsibilities – particularly women – will be subject to career penalties. Bias avoidance therefore represents an attempt to evade such penalties.

This chapter addresses the question of whether or not work–family policies are associated with reduced levels of bias avoidance behaviors. To do so, we use data from national surveys of institutions and of faculty in the chemistry and English departments of those same institutions.

Theory and Hypotheses

Work–Family Policies and Employee Behavior

To link bias avoidance and work–family policies requires that we under-stand how work–family policies alter employee behavior. Hochschild's (1997) study of a corporation found that work–family policies were rarely utilized, a phenomenon echoed in other research.[3] Somewhat differently, Eaton (2003) found that formal flexibility policies had no significant association with organizational commitment, though "usable" policies did exhibit a positive and significant correlation. Most directly, Behson (2004) found that informal means of work–family support accounted for more than 95 percent of the explained variance in job satisfaction, work–family conflict, stress and turnover intent, with formal policies accounting for less than 5 percent of the variance. However, Thompson, Beauvais, and Lyness (1999) report formal policy associations with affective commitment and turnover intent that are close to those for (informal) work–family culture.

Less directly, there is evidence that supervisors supportive of work–family commitments exert a strong influence over an employee's ability to balance work and family (Thomas & Ganster, 1995), as does the organ-izational climate around these issues (Bond, Galinsky, & Swanberg, 1998), with supervisor support perhaps exerting stronger effects (Warren & Johnson, 1995). For both supervisor support and organizational climate, these phenomena may be interpreted as informal practices, implicitly suggesting that formal policies are not that important.

Theoretically, formal policies might alter employee behavior and attitudes through three channels. First, the policies may increase opportunities for employees to change their work patterns to better fit family circumstances. Eaton (2003) suggests that formal policies are necessary but not sufficient. A second channel is symbolic, wherein work–family policy implementa-tion represents an expression of organizational commitment to employees (Grover & Crooker, 1995). Thus, policies may enhance the climate around work and family, thereby inducing policy utilization. A third linkage is that of stigma, wherein policies generate divisions between the serious and committed employees who do not use the policies, and the substandard employees who do (Bailyn, 1993; Williams, 2000). In this view, formal policies may exacerbate the very problems they are intended to solve: employees might be better off working informally with their supervisors to facilitate dual commitments. The stigma argument suggests that pol-icies will have minimal effects on employee behavior.

Finally, work–family policies will exert few effects if employees are unaware of them. Although research on this is slight, a British study using matched employer-employee surveys found employees were only about half as likely as managers to claim that various work–family policies existed (Budd & Mumford, 2004).[4] Assuming the managers' information to be more accurate, this evidence suggests that employee ignorance is widespread, and that policy impacts on employee behavior will, therefore, be weak.

Bias Avoidance and Gender

The literature suggesting that employees who use work–family policies will be stigmatized is based on the notion of widespread biases against caregiving for professional employees (Bailyn, 1993; Williams, 2000). Employees may encounter such bias when they admit to family caregiving, such as when a talented accountant is told that her "career is over" when she announces that she is pregnant.

Bias avoidance (BA) strategies are defined as purposeful behaviors intended to minimize the appearance or reality of family commitments in order to enhance the probability of career success (Drago & Colbeck, 2003). BA strategies are a logical response to bias against caregiving: if an employee believes such biases exist, he or she may strategize to escape penalties flowing from the making or admission of family commitments.

There are two types of BA behaviors: productive and unproductive. Productive BA minimizes family commitments to improve work performance, thereby facilitating career success. For example, a manager might forego having children in order to devote more time to the job. Unproductive BA strategies hide caring responsibilities in order to preserve the appearance of job commitment. For example, an individual may make excuses for missing a meeting rather than admitting that caregiving is responsible. The behavior is not enhancing productivity *per se*, but is establishing the appearance of commitment.

We expect to find both productive and unproductive forms of BA concentrated among women (Drago et al., 2006). For productive BA, gender inequality is predicted due to conditions in the home and workplace. We expect women to exhibit productive BA at higher rates than men due to an unequal division of labor in the home. Although fathers, and particularly educated ones, have increased their contributions to child care in recent decades, mothers still perform significantly more child care (Sandberg & Hofferth, 2001). Therefore, for otherwise equivalent women and men, women's professional work may be compromised more severely by the demands of children. Women may, therefore, rear fewer children as a form of productive BA. Gender inequality in the domestic division of labor extends to housework regardless of children (Bianchi, Milkie, Sayer, & Robinson, 2000). Women may, therefore, stay single more often than men as a form of productive BA. In the workplace, women may experience sex discrimination, regardless of family commitments (MIT, 1999). If higher levels of effort are required for women to achieve career success, then they may sacrifice family commitments more often than men.

Neither the division of labor nor sex discrimination can explain the gendered character of unproductive BA – the hiding of family commitments. Bailyn (1993) and Williams (2000) trace these behaviors to norms concerning the ideal worker and motherhood. The ideal worker norm involves internally and externally held expectations that employees will be committed to the job for long hours, with minimal breaks, for periods of years or decades. Although historically applied to professional and managerial men, the norm is now applied to women in relevant careers (Bailyn, 1993; Williams, 2000). Accordingly, signs of non-work commitments may be viewed as symptomatic of low commitment and poor job performance, motivating unproductive BA. To the extent it is more difficult for coworkers and superiors to see women as ideal workers, we would, therefore, expect women to exhibit higher levels of unproductive BA.

The norm of motherhood is an expectation that women will care for children and others without compensation (Folbre, 2001). The norm implies that admission of caregiving commitments will be viewed more negatively if the employee is a woman. Women face strong incentives to engage in unproductive BA because public admissions of caregiving commitments tend to generate wage penalties (Waldfogel, 1998) and slow career advancement (Judiesch & Lyness, 1999).

Previous research, including the studies cited above as well as an earlier analysis of the data on academic faculty used here, consistently supports the claim that women rely more heavily than men on both productive and unproductive BA strategies.

Bias Avoidance and Work–Family Policies

Recalling the various theoretical linkages between policies and employee behavior, BA behaviors should be negatively correlated with work–family policies. For example, if paid parental leave policies have a direct, intended effect, then their introduction should reduce the probability that employees avoid taking parental leave to achieve career success, or have fewer children than desired. If policies exert a symbolic effect, the causal chain is slightly longer, since policies should improve the work–family climate, thereby reducing the likelihood of career penalties flowing from either making or admitting family commitments, hence reducing BA behaviors. However, to the extent policy utilization leads to stigma, or employees are unaware of policies, then the hypothesized negative correlation would either be weak or non-existent.

Complicating this hypothesis is the possibility that organizations with greater resources may have both stronger policies and higher levels of BA. Organizations with substantial means may be better poised to hire work–family experts to develop policies and to afford any policies that are costly (e.g., paid parental leave or on-site child care). The BA correlation then is that those same organizations hire, retain and motivate employees who are the most ideal of ideal workers – and hence make and admit fewer family commitments. This argument is consistent with the fact that the only universities on the *Working Mother* magazine Top 100 list of family-responsive organizations are Harvard, MIT, and Stanford. These institutions are heavily resourced, as is true of virtually all organizations in the Top 100 list, and place extreme work demands on their faculty. Therefore, any attempt to identify a negative correlation between work–family policies and BA behaviors should control for institutional resources.

We may therefore state the simplest hypothesis as follows:

Hypothesis 1: A greater number of work–family policies will be associated with lower levels of bias avoidance behaviors, ceteris paribus.

A further complication for the analysis is inherent in the notion of BA. Specifically, some forms of BA require that a specific work–family policy exist. For example, suppose a faculty member were asked whether he or she "Did not ask for a reduced teaching load when I needed it for family reasons, because it would lead to adverse career repercussions." A negative response could mean that the respondent did not request a reduced load when needed, never needed a reduced load, or needed but did not ask for a reduced load for some reason other than potentially adverse career repercussions. Additionally, we would expect negative responses from individuals employed in organizations that have no reduced load policy.

These considerations suggest the following:

Hypothesis 2: A greater number of work–family policies will be associated with reduced levels of bias avoidance around a specific policy where the specific policy already exists, ceteris paribus.

The Academic Setting

Motivations for bias avoidance among faculty at U.S. colleges and universities are not difficult to locate. The prototypical career path finds a student going to college, receiving the terminal degree (usually a PhD), and in many fields completing a post-doctoral fellowship in their late 20s. The individual takes a full-time position as an assistant professor on the tenure track. Typically, at the beginning of the sixth year, the faculty member documents her or his accomplishments, which are reviewed by faculty inside and outside the school. The review uses the three criteria of research, teaching, and service, with an almost exclusive weight placed on research at elite schools, but with more weight on teaching at liberal arts institutions. Finally, the faculty member is told whether he or she will be promoted to associate professor with tenure, or released at the end of the seventh year of employment.

This system creates an institutional bias against caregiving up through the tenure point. Productive BA represents a strategic response to such biases. To obtain tenure, faculty may choose to delay partnering or marriage, delay childrearing, or limit the number of children reared. To the extent there is continuing sex discrimination in the workplace, and an unequal division of labor in the home, pressures to engage in productive and unproductive BA will be strongest among women.

It is not obvious how the academic context would affect any linkage between work–family policies and BA. Because academics are frequently inundated with information and may filter it more heavily, they may be unaware of institutional policies. Information overload would weaken any connection between BA and work–family policies. Very differently, academic jobs often provide a high degree of autonomy, and autonomous workers may be less likely to engage in BA since pressure from peers and superiors may appear less frequently and job autonomy may limit the need for formal work–family policies. On the other hand, the pressures involved in attempting to gain tenure may provide a much stronger incentive to avoid policy utilization while on the tenure track, relative to other professions. These considerations suggest that findings here may not generalize to managerial and professional careers.

The specific disciplines of chemistry and English were selected for the current study in part because they are relatively gender imbalanced. As of 1999, 19.5 percent of college level chemistry teachers and 60.1 percent of English teachers were women.[5]

In a faculty survey described later, it was found that men in chemistry tend to be partnered and to parent more frequently than men in English departments. For the women in chemistry, they tended to return sooner from parental leave than preferred relative to women in English departments (Drago et al., 2006). The prior results might stem from the higher salaries associated with chemistry relative to English, while the latter is consistent with more substantial "face time" requirements in chemistry.

Could discipline of employment mediate the relationship between BA and work–family policies? This seems worth exploring for two reasons. First, given there are more women in English, the likelihood of achieving a critical mass to effectively challenge BA seems greater. In this case, BA should be more closely (and negatively) correlated with work–family policies within English departments. Second, given the higher wages and status of chemistry faculty, they may be in a stronger position to challenge biases against caregiving, suggesting greater use of work–family policies. This suggests we should test for the possibility of any mediating effects.

Finally, research suggests that unions may play a role in the creation and effectiveness of work–family policies. Using British data, Budd and Mumford (2004) find that union membership is positively associated with work–family policies and positively correlated with their perceived availability, where the latter effect may either be due to enhanced information flows in unionized workplaces or to union facilitation of program use. Firestein (2000) documents various U.S. cases where union–management partnerships have produced substantive improvements in work–family benefits, such as child care or alternative work schedules. Using interview data from U.S. unions, Gerstel and Clawson (2002) argue somewhat differently that unions respond to the preferences of their members, which may or may not place a high priority on work–family benefits.

Unions may also reduce the perceived need for employees to use BA strategies to the extent unions protect the rights of employees. Finally, if unions alter the climate around work–family policies by making them appear less as a managerially provided benefit (or façade) and more as a right of employees, then unions may mediate the effect of work–family policies on BA behaviors.

Method

To understand any linkage between formal work–family policies and employee behavior, matched employer-employee data are required. In this study, we used a matched sample of surveys administered to over 2,000 faculty and their administrations at over 250 colleges and universities to analyze any linkages between bias avoidance behaviors among employees and the work–family policies of their institutions.

Faculty Survey

Because BA behaviors are strategic, relevant survey items were difficult to construct. Therefore, a total of 13 survey questions were developed through a series of four pilot surveys (see Drago & Colbeck, 2003). Five of these questions are excluded from the present analysis because their interpretation as BA behaviors is questionable.[6]

We structured the survey and survey administration to maximize responses and so we would not overstate levels of BA due to any overrepresentation of parents and particularly of mothers (see Drago & Colbeck, 2003). The survey was brief (36 items), accessible by clicking on an address in an email sent to prospective participants, and took approximately five minutes to complete. Six initial items on bias avoidance were written such that any faculty member could respond. Eight items were specific to parents, with non-parents asked to skip these questions, with the remaining items designed such that anyone could respond. All respondents were able to have a $2 donation made to the charity of their choice, an incentive that did not distinguish by caregiving status.

The sampling frame for the survey was a stratified, random sample of 702 institutions on the 2000 Carnegie list of U.S. colleges and universities, where stratification used the 1994 Carnegie categories.[7] The Carnegie categories included Research, Doctoral, Bachelor's and Associate's degree granting institutions. We also included all institutions in the College and University Work/Family Association, and all work–family "leadership institutions" identified in an earlier study (Friedman, Rimsky, & Johnson, 1996). To the extent these schools are responsive to family commitments, their inclusion should lead us to understate levels of BA.

Once the sample was drawn, email addresses were gathered from chemistry and English faculty in these institutions. This resulted in a sample of 507 institutions, since 195 colleges and universities did not provide publicly available email addresses. Most excluded institutions were from low tiers of the Carnegie rankings where we suspect that levels of BA tend to be higher, such that our results may understate the extent of the behavior.[8]

Excluding 1,264 emails that bounced or where the respondent was on sabbatical, the prospective sample was 14,634 respondents who were contacted between October 2001 and March 2002. Of those, 5,087 individuals returned the survey either on-line or in writing, yielding an overall response rate of 34.8 percent. Only 4,188 respondents completed all items relevant to all respondents, yielding a net response rate of 28.6 percent. Response rates did not vary much across institutions, nor by the percentage of women or of immigrants on the faculty. The latter finding effectively countered any pro-natalist bias in the survey (see Drago et al., 2006).

Excepting work–family policy measures and the measure of faculty unionization discussed below, data on other institutional characteristics were obtained from the Integrated Postsecondary Education Data System from the fall of 1997 (National Center for Education Statistics, 1998).

Institutional Survey

The Faculty Work–Family Policy Study (Hollenshead, Sullivan, Smith, August, & Hamilton, 2005), conducted by the University of Michigan's Center for the Education of Women (CEW), analyzed policies and programs using the same initial sample of institutions used for the Drago and Colbeck faculty survey. The study included two instruments: a web survey and a follow-up telephone survey of a subset of the on-line respondents. (For the purposes of this chapter, only results from the web survey were relevant.) The work–family policies examined were tenure clock stop, modified duties, paid leave while recovering from childbirth, paid dependent care leave, unpaid dependent care leave in excess of the 12 weeks mandated by the Family Medical Leave Act, reduced appointments for dependent care needs, and part-time and job-share appointments. The study also probed the existence of individuals or units designated to assist faculty with work–family issues, as well as employment assistance to spouses or partners of faculty. (While the study's authors understood that a good deal of policy implementation, especially when informal practice is considered, is decided at the unit level within colleges, they chose to focus on policy development and administration from the institution's perspective.)

Data collection began with calls to each institution's office of academic affairs to identify a contact person knowledgeable and willing to complete the survey. If the respondent preferred to respond to a hard copy version of the survey, one was faxed to him/her. From the initial sample of 702 schools, the list of prospective respondents was reduced to 648, primarily due to institutions' unwillingness to provide an assigned respondent for the survey.

From these 648, CEW received 255 responses to the web-based survey, which was fielded in the fall of 2002. The overall response rate was 39 percent. Response rates across the sample varied by Carnegie Classification (see

Table 3.1   Description of the CEW sample.

	Research I & II	Doctoral I & II	Masters I & II	Bacc I & II	Assoc	Total
Number surveyed	123	38	180	198	109	648
Number returned	73	16	66	70	30	255
Response rate (%)	59	42	35	35	28	39

Table 3.1). The institutions with more policies – the research institutions – chose to respond to the survey in greater numbers than other types of institutions. The small number of respondents from the doctoral category cannot be generalized to the initial sample of such institutions.

Methods

The analysis of BA needs to account for the binary character of the BA variables, the fact that we include both individual and institutional level data, the potential for heavily resourced institutions to exhibit both work–family policies and high levels of BA, and the potential for sample selection bias where positive responses regarding BA behavior require that a specific policy already be in place. The BA items are described in Table 3.2.

Five productive BA items are listed first. Some minimize family commitments: staying single to achieve career success, having fewer children than desired, or postponing a second child until after tenure. The other two are slightly less clear-cut. In these cases – not asking for a reduced teaching load when needed and not taking parental leave for a new child – time for career is explicitly maintained in the face of heightened family responsibilities. Because these decisions place a relatively greater weight on faculty production, we cast them as productive BA.

The next three items address unproductive BA, wherein family commitments are strategically hidden. Not stopping the tenure clock contributes nothing to academic performance. The other two items, regarding missing important events in the lives of young children and taking shorter parental leave than desired, arguably involve minimal impacts on performance (particularly relative to an entire faculty career), so are classified as unproductive BA.

Also found in that table is a list of the items included in the additive work–family policy scale ($\alpha = .686$). Although the α is slightly lower than

Table 3.2   Bias avoidance and work–family policy items.

	Mean (S.D.)	Corr.
Productive BA		
Stayed single because I did not have time for a family and a successful academic career: **Single**	.126 (.331)	−.009
To achieve academic success, I had fewer children than I wanted: **<Kids**	.178 (.382)	.036
Did not ask for a reduced teaching load when I needed it for family reasons, because it would lead to adverse career repercussions, **Noreduce**	.246 (.430)	−.044
Had one child, but delayed considering another until after the tenure decision, **Delay** [par.]	.088 (.283)	.062
Did not ask for parental leave even though it would have helped me to take it, **Noleave** [par.]	.274 (.446)	.008
Unproductive BA		
Did not ask to stop the tenure clock for a new child even though it would have helped me to take it, **Noclockstp** [par.]	.161 (.368)	.000
Missed some of my children's important events when they were young, because I did not want to appear uncommitted to my job, **Missedevnts** [par.]	.375 (.484)	−.012
Came back to work sooner than I would have liked after having a new child because I wanted to be taken seriously as an academic, **Shrtleave** [par.]	.212 (.409)	−.016
Work–Family Policies (institution-wide)		
Unpaid leave to care for dependents beyond the 12 weeks required under FMLA	.600 (.491)	
Paid leave to care for dependents, apart from sick or vacation leave	.190 (.390)	
Policy allowing temporary relief from teaching or other modification of duty with no reduction in pay for dependent care	.350 (.478)	
Policy allowing stoppage of the tenure clock	.760 (.428)	
Policy allowing reduced appointment with corresponding reduction in pay for ordinary dependent care responsibilities	.360 (.481)	
Policy allowing faculty a part-time appointment or job sharing	.300 (.458)	
Provide employment assistance for spouses/partners of faculty	.450 (.498)	
Policy scale, **Policy** ($\alpha = .686$)	3.01 (1.91)	

Notes: Sample size approximately 2343. Corr. is the simple correlation coefficient for BA items and the Policy scale. [par.] denotes question only asked of parents. BA data from the Mapping Project, National Survey of Faculty, 2002.

is desirable, a factor analysis suggests it is not multi-dimensional,[9] so it is used as a single scale.

The simple correlations between the policy scale and the individual measures of BA are reported in the far right-hand column of the table. No overall pattern is discernable from the simple correlations, with four being negative and four positive. The latter are contrary to Hypothesis 1.

The probit regression method is appropriate for binary dependent variables and therefore applied here. To understand relevant effect sizes, we report predicted probability changes in the dependent variable for a one unit change in each independent variable (dF/dx), reflecting a shift from zero to unity for dummy variables. The main independent variable of interest is the work–family policy scale. Hypothesis 1 predicts a negative association between the policy scale and BA behaviors.

Given that the BA data were collected at the level of the individual faculty member, while work–family policies were measured at the institutional level, the standard errors for any institutional-level coefficients will tend to be biased downward. In response, all regressions reported here employ robust standard errors clustered by institution.

The baseline regressions respond to the possibility that substantial institutional resources may be positively correlated with both BA and work–family policies. To isolate the effects of policies, dummy control variables are included for the six Carnegie categories (with Research institutions serving as the omitted category), and for the private status of the institution, with a continuous variable for enrollment size also serving to control for institutional resources. (See Table 3.3 for descriptions of all control variables.) We also control for a few relatively independent variables that might confound the relationship between policy and BA behaviors, including dummy variables for women and for employment in chemistry, along with an age quadratic (see Drago et al., 2006).

As discussed earlier, gender is highly correlated with BA behaviors, with women significantly more often reporting the behavior. It seems possible that the effects of work–family policies might diverge by gender, such that the inclusion of both men and women in the same regressions might mask the effects of policies on BA behaviors. Therefore, alternative specifications begin with the baseline regressions replicated for the subsample of women respondents.

Given the cross-sectional character of the data, it is possible that other facets of individuals or the workplace might be linked to both BA and to work–family policies, resulting in spurious correlation. Somewhat differently, heterogeneity across institutions in terms of demographic and

Table 3.3   Control variables for the analysis.

	Mean (S.E.)
Baseline control variables	
Research I or II institution (ommitted category for regressions)	402 (.490)
Doctoral institution[I]	.080 (.271)
Master's institution[I]	.244 (.429)
Bachelor's I institution[I]	.074 (.262)
Bachelor's II institution[I]	.114 (.318)
Associate's Degree institution[I]	.076 (.265)
Technical Specialty institution[I]	.010 (.101)
Enrollment at institution[I]	13442 (11783)
Private	.352 (.478)
Women	.400 (.490)
Chemistry department	.389 (.487)
Age in years	48.7 (10.7)
Age squared	2488 (1066)
Extended controls	
Tenured	.650 (.477)
U.S. born	.871 (.335)
Parent	.622 (.485)
Supervisor Support scale (α = .876)	10.5 (3.44)
Organizational Work–Family Climate scale (α = .818)	34.1 (2.98)
Positive affect variable	−34.1 (6.80)
Prop. of women among tenure-track faculty[I]	.409 (.148)
Pipeline: Prop. women among tenured faculty divided by Prop. of women among tenure-track faculty[I]	.591 (.214)

Notes: Data from the Mapping Project, National Survey of Faculty, 2002, except (I) variables from IPEDs data (NCES 1998).

institutional characteristics might mask any linkages. A straightforward response to both problems required that we repeat the regressions after including extensive control variables, such as whether respondents are tenured, born in the US, or are parents, scales for supervisor support and organizational climate regarding work and family, a control for positive affect, and controls for the success of the institution in hiring and promoting women in tenure-track positions.

As mentioned earlier, Hypothesis 2 suggests the need to control for policy existence where the specific BA item requires the policy be present in

order for respondents to report the behavior. We therefore considered four
of the BA variables. Specifically, whether the individual avoided asking for
a reduced teaching load when needed for family reasons may require that
a modified duties policy be in place before the individual could ask for it.
Similarly, where individuals avoid asking for parental leave, but no paid
leave policy is in place, the reason for the behavior may be financial rather
than connected to bias avoidance. The question of stopping the tenure clock
following the birth of a child may be moot where tenure clock stop policies
do not exist, while taking a short parental leave following the arrival of a
new child may be more meaningful where paid leave policies exist. In each
of these four cases, the baseline regressions are replicated for the subsample where the relevant policy is in place. Hypothesis 2 then predicts that
the policy scale will be negatively correlated with the four BA variables.[10]

Other tests suggested by our earlier discussion concern disciplinary differences and union effects. To test for any mediating effects of discipline
on the relationship between policies and BA behaviors, we replicate the
baseline regressions for subsamples of faculty in chemistry and English. For
union effects, we first add a union variable to the baseline regressions to
ascertain whether the direct effect is negative. We then check for any correlation between unionization and work–family policies to see if unions
are promoting the policies. Finally, we introduce an interaction term to
check whether unions mediate the relationship between policies and reports
of BA behaviors.

Results

Results for the baseline regressions and the indicators of productive bias
avoidance are reported at the top of Table 3.4. Three of the five policy scale

Table 3.4 Work–family policies and productive bias avoidance, probit
regressions.

Regressions	Single	<Kids	Noreduce	Delay	Noleave
Baseline[a]					
Policy coef.	−.0011	.0042	−.0088	.0029	−.0025
(stand. error)	(.0039)	(.004)	(.005)	(.004)	(.008)
X^2	80.6**	125.9**	82.3**	67.1**	41.0**
Pseudo-R^2	.039	.078	.032	.089	.026
N	2203	2183	2152	1365	1448

Table 3.4 *(Con't)*

Regressions	Single	<Kids	Noreduce	Delay	Noleave
Baseline, women subsample[b]					
Policy coef.	−.0076	−.0084	−.0139	.0061	.0068
(stand. error)	(.007)	(.007)	(.007)	(.009)	(.013)
X^2	37.5**	63.8**	26.7**	36.9**	10.75
Pseudo-R^2	.032	.050	.019	.082	.014
N	903	894	884	485	516
Extended controls[c]					
Policy coef.	−.0011	.0064	−.0069	−.0017	−.0035
(stand. error)	(.004)	(.005)	(.005)	(.004)	(.009)
X^2	166.7**	324.3**	407.0**	94.0**	152.9**
Pseudo-R^2	.114	.128	.155	.114	.092
N	1929	1912	1895	1134	1258
Baseline regressions w. selection			*Modified*		*Paid*
on existence of policy for:			*duties*		*leave*
Policy coef.			−.0148		−.0437**
(stand. error)			(.010)		(.014)
X^2			.		.
Pseudo-R^2			.032		.060
N			751		273
Baseline with union var					
Policy coef.	.0001	.0033	−.0088	.0035	−.0014
(stand. error)	(.004)	(.004)	(.005)	(.005)	(.008)
Union coef.	−.0219	.0216	−.0001	−.0072	−.0170
(stand. error)	(.018)	(.020)	(.021)	(.017)	(.030)
X^2	89.0**	127.5**	82.9**	67.6**	42.6*
Pseudo-R^2	.039	.079	.032	.090	.027
N	2200	2180	2149	1363	1447

Notes: * significant at the 5% level, ** significant at the 1% level.
[a] Regression includes as controls six Carnegie classification dummies, excluding Research universities, number of students enrolled, a dummy for private school status, a dummy for women, and for Chemistry department, and an age quadratic.
[b] Baseline controls except gender variable excluded.
[c] Extended controls include those in the baseline plus dummy variables for whether the respondent is tenured, born in the US, or a parent, with relatively continuous measures of supervisor support, the organizational climate around work and family, positive affect, the percent of women among tenure-track faculty, and a pipeline variable for the ratio of the percentage of women among tenured faculty divided by the percentage of women among the tenure-track faculty.

coefficients are negative as predicted, and the largest coefficient in absolute terms – whether the individual avoided asking for a reduced teaching load – is over twice as large as the other coefficients. The effect size is, nonetheless, not large: for the introduction of two additional work–family policies,[11] the probability of reporting this type of BA behavior only declines by around 2 percent.

For the baseline regressions replicated for the subsample of women respondents, we again find three of the five coefficients being negative, and again without significance. Note also that two coefficients switched signs: the indicator for having fewer children than desired is now negatively correlated with the policy scale, while the indicator for not taking parental leave becomes positive. Note that the sizes of the coefficients are around two to three times as large as those for the baseline regressions, with the coefficient for avoiding asking for a reduced teaching load remaining the largest in absolute terms.

Once the extended control variables are introduced, a full four of the coefficients are found to be negative as predicted, although again no statistical significance is found. The only coefficient that remains positive is for the relationship between the policy scale and having fewer children than wanted. From the regressions thus far, we might conclude that support for Hypothesis 1 regarding the negative association between work–family policies and BA behaviors is mixed or at most mildly supportive.

For testing Hypothesis 2, two of the baseline regressions were replicated with subsamples where the policy most relevant to the BA behavior is in place. In both cases, the resulting coefficients are negative as predicted: for no reduction of teaching load and for no parental leave. The latter coefficient is not only negative, but also significant at conventional levels. Further, the effect size is notable, with the introduction of two additional policies reducing estimated reports of avoiding parental leave by over 8 percent. These results are consistent with Hypothesis 2.

Turning to results for unproductive BA, these are reported in Table 3.5. For each of the three types of BA behavior – not asking for a stoppage of the tenure clock for a new child, missing important events in a young child's life, and returning sooner than desired from parental leave – the coefficients are negative as predicted. Statistical significance is absent, however, and the largest coefficient – returning soon from leave – suggests an estimated effect from two additional policies of only a three percentage point reduction in reports of the behavior.

For the subsample of women, again statistical significance is absent. The smallest coefficient – missing events in young children's lives – becomes positive, while the other two remain negative and are again larger in size,

Table 3.5 Work–family policies and unproductive bias avoidance, probit regressions.

Regressions	Noclockstp	Missedevnts	Shrtleave
Baseline[a]			
Policy coef.	−.0085	−.0018	−.0144
(stand. error)	(.006)	(.008)	(.006)*
X^2	50.46**	37.40**	272.92**
Pseudo-R^2	.029	.018	.186
N	1429	1455	1429
Baseline, women subsample[b]			
Policy coef.	−.0125	.0042	−.0162
(stand. error)	(.011)	(.012)	(.014)
X^2	12.6	16.31	29.43**
Pseudo-R^2	.019	.022	.037
N	501	514	510
Extended controls[c]			
Policy coef.	−.0067	−.0032	−.0127
(stand. error)	(.006)	(.008)	(.006)*
X^2	122.8**	226.5**	329.6**
Pseudo-R^2	.096	.113	.291
N	1242	1258	1242
Baseline regressions w. selection on existence of policy for:	Tenure clock stoppage		Paid leave
Policy coef.	−.0090	−.017	
(stand. error)	(.008)	(.014)	
X^2	46.2**	95.5**	
Pseudo-R^2	.027	.230	
N	1077	265	
Baseline with union var			
Policy coef.	−.0061	−.0004	−.0104
(stand. error)	(.006)	(.008)	(.006)
Union coef.	−.0342	−.0187	−.0597
(stand.error)	(.021)	(.031)	(.024)*
X^2	56.1**	38.2**	282.8**
Pseudo-R^2	.031	.019	.190
N	1428	1454	1428

Notes: * significant at the 5% level, ** significant at the 1% level.
[a] Regression includes as controls six Carnegie classification dummies, excluding Research universities, number of students enrolled, a dummy for private school status, a dummy for women, and for Chemistry department, and an age quadratic.
[b] Baseline controls except gender variable excluded.
[c] Extended controls include those in the baseline plus dummy variables for whether the respondent is tenured, born in the US, or a parent, with relatively continuous measures of supervisor support, the organizational climate around work and family, positive affect, the percent of women among tenure-track faculty, and a pipeline variable for the ratio of the percentage of women among tenured faculty divided by the percentage of women among the tenure-track faculty.

as happened in the productive BA baseline regressions when the sample was restricted to women.

Once the extended controls are introduced, the coefficients are again negative as predicted, and the coefficient for returning sooner than desired after parental leave achieves significance. The sizes of the coefficients are not, however, markedly different from those for the baseline regressions. Overall, these results are mildly supportive of Hypothesis 1.

For the tests of Hypothesis 2, two regressions were performed using baseline controls and relevant subsamples of respondents. For respondents in institutions with tenure clock stoppage policies, the effects of policies on avoiding stopping the tenure clock are estimated to be negative, although the size of the coefficient is similar to that for the baseline regression for the complete sample. For individuals at institutions with paid leave policies, returning sooner than desired from parental leave is negatively associated with the policy scale although, again, the size of the effect is similar to that found in the original baseline regression.

In general, the regression results presented here provide some support for Hypothesis 1, that institutional work–family policies will be negatively correlated with faculty reports of bias avoidance behaviors. In contrast to the simple correlations, where half were negative and half positive, results reported in Tables 3.4 and 3.5 show 18 of 24 coefficients (75 percent) as negative, although statistical significance was achieved for only one coefficient. For Hypothesis 2, regarding a negative correlation where relevant policies exist, the evidence is consistently supportive, since all four coefficients are negative, and the effect size in the one case where significance was found may be sufficiently large to warrant consideration in policy discussions.

As discussed earlier, we tested whether policy effects on BA vary across the disciplines of English and chemistry. The baseline regressions for the subsample of faculty in English departments yielded results that are identical in sign and similar in size to those reported for the baseline regressions for the subsample of women (see Tables 3.6 and 3.7). Given that women in the sample are concentrated within English departments, it seems reasonable to conclude that the stronger, and typically negative, association between BA and work–family policies we found for women may in fact be confounded by a related effect for English departments.

The results for chemistry faculty were generally quite weak with regard to productive BA, except for a larger negative coefficient on the variable for not taking parental leave (−.014). For unproductive BA, the chemistry results basically mirrored those for the overall sample (consistently negative coefficients), except the effect sizes were estimated to be around twice

Table 3.6 English and chemistry subsample results, work–family policies and productive bias avoidance, probit regressions.

Regressions	Single	<Kids	Noreduce	Delay	Noleave
Baseline, English subsample					
Policy coef.	−.0028	−.001	−.0120	.0031	.0083
(stand. error)	(.005)	(.005)	(.007)	(.005)	(.010)
X^2	47.5**	102.3**	59.2**	47.6**	18.0
Pseudo-R^2	.049	.080	.036	.085	.020
N	1335	1322	1311	776	830
Baseline, Chemistry subsample					
Policy coef.	.0027	.0123	.0003	.0030	−.0138
(stand. error)	(.007)	(.008)	(.009)	(.006)	(.012)
X^2	32.8**	76.6**	36.7**	56.1**	38.0**
Pseudo-R^2	.038	.087	.037	.107	.054
N	868	861	841	861	618

Notes: Data from the Mapping Project, National Survey of Faculty, 2002, except (I) variables from IPEDs data (NCES 1998).

Table 3.7 English and chemistry subsample results, work–family policies and unproductive bias avoidance, probit regressions.

Regressions	Noclockstp	Missedevnts	Shrtleave
Baseline, English subsample			
Policy coef.	−.0043	.0003	−.0071
(stand. error)	(.008)	(.010)	(.008)
X^2	19.5	36.5**	181.3**
Pseudo-R^2	.028	.028	.186
N	816	830	822
Baseline, Chemistry subsample			
Policy coef.	−.0117	−.0069	−.021
(stand. error)	(.008)	(.014)	(.010)*
X^2	29.6**	7.9	120.8**
Pseudo-R^2	.044	.010	.203
N	613	625	607

Notes: Data from the Mapping Project, National Survey of Faculty, 2002, except (I) variables from IPEDs data (NCES 1998).

as large. Why chemistry departments would help work–family policies reduce the degree of unproductive BA is not obvious.

Finally, turning to union effects, results reported at the bottom of Tables 3.4 and 3.5 replicate the baseline regressions after adding a variable for faculty unionization. For six of the eight regressions, the coefficient for the policy scale shrinks after the union variable is included, and the coefficient for staying single even switches from negative to positive (albeit a tiny positive). The union coefficient is negative across seven of the eight regressions, although only one coefficient achieves statistical significance. Further, given that the union coefficient expresses the estimated probability change for movement from not unionized to unionized, union effects are generally larger than those found for work–family policies, with three of the negative coefficients for productive BA suggesting effect sizes of around 2 percent, and the coefficients for unproductive BA ranging from about 2 percent to almost 6 percent.

These results suggest that some sort of interaction is at work. As a check, we regressed the policy scale against unionization using ordinary least squares since the scale is relatively continuous and found an estimated positive coefficient of 1.161, which is statistically significant.[12] This figure implies that unionized colleges and universities in the sample averaged over one additional work–family policy compared to their non-union counterparts.

To test for mediating effects, an additional term for the interaction of unions and the policy-scale was added to the regressions just discussed. The results (not reported) showed the interaction coefficient taking the opposite sign of the union and policy scale coefficients in six of the eight regressions, suggesting the results are not very meaningful due to collinearity between the variables. A reasonable conclusion here is that faculty unions tend to promote work–family policies and may mitigate BA behaviors either directly or indirectly by leveraging policies.

Discussion

Using data from thousands of faculty and the hundreds of institutions where they are employed, we provide the first analysis of the potential linkage between work–family policies and bias avoidance behaviors. Bias avoidance behaviors involve the strategic minimizing or hiding of family commitments and would not be necessary in an ideal workplace. More troubling, bias avoidance behaviors disproportionately affect women, and are indicative of gender inequality in the workplace. To move towards gender equity will almost certainly require the alleviation of conditions promoting bias avoidance behaviors.

At present, there is a virtual explosion of work–family policies within academe. As earlier studies suggest, these policies will likely have salutary effects on faculty commitment, job satisfaction, and retention. Will they also reduce the incidence of bias avoidance behaviors?

Given the evidence presented here, it appears that work–family policies typically exert a small negative effect on the prevalence of bias avoidance behaviors. It seems safe to conclude that work–family policies alone will be insufficient to induce substantial reductions in bias avoidance behaviors. Earlier research using the faculty data analyzed here suggests that supportive supervisors exert a far stronger effect on BA behaviors, while the results presented here suggest that faculty unions may help both in terms of directly mitigating the behaviors and by promoting policy development.

In terms of gender, the results suggest that policies are slightly more effective for reducing the incidence of bias avoidance among women. However, disciplinary results suggest that the gender effect might be driven by behavior in departments with large numbers of women (e.g., in English) rather than by the behavior of individual women per se.

We do not know whether these results would generalize to other professions and industries. The theoretical construction of the notion of bias avoidance suggests it is mainly limited to managers and professionals. Without further research, we cannot provide even an informed estimate of the likely effects of work–family policies on bias avoidance in other employment arenas.

The bias avoidance items included here cover only a small portion of relevant behaviors. For example, we did not ask about absenteeism for family purposes and how often faculty attribute these absences to personal illness. Nor did we ask about faculty pretending to work at home while engaging in day-to-day child care. Indeed, because bias avoidance behaviors are strategic, they are practically limitless in scope. We cannot, therefore, conclude that we have provided a definitive answer to the question of the relationship between work–family policies and bias avoidance behaviors.

Further research to define this relationship could proceed in two very different directions. On the one hand, qualitative research might help to better understand how faculty or other employees view work–family policies and any linkages to bias avoidance behaviors. Simply asking people about these issues could shed much light on the question. On the other hand, survey research might explore employees' beliefs regarding biases against caregiving. A relatively small set of survey items could illuminate different types of bias and thereby the sources of bias avoidance behaviors.

Regardless of the caveats just expressed, it seems safe to conclude that work–family policies are worthwhile, but other aspects of the academic workplace also need to change if bias avoidance behaviors are to be eliminated and gender equity achieved.

Acknowledgements

We thank the Alfred P. Sloan Foundation for funding this research, and particularly Kathleen Christensen of the Foundation for her support and insights.

Notes

1   See "Joint Statement by the Nine Presidents on Gender Equity in Higher Education," December 6, 2005 [http://ucfamilyedge.berkeley.edu].
2   See Bhattacharjee (2005) and Williams (2005), respectively.
3   On low utilization rates for formal policies, see Bailyn (1993), Kossek, Noe and DeMarr (1999) and Williams (2000).
4   Specifically, Budd and Mumford (2004) found, for comparable matched samples, that 42 percent of managers, but only 27 percent of employees report that parental leave is available, while 12 percent of managers but only 4 percent of employees report the availability of a workplace nursery or child care subsidy, with 18 percent of managers but only 9 percent of employees reporting that working at home is available (see Budd & Mumford, 2004, Table 1).
5   The Population Research Institute at Penn State calculated these figures from data provided by the NCES for tenure- and non-tenure-line teachers.
6   For a list and discussion of excluded questions, see Drago et al. (2006).
7   We undersampled the numerous, though typically small, institutions in the lower tiers of the Carnegie categories. See Drago and Colbeck (2003) for a complete discussion and the number of schools sampled within each category.
8   The lack of email directories may either signal privacy policies, and hence an exclusive organizational climate, or a scarcity of financial resources, in either case motivating high levels of BA. Case study results from an excluded school supports both possibilities (see Drago & Colbeck, 2003, Chapter 3, Case Study 5).
9   Exclusion of the item on paid dependent care leave raises the α to .709. However, given that this particular item is the lone high-cost policy included in the list, it seemed important to retain it. In a factor analysis, all items loaded most heavily, and positively, on a single factor, excepting the paid dependent care leave item, which loaded most heavily on a second factor. Note that two questions were included in the survey regarding reduced time appointments for faculty, one regarding such appointments under ordinary circumstances

and the other for extraordinary circumstances. The inclusion of both items would have arguably double-counted the importance of this type of policy, so only the item on the availability of reduced time appointments in ordinary circumstances was included. Use of the alternative item reduces the scale reliability only slightly, to .684. The survey also permits the construction of a scale based on formal policy existence, although the α for that scale is only .649, suggesting it not be used in the present analysis.

10 Since the sample selection process makes one particular policy a constant within the policy scale, we are actually using variance among the other items in the policy scale to drive any negative correlation between BA behaviors and policies.

11 A two-unit change in the policy scale is close to the standard deviation for the variable, hence is a reasonable approximation to variability actually found across the institutions in the sample (see Table 3.1).

12 As in the main regressions, robust standard errors were calculated. That figure for the union coefficient is .419, yielding significance at the 1 percent level.

References

American Council on Education (2005). *An agenda for excellence: Creating flexibility in tenure-track faculty careers.* Washington, DC: Ace.

Bailyn, L. (1993). *Breaking the mold.* New York: Free Press.

Behson, S. J. (2004). The relative contribution of formal and informal organizational work–family support. *Journal of Vocational Behavior, 66,* 487–500.

Bhattacharjee, Y. (2005). Princeton resets family-friendly tenure clock. *Science, 309,* 1308.

Bianchi, S. M., Milkie, M. A., Sayer, L. C., & Robinson, J. P. (2000). Is anyone doing the housework? Trends in the gender division of household labor. *Social Forces, 79,* 191–228.

Bond, J. T., Galinksy, E., & Swanberg, J. E. (1998). *The 1997 national study of the changing workforce.* New York: Families and Work Institute.

Budd, J. W., & Mumford, K. A. (2004). Trade unions and family-friendly policies in Britain. *Industrial and Labor Relations Review, 57,* 204–222.

Drago, R., & Colbeck, C. (2003). *Final report for the mapping project.* Retrieved January 25, 2007 from Pennsylvania State University, University Park Work/ Family Newsgroup Web site: http://lsir.la.psu.edu/workfam/mappingproject.htm

Drago, R., Colbeck, C., Stauffer, K. D., Pirretti, A., Burkum, K., Fazioli, J. et al. (2006). The avoidance of bias against caregiving: The case of academic faculty. *American Behavioral Scientist, 49,* 1222–1247.

Eaton, S. C. (2003). If you can use them: Flexibility policies, organizational commitment, and perceived performance. *Industrial Relations, 42,* 145–167.

Firestein, N. (2000). Labor unions speak for working families. In E. Appelbaum (Ed.), *Balancing acts: Easing the burdens and improving the options for working families* (pp. 127–138). Washington, DC: Economic Policy Institute.

Folbre, N. (2001). *The invisible heart: Economics and family values*. New York: New Press.

Friedman, D. E., Rimsky, C., & Johnson, A. (1996). *College and university reference guide to work–family programs*. New York: Families & Work Institute.

Gerstel, N., & Clawson, D. (2002). Unions' responses to family concerns. In N. Gerstel, D. Clawson, & R. Zussman (Eds.), *Families at work: Expanding the bounds* (pp. 317–342). Nashville, TN: Vanderbilt University Press.

Grover, S. L., & Crooker, K. J. (1995). Who appreciates family-responsive human resource policies: The impact of family-friendly policies on the organizational attachment of parents and non-parents. *Personnel Psychology, 48,* 271–288.

Hochschild, A. R. (1997). *The time bind: When work becomes home and home becomes work*. New York: Henry Holt.

Hollenshead, C., Sullivan, B., Smith, G., August, L., & Hamilton, S. (2005). Work–family policies in higher education: An analysis of survey data and case studies of policy implementation. In J. Curtis (Ed.), *The challenge of balancing faculty careers and family work* (pp. 41–65). New Directions for Higher Education, no. 130. San Francisco: Wiley Periodicals, Inc.

Integrated Postsecondary Education Data System – Fall Staff: 1997 [Data file]. Washington DC: National Center for Education Statistics.

Judiesch, M. K., & Lyness, K. (1999). Left behind? The impact of leaves of absence on managers' career success. *Academy of Management Journal, 42,* 641–651.

Kossek, E. E., Noe, R. A., & DeMarr, B. J. (1999). Work–family role synthesis: Individual and organizational determinants. *International Journal of Conflict Management, 10,* 102–129.

MIT (Massachusetts Institute of Technology). (1999). A study on the status of women faculty in science at MIT. Cambridge, MA: MIT.

Sandberg, J. F., & Hofferth, S. L. (2001). Changes in children's time with parents, United States, 1981–1997. *Demography, 38,* 423–436.

Thomas, L. T., & Ganster, D. C. (1995). Impact of family-supportive work variables on work–family conflict and strain: A control perspective. *Journal of Applied Psychology, 80,* 6–15.

Thompson, C. A., Beauvais, L. L., & Lyness, K. S. (1999). When work–family benefits are not enough: The influence of work–family culture on benefit utilization, organizational attachment, and work–family conflict. *Journal of Vocational Behavior, 54,* 392–415.

Waldfogel, J. (1998). Understanding the "Family gap" in pay for women with children. *Journal of Economic Perspectives, 12,* 137–156.

Warren, J. A., & Johnson, P. J. (1995). The impact of workplace support on work–family role strain. *Family Relations, 44,* 163–169.

Williams, J. (2000). *Unbending gender*. New York: Oxford University Press.

Williams, J. (2005). Are your parental-leave policies legal? *The Chronicle of Higher Education, 51*(23), C1.

Part II

Culture, Age, and Sexual Orientation: How Does Society Deal with Diversity?

Part II

Introduction

Amy Marcus-Newhall

The majority of research on mothers employed outside of the home has focused on the experiences of white, middle and upper-middle class, heterosexual women (Casad, this volume; LeMaster, Marcus-Newhall, Casad, & Silverman, 2004). Findings from this privileged subset of women have been overgeneralized to the more diverse group of women.

The *American Heritage Dictionary of the English Language* (1978) defines privilege as "a special advantage, immunity, permission, right, or benefit granted to or enjoyed by an individual, class, or caste." Social norms are derived from privilege such that what is normal in society is created by those who have privilege (Wildman & Davis, 2000). This normalization of privilege leads to others who do not match the privilege to be judged by these standards and measured against the characteristics that are held by those who are privileged.

"Whiteness" refers to those who have privilege and can include such categories as males, heterosexuals, European Americans, and those of middle to higher socioeconomic status; all of those who are outside of "Whiteness" are viewed as the "Other" (McIntosh, 2007). Within work-family research, a form of "Whiteness" is being used as the norm to judge all others. The use of this "typical" mother employed outside of the home limits our ability to understand the similarities and differences experienced by groups who do not represent this privilege. Although certain aspects of the work-family intersection may be common to working mothers of differing demographic variables (e.g., ethnicity, race, sexual orientation, age), there likely are important differences in the ways that groups experience the work-family interface. By having "whiteness" as the norm, other important variables are missing. It is imperative to extend the research to include different categories, as well as variables of importance to these different categories, that may influence the conditions of the work-family intersection on outcome variables such as quality of life, work stress and overall satisfaction.

In Part II, researchers discuss, both theoretically and empirically, variables that have not been addressed sufficiently within the research literature or the broader public sphere. First, Barnett and Gareis introduce community as the critical missing link in work-family research. They discuss the importance of community and community resources to meet the demands of families' complicated lives with both work and family. Their new measure, Community Resource Fit, assesses the extent to which the resources of a residential community (e.g., work, public transportation, school, school transportation, after-school program, and after-school transportation) meet the needs of its working families with school-age children. They studied families with two full-time employed parents, families with one full-time employed parent and one part-time or non-employed parent, and families with a full-time employed single parent and concluded that school and work resource fit were related to several quality of life and well-being outcomes.

Marcus-Newhall, Casad, LeMaster, Peraza, and Silverman studied how race and socioeconomic status (SES) influence the work-family experience. They collected quantitative and qualitative data from mothers employed outside of the home who were Latina or White and were from higher or lower socioeconomic status. In addition, they examined two psychological factors, machismo and religiosity, that moderate the experiences of employed mothers. Interesting patterns of results were found for each of these variables on outcome measures such as work stress, job satisfaction, and overall satisfaction. Regardless of race, SES, machismo, or religiosity, one similarity shared by these mothers employed outside of the home was that they needed many of the same resources to better juggle the demands of home and work such as help from their spouse, family members, and friends as well as access to affordable high quality daycare.

Cleveland reviews the literature and stresses the importance of understanding the meaning of age within both the work and family domains. Society is changing such that family sizes are smaller, people are living longer, and the workforce is aging. These trends have a number of effects on how work and family issues are framed. One such effect is that as the proportion of the population over 65 increases, there are an increasing number of workers that need to care for their aging parents or relative in addition to their children. In order to address these changes and subsequent effects, the author reviews what it means to be old at work, the stereotypes associated with older people, actual changes associated with increasing age, actual and perceived age changes in the work and family context, and linkages among work and family as aging occurs.

Badgett frames the workplace issues encountered by gay, lesbian, and bisexual (GLB) people within the work-family intersection rather than solely within the more traditional civil rights approach. She reviews what is known about GLB families and workers as well as discussing how the workplace for GLB people has improved but remains far from equal. The author discusses how GLB workers experience the same challenges in balancing work and family responsibilities as heterosexual workers but they do so in the context of sexual orientation discrimination. Moreover, GLB workers also encounter compensation discrimination because their domestic partners and children are rarely included in health care or survivor benefits. This chapter emphasizes the costs to employees and to employers of the differential treatment of GLB workers and their families and develops a business case for change.

References

LeMaster, J., Marcus-Newhall, A., Casad, B. J., & Silverman, N. (2004). Life experiences of working and stay-at-home mothers. In J. L. Chin (Ed.), *The psychology of prejudice and discrimination: Gender and sexual orientation* (Vol. 3., pp. 61–91). Westport, CT: Greenwood Press.

McIntosh, P. (2007). White privilege: Unpacking the invisible knapsack, reprinted in Paula S. Rothenberg (Ed.), *Race, Class, and Gender in the United States* (7th ed., pp. 177–182). New York: Worth Publishers.

Wildman, S. M., & Davis, A. A. (2000). Language and silence: Making systems of privilege visible. In M. Adams, W. J. Blumenfeld, R. Castaneda, H. W. Hackman, M. L. Peters, & X. Zuniga (Eds.), *Readings for diversity and social justice* (pp. 50–60). New York: Routledge.

4

Community: The Critical Missing Link in Work–Family Research

Rosalind Chait Barnett and
Karen C. Gareis

Work–family research is a relatively new and interdisciplinary field; to date, much work–family research has focused on workplace stressors (e.g., Fox & Dwyer, 1999; Kossek & Ozeki, 1998). This focus has yielded important insights and has even led to changes in policies and benefits. For example, flexible work arrangements and parental leave policies derived from research on work hours; research on supervisor and coworker support prompted the development of Employee Assistance Programs (EAP) services; and on-site day care and family referral services derived from research on and advocacy for workers' dependent care needs.

As with all emerging fields, some norms and assumptions have influenced the direction of theory and research. In U.S. work–family research, there is a growing consensus that corporations alone cannot meet the many needs of working families, especially those with children. It is time to explore the role of community – not only as a context outside of work, but as a provider of resources essential to the well-being of working families.

Community resources are key to the well-being of resident families, regardless of socioeconomic class or geographic location. The presence of adequate resources can facilitate the lives of working families, whereas inadequate resources constitute a hindrance. We argue that the distress that working parents experience in striving to meet family needs contributes to their overall distress, net of the effect of such well-studied stressors as job demands and job control (Karasek & Theorell, 1990). These newly identified stressors are important because they may significantly increase employees' health risks and decrease their productivity on the job.

Family Structure and Community Life

The two-earner family is now the modal American family. As of 2005, 61.3 percent of U.S. couples with children were dual-earner families (U.S. Bureau of Labor Statistics, 2006a). Parents of minor children constituted 35.2 percent of the labor force – close to 50 million employees – in 2005 (percentage computed by the authors from data in U.S. Bureau of Labor Statistics, 2006a, 2006b). Yet major aspects of work and community life remain organized as though all households were families with an adult available to participate in household-sustaining but non-earning activities. The breadwinner-homemaker family no longer prevails, but much local commerce and many public services do not accommodate this reality. This disjuncture burdens dual-earner families, single parents with substantial custodianship, and even those without dependents who work full-time.

Workers and their families reside in communities, and their lives are structured in part by the resources that are available to them in those communities. Full-day kindergarten is unavailable in most locales. School days end between 2:00 p.m. and 3:00 p.m.; school conferences and parent-teacher meetings are often scheduled during the workday. Most doctors and dentists see patients only during regular work hours. Retail and local service businesses often do not open until 10:00 a.m., and many are closed on Sundays. Public transit authorities run limited holiday schedules on many workdays each year. Home repairs and deliveries can usually be scheduled only during regular work hours. Although there has been some movement toward aligning working adults' needs and community resources – for example, post offices and banks are now routinely open half-days on Saturdays – the needs of working adults (and their children) are often left unfulfilled or are inadequately met by their communities.

Of course, communities vary in the resources they provide to their residents, thereby affecting the ability of resident families to thrive. "Community resources" may encompass a broad array of assets – good schools, libraries, well-lit playgrounds, sidewalks, bike trails, community facilities for teens and elders, accessible healthcare services, safe and adequate transportation, preschool programs, after-school programs, cultural events sponsorship, and accessible retail business zones.

Workers residing in communities with abundant resources are likely to report better quality-of-life and well-being outcomes than those who reside in communities with meager community resources. Community resources can function as supports for working families in a number of ways. For example, if a state or the federal government does not mandate the provision of maternity leave, women may be forced to leave their jobs when they give birth unless their community has infant day care resources that they can easily use. Workers who lose their jobs in a poor economy may be better able to find new employment if their communities provide commuting options to areas with more employment opportunities. The impact of work schedule changes on the employee's work-social system will vary depending on how well communities meet the needs of the family. Thus, community resources have both direct and indirect effects on work–family outcomes. When the resources of a community are well matched to the needs of a working family, that family's "community resource fit" is good. When the resources are poorly matched to a family's needs, their community resource fit is poor.

Theoretical Background

"Community" in Work–Family Thought

In contrast to fields such as child development and crime prevention, until recently, "community" has not had a conceptual presence in the work–family literature. However, despite growing interest in community among work–family scholars (e.g., Bookman, 2004, 2005; Lewis & Cooper, 1999; Voydanoff, 2001a, 2001b), research to date has been scattered and non-cumulative. One important reason for the current state of affairs is the absence of an agreed-upon definition of community.

What do we mean by community? Most of us are members of several communities: communities of shared interests, religious faith, political leanings, professional identification, employment, interpersonal commitments, common history, shared values, shared practices, and common territory. Each of these communities has its own resources (e.g., a holy book, a set of traditions, a political platform). The focus of this chapter is on residential communities and the resources available within them, building on Bookman's definition of community as a "real geographical community that shape[s] family life and work" (2005, p. 144). We also build on Voydanoff's (2001a) analysis of community. She identifies six different aspects: (1) community social organization; (2) social networks; (3) social capital; (4) formal volunteering and informal helping; (5) sense of community; and (6) community satisfaction. Our approach is linked to the satisfaction aspect of community. In contrast to researchers who focus on community-level resources such as crime rate, poverty level, academic performance of the school system, (e.g., Sampson & Groves, 1989), we assess individual community members' perceptions of how well community resources meet their needs using a newly developed quantitative measure.

The Community-Families-Work Model

In the Community-Families-Work Model, decisions about one's work and family arrangements are influenced by such factors as: (1) regional economic welfare, social structures, and cultural norms; (2) the availability of community resources that support family life (for example, after-school arrangements and transportation to and from those arrangements); (3) workplace policies and practices; and (4) objective job characteristics and actual work conditions (e.g., flexibility, expectations about productivity, and task discretion). This model is dynamic and recursive. When economic conditions are good, the job environment is favorable, and workers may need fewer services from the community. At the same time, a healthy tax base arising from high rates of employment means that communities have more resources with which to provide working families with the services they need. When economic times are bad, job conditions are less favorable, while communities concomitantly have fewer resources to allocate.

Additionally, and independently of the state of the economy, workers' needs for community resources vary as a function of the life stage of members of their social system. For example, families with young children seek day care services; families with older children need after-school activities and programs; families with older or otherwise vulnerable adult dependents may need visiting nurses, physical therapists, or social workers. When families' communities fail to meet their needs – because the needed resource is either unavailable or inaccessible – individuals may have to alter their labor force participation in order to provide more direct care.

The resources that communities direct toward working families are not only a reflection of socioeconomic factors; social philosophy informs priorities at many levels. In tight economic times, some communities raise taxes to preserve such services as full-day kindergarten and after-school programs. Other communities choose to cut services. Thus, communities differ in the extent to which the needs of working families are a priority, and they allocate their resources accordingly.

Unavailable or inaccessible community resources may result in increased distress and in disruptions and ultimately, lower productivity at work.

Reduced productivity, especially reduced work hours, generally means fewer economic resources, making it even harder for working parents to obtain the community resources they need. Again, these effects are complex and recursive – inadequate community resources create strains for working parents (Maguire, 2003), and distressed working parents create demands for community resources.

The Family Schedule Coordination Study

Our recently completed Family Schedule Coordination Study had two major aims: (1) to develop a psychometrically sound measure of community resource fit; and (2) to discover how community resource fit is related to quality-of-life and well-being outcomes in a sample of working families with at least one school-aged child. For the purposes of this study, we defined working families as those in which at least one parent is employed full-time.

Developing a Measure of Community Resource Fit

For the first phase of the study, we conducted and audiotaped open-ended telephone interviews with 17 parents and guardians of at least one school-aged (i.e., in grades K-12) child about each family member's work or school schedule and transportation needs and asked them about what factors in the community, the children's schools, and the parents' workplaces made it easier or more difficult to coordinate family schedules and transportation. The audiotapes were transcribed and analyzed to develop a measure of community resource fit.

Content analysis of the responses to the open-ended questions yielded a 36-item community resource fit measure (see Appendix). The items ask participants to rate their level of satisfaction with 36 aspects of community resources clustering into six categories of resources: work, public transportation, school, school transportation, after-school programs, and after-school transportation. (As shown in the Appendix, we suggest cutting the measure to 31 items by combining several of the after-school transportation items and dropping two of the less relevant after-school program items.)

The overall community resource fit scale has excellent psychometric properties (see Table 4.1), with Cronbach's alphas of .86 for mothers and .90 for fathers. Cronbach's alphas for the subscales were within the moderate to high range (alphas ranged from .73 to .95 for mothers and from .69

Table 4.1   Cronbach's alphas for community resource fit scale and subscales.

	Mothers $(n = 86)$	Fathers $(n = 59)$
Global score	.86	.90
Work	.77	.80
Public transportation	.91	.81
School	.73	.69
School transportation	.77	.73
After-school programs	.88	.85
After-school transportation	.95	.91

to .91 for fathers). There were no significant differences in global community resource fit scores by gender; $t(143) = 0.65$, $p = .515$ or by family type; $F(2,79) = 0.05$, $p = .955$. Overall, the means for mothers (*Mean* = 4.90, *SD* = 0.73) and fathers (*Mean* = 4.97, *SD* = 0.64) were almost one point above the midpoint of the 7-point scale from 1 (*completely dissatisfied*) to 7 (*completely satisfied*), or close to *slightly satisfied*.

Preliminary Findings Linking Community Resource Fit to Outcomes

For the second phase of the study, we conducted face-to-face quantitative interviews with parents in three different types of families defined by parent marital status and employment pattern: (1) dual-earner families had one parent who was employed full-time and a second parent who was employed at least 20 hours per week ($n = 29$ families, or 58 individual parents); (2) one-main-breadwinner families had one parent who was employed full-time and a second parent who was not employed or who was employed for fewer than 20 hours per week ($n = 29$ families, or 58 individuals); and (3) single-parent families had one parent who was employed full-time ($n = 29$ families, or 29 individuals). Thus, we interviewed a total of 145 parents from 87 families.

All of the families have at least one school-aged (i.e., in grades K-12) child and reside in an urban community near Boston. The city has a broad range on socioeconomic status, with a median household income of $54,000. It has a fairly small poverty population: 7.0 percent of the population live below the poverty line, and 1.9 percent receive public assistance. Almost

Table 4.2 Descriptive characteristics of sample.

	Dual-earner[a] (n = 29) Mean (SD)	One main breadwinner[b] (n = 29) Mean (SD)	Single parent[c] (n = 29) Mean (SD)
Mother's work hours	37.5 (11.6)	10.6 (16.2)	43.0 (8.8)
Father's work hours	47.6 (9.3)	41.2 (24.4)	50.0 (—)
Per capita household income	$24,371 (9,889)	$19,044 (7,149)	$15,956 (10,261)
Number of children at home	2.1 (0.8)	2.4 (0.7)	1.8 (0.7)

Notes: [a] In dual-earner families, 20 mothers were full-time employed and 9 mothers were part-time employed (at least 20 hours per week). All 29 fathers were full-time employed.
[b] In one-main-breadwinner families, 6 mothers were full-time employed, 5 mothers were part-time employed (fewer than 20 hours per week), and 18 mothers were not employed. In these same families, 23 husbands were full-time employed, 1 father was part-time employed (fewer than 20 hours per week), and 5 fathers were not employed.
[c] Of the single-parent families, 28 were headed by mothers and 1 was headed by a father; all single parents were full-time employed.

one-fifth (17.1 percent) of residents are minorities. Table 4.2 shows descriptive data on this sample.

In this preliminary analysis, we focus on *work resource fit* and *school resource fit* because, as the places where parents and children spend the largest chunk of their weekdays, these seem to be the most crucial aspects of community resource fit for working families of school-aged children. In addition, because employed parents work in all types of settings and under all types of conditions, and because the community we studied has nine different public schools as well as several private schools, there should be substantial variability on these aspects of community resource fit. We predict that high levels of work and school resource fit should be associated with positive quality-of-life and well-being outcomes for employed parents.

There were few significant correlations between the two community resource fit subscales and the parents' demographics (i.e., number of work hours, size of employing company, number of children at home, parents' education, and household income). However, not unexpectedly, mothers who worked longer hours reported lower school resource fit and fathers with higher household incomes reported higher work resource fit. Surprisingly, for both mothers and fathers, having more children at home was associated with reporting higher school resource fit. Future research is needed to determine whether this unexpected finding replicates and, if so, to determine what the mechanism of this effect might be.

In preliminary analyses, we tested whether work and school resource fit were related to seven quality-of-life and well-being outcomes: psychological distress, work-to-family conflict, family-to-work conflict, job disruptions, job-role quality, marital-role quality, and parent-role quality. We computed partial correlations controlling for negative affectivity, a mood-dispositional trait to view the world negatively that is thought to account for spuriously high correlations between self-report measures of predictor and outcome variables, especially in cross-sectional analyses (Brennan & Barnett, 1998; Barnett & Gareis, 2007a, b).

Because work resource fit and four of the seven outcome variables are only available for parents who are employed, we focus on three groups of parents in these analyses: employed mothers in two-parent families ($n = 40$), employed fathers in two-parent families ($n = 53$), and employed single mothers ($n = 28$; there was only one single father in the sample). It is important to note that this is an exploratory study: Our sample is located in a single community, and our sample size is fairly small, especially when further subdivided by gender, employment status, and single-parent vs. two-parent families. Therefore, results should be interpreted with caution.

Partial correlations for the three groups of parents are shown in Table 4.3. Overall, stronger results were found for married mothers than for married

Table 4.3 Partial correlations linking work and school resource fit to outcomes among employed parents.

Resource fit	Married mothers ($n = 40$)		Married fathers ($n = 53$)		Single mothers ($n = 28$)	
	Work	School	Work	School	Work	School
Distress	−.54*	.03	−.16	−.42*	−.26	.19
Work-to-family conflict	−.74*	−.04	−.40*	−.01	−.10	−.05
Family-to-work conflict	−.34*	−.24	−.06	−.04	−.29	−.04
Job disruptions	−.23	−.34*	.00	−.00	−.34†	−.07
Job-role quality	.51*	−.08	.69*	.33*	.61*	.17
Marital-role quality	.11	.33*	−.12	.09	−	−
Parent-role quality	−.02	.31†	−.16	.11	.02	.05

Notes: * $p < .05$, † $p < .10$; All correlations controlled for negative affectivity.

fathers. This pattern of findings may reflect the fact that mothers, who tend to take more responsibility for child care, may be more reliant on their community's resources than are fathers. Specifically, we found that when married mothers are satisfied with the extent to which their workplaces are meeting their needs, they report significantly lower work-to-family and family-to-work conflict and psychological distress and significantly higher job-role quality. If they are satisfied with the extent to which their child's school is meeting their needs, they report significantly fewer job disruptions, significantly higher marital-role quality, and marginally higher parent-role quality.

For married fathers, those with high work resource fit report significantly lower work-to-family conflict and significantly higher job-role quality. To the extent that married fathers are satisfied with the way their children's schools meet their needs, they report significantly lower psychological distress and significantly higher job-role quality. Thus, for work resource fit, married fathers show some of the same patterns of outcomes as married mothers, but school resource fit appears to be related to different outcomes for them than for the married mothers.

It is easy to imagine that single mothers might be more dependent on community resources than are their married counterparts. Surprisingly, however, there were few relationships linking resource fit to quality-of-life and well-being outcomes among the single mothers. Like the married mothers and fathers, those with high work resource fit reported significantly higher job-role quality. They also reported marginally lower levels of job disruptions. Inspecting the magnitude of the correlation coefficients in Table 4.3 suggests that some of the relationships between work resource fit and other outcomes found among the married mothers might be replicated among the single mothers if the sample size were larger. However, this does not appear to be the case for school resource fit, where there is little evidence of links to the outcomes we assessed.

These counterintuitive findings appear to be at least partially due to the fact that single mothers report that their children and unspecified "others" take more responsibility for household and child-care labor and for planning, coordinating, and keeping track of family members' day-to-day schedules than is reported by mothers in the other two family types. Even after correcting for the average age of the children in the household, single mothers report getting significantly more help from others with child care; $F(2,82) = 3.53$, $p = .034$ and marginally more help from their children with household tasks; $F(2,82) = 2.50$, $p = .089$ than do married mothers.

Conclusions

To summarize, we have developed a 36-item measure of community resource fit with good psychometric properties that warrants further study. The measure is comprised of six moderately intercorrelated subscales assessing resource fit in the areas of work, public transportation, school, school transportation, after-school program, and after-school transportation resources.

Even with very small samples, we found interesting patterns of results linking two aspects of community resource fit, work and school resource fit, to a variety of quality-of-life and well-being outcomes among employed parents. We plan to conduct further, more sophisticated regression analyses to look more closely at the process by which various aspects of community resource fit may act as safety valves for working parents. We also plan to look at couple-level effects, including crossover effects from one spouse to the other, among the families that are headed by married couples.

Directions for Future Research

Previous models of the work–family relationship should be expanded to include the direct and indirect effects of the availability and adequacy of community resources. Our findings suggest the need to more fully identify the range of community resources that impact worker distress. The scale could easily be modified to add or subtract modules assessing resource fit in areas of concern to different types of families or to families in different stages of the life cycle. For example, families with preschoolers could be asked about community resource fit in the area of day care, while families with adult- or elder-care responsibilities could be asked about similar aspects of community-based resources for adults and elders.

In addition, our findings suggest that community-level policies and practices can act as resources that alleviate stress for working parents. Given the pattern of results we found, such community resources appear to have consequences for individuals (e.g., psychological distress), for families (e.g., marital-role quality, parent-role quality), and for workplaces (e.g., job disruptions, job-role quality). Such community-level policies and practices might include, for example, coordinated start and end times for elementary, middle, and high schools in the community; engaging, high-quality after-school programs that are located in schools to avoid the need for transportation, or in central locations with safe, reliable transportation provided;

and workplaces that allow for flex-time and flex-place scheduling, such as programs allowing parents to work in the office during school hours and then from home during the after-school hours.

Further research into the impact of community resources on worker outcomes is clearly needed. Future research should be longitudinal in design and include employees from a wider range of workplaces and residential communities – inner city, exurban, suburban, and rural – with a broader range of community resources. With a larger and more heterogeneous sample, we will be better able to detect relationships between the full range of community resource fit subscales and outcomes of interest.

Finally, the community resource fit measure can provide information useful to community leaders as they decide how to allocate tax revenues. The subscales can help decision makers determine which community aspects need to be better designed to meet the needs of the working families the town wants to attract. The measure also could be used to evaluate the success of community initiatives aimed at attracting working families. Finally, communities and businesses in communities can use scores on the community resource fit measure to recruit residents and workers. A town that scores high on meeting the needs of working families has a powerful marketing tool. In a competitive world, being able to justifiably claim that your community has designed its services to make the lives of working families easier to manage might prove to be a winning strategy.

Acknowledgements

Data for this analysis were gathered under a grant from the Alfred P. Sloan Foundation to the first author. We gratefully acknowledge the contributions of Claudia Morgan, PhD, to an earlier draft of this chapter. Correspondence concerning this analysis should be addressed to Rosalind Chait Barnett, Brandeis University, Women's Studies Research Center, Mailstop 079, 515 South Street, Waltham, MA 02453-2720, rbarnett@brandeis.edu, (781) 736-2287, fax (781) 736-4881.

Appendix: Community Resource Fit Measure[1]

Work Resources

1   The way your work schedule fits with your child(ren)'s schedule(s)
2   The flexibility available at your workplace to handle emergencies

3   The flexibility available at your workplace to attend to family needs
4   Your ability to work at home if necessary
5   Your ability to bring child(ren) to work if necessary

Public Transportation Resources

6   The way the public transportation schedule fits with your own travel
    needs
7   The way the public transportation schedule fits with your child(ren)'s
    travel needs
8   The convenience of your own access to public transportation
9   The convenience of your child(ren)'s access to public transportation
10 The way that the available public transportation routes meet your
    own travel needs
11 The way that the available public transportation routes meet your
    child(ren)'s travel needs

School Resources

12 The time(s) your child(ren)'s school(s) start(s) in the morning
13 The time(s) your child(ren)'s school(s) let(s) out in the afternoon
14 The way different schools in the community coordinate their schedules
    with each other
15 The scheduling of school meetings, parent conferences, and events
16 Communication between the school(s) and parents
17 Scheduling of extracurricular activities

School Transportation Resources

18 Where the children wait to be picked up by the school bus in the
    morning
19 Where the children wait to be picked up by the school bus in the
    afternoon
20 The reliability of school bus transportation to and from school
21 The availability and scheduling of late buses

After-School Program Resources[2]

22 The availability of after-school programs
23 The cost of after-school programs

24   The location of after-school programs
25   The scheduling of after-school programs
26   The availability of supervised programs for children on early release days
27   The availability of supervised programs for children during school vacations
28   Communication between after-school program providers and parents
29   The expectations of after-school program providers for parental involvement

After-School Transportation Resources[3]

30   The availability of transportation between school and after-school activities
31   The scheduling of transportation between school and after-school activities
32   The reliability of transportation between school and after-school activities
33   The availability of transportation between after-school activities and home
34   The scheduling of transportation between after-school activities and home
35   The reliability of transportation between after-school activities and home
36   The cost of transportation to and/or from after-school activities

Notes

1   Response scale ranged from 1 (*completely dissatisfied*) to 7 (*completely satisfied*).
2   We suggest dropping items 26 and 27 in the interests of shortening the measure.
3   We suggest combining items 30 and 33, items 31 and 34, and items 32 and 35 into three items about the availability, scheduling, and reliability of transportation "to and from after-school activities" in the interests of shortening the measure.

References

Barnett, R. C., & Gareis, K. C. (2007a, April). *Does community resource fit matter to fathers? A Study of employed fathers of school-aged children.* Paper presented at the 2nd International Conference on Community, Work and Family, Lisbon, Portugal.

Barnett, R. C., & Gareis, K. C. (2007b, April). *The importance of satisfactory work arrangements: A study of employed women with school-aged children.* Paper presented at the 2nd International Conference on Community, Work and Families, Lisbon, Portugal.

Bookman, A. (2004). *Starting in our own backyards: How working families can build community and survive the new economy.* New York: Routledge.

Bookman, A. (2005). Can employers be good neighbors? Redesigning the workplace–community interface. In S. M. Bianchi, L. M. Casper, & R. B. King (Eds.), *Work, family, health, and well-being* (pp. 141–156). Mahwah, NJ: Lawrence Erlbaum Associates.

Brennan, R. T., & Barnett, R. C. (1998). Negative affectivity: How serious a threat to self-report studies of psychological distress? *Women's Health: Research on Gender, Behavior, and Policy, 4*(4), 369–383.

Fox, M. L., & Dwyer, D. J. (1999). An investigation of the effects of time and involvement in the relationship between stressors and work–family conflict. *Journal of Occupational Health Psychology, 4*(2), 164–174.

Karasek, R., & Theorell, T. (1990). *Healthy work: Stress, productivity, and the reconstruction of working life.* New York: Basic Books, Inc.

Kossek, E. E., & Ozeki, C. (1998). Work-family conflict, policies, and the job-life satisfaction relationship: A review and directions for organizational behavior–human resources research. *Journal of Applied Psychology, 83*(2), 139–149.

Lewis, S., & Cooper, C. L. (1999). The work-family research agenda in changing contexts. *Journal of Occupational Health Psychology, 4*(4), 382–393.

Maguire, K. (2003, April 16). Bus fees eyed for K-6 school kids. *Associated Press State and Local Wire.*

Sampson, R. J., & Groves, W. B. (1989). Community structure and crime: Testing social-disorganization theory. *American Journal of Sociology, 94*(4), 774–802.

U.S. Bureau of Labor Statistics (2006a). *Employment characteristics of families in 2005* (News Release, April 27, 2006). Retrieved August 31, 2006, from http://www.bls.gov/news.release/pdf/famee.pdf

U.S. Bureau of Labor Statistics (2006b). *State and regional unemployment, 2005 annual averages* (News Release, March 1, 2006). Retrieved August 31, 2006, from, http://www.bls.gov/news.release/pdf/srgune.pdf

Voydanoff, P. (2001a). Conceptualizing community in the context of work and family. *Community, Work & Family, 4*(2), 133–156.

Voydanoff, P. (2001b). Incorporating community into work and family research: A review of basic relationships. *Human Relations, 54*(12), 1609–1637.

5

Mothers' Work-Life Experiences: The Role of Cultural Factors

Amy Marcus-Newhall, Bettina J. Casad, Judith LeMaster, Jennifer Peraza, and Nicole Silverman

Despite the prevalence of dual-earner families (White & Rogers, 2000), societal views continue to reflect expectations characteristic of the traditional family type of the breadwinning father and stay-at-home mother (Ganong & Coleman, 1995). Society's expectation for women to focus primarily on family rather than career has been coined the "motherhood mandate" (Russo, 1976). The motherhood mandate states that motherhood is the ultimate form of femininity and should be the center of women's identities, leaving career aspirations as a secondary aspect of identity. According to the motherhood mandate, the best mothers are constantly available to their children and happily sacrifice their own needs and career aspirations to meet the needs of their families. In addition to the view that mothers should stay at home with their children, mothers who choose to work outside of the home are evaluated more negatively than their stay-at-home counterparts (Bridges & Orza, 1993; Marcus-Newhall, LeMaster, Casad, & Shaked, 2007). Moreover, employed mothers experience role strain, which occurs when multiple roles create incompatible pressures such that participation in one role is made more difficult by participation in another role (Greenhaus, Parasuraman, Granrose, Rabinowitz, & Beutell, 1989).

Social role theory (Eagly & Steffen, 1984) provides one explanation for traditional expectations for families, which linger despite changes in families' realities. It is the historical social roles of men as breadwinners and women as caretakers that are largely responsible for the strong association between men and work and women and motherhood (Eagly, Wood, &

Diekman, 2000). When men and women violate their social roles by being a stay-at-home father or career-oriented mother, negative evaluations are likely to result (e.g., Doherty, 1998).

Spillover theory (Barnett, 1994; Kanter, 1977) provides an alternative to social role theory by suggesting that the work and family domains are not separate spheres. Rather, each domain affects the other in both positive and negative ways. Satisfaction (or dissatisfaction) with one aspect of a woman's life, such as marriage and motherhood, is likely to influence her satisfaction (or dissatisfaction) in another aspect of her life, such as the workplace. The work-family interface is interactive and affected by psychological moderating variables such as coping skills, gender role ideologies, self-esteem, and perceived control.

The purpose of the present research was to examine several cultural moderating variables for employed mothers outside of the home. Although the topic of working mothers has received much attention in the past few decades (e.g., Friedman & Greenhaus, 2000; Halpern & Murphy, 2005; Halpern & Riggio, 2006; Riggio & Halpern, 2006), most research has focused on the experiences of white, middle and upper-middle class women, to the exclusion of women from other groups (Casad, this volume; LeMaster, Marcus-Newhall, Casad, & Silverman, 2004). Therefore, we focused on the race (Latina and White) and socioeconomic status (higher and lower) of employed mothers as well as two psychological variables we expected to moderate the work experiences of married women – machismo (higher and lower) and religiosity (higher and lower). Specifically, we were interested in the following questions: Do Latina and White mothers employed outside of the home differ in their experiences with work-family interaction? That is, do they experience similar or different levels of satisfaction and stress? Are machismo and religiosity cultural determinants that differentially influence the experiences of working mothers? What is the relationship between socioeconomic status and their experiences? Finally, based on the answers to these questions, do different ethnic groups need culturally relevant programming and resources?

Latina American Mothers Employed Outside of the Home

The literature on work-family balance has focused primarily on those who are European American and middle class (LeMaster et al., 2004). However, a growing body of research concerning the experiences of Latina working mothers serves to remind us of the ongoing negative effects of prejudice and discrimination. For example, many Latina women have experienced discrimination in their jobs (Amaro, Russo, & Johnson, 1987); such negative experiences in the workplace have been associated with decreased psychological well-being and increased role strain (Amaro et al.), The researchers also identified an in-home contributor to Latina women's experiences with role strain – having a Latino partner. Latino partners tended to be less supportive when their wives or female partners work outside the home. Some researchers have suggested that traditional sex-role beliefs and cultural expectations may increase the role burdens of Latina women (e.g., Amaro et al.; Hondagneu-Sotelo & Avila, 1997).

However, Latina mothers do not necessarily succumb to the pressures of cultural stereotypes (e.g., Herrera & Del Campo, 1995). In one study, Latina mothers did not believe they should be solely responsible for maintaining the household while also working outside of the home. Instead, they valued egalitarianism in their relationships and expected their husbands to help with household tasks and childcare responsibilities (Herrera & Del Campo). Further, married Latina women tend to be less satisfied working outside of the home if they hold traditional gender-role beliefs (e.g., Krause & Markides, 1985).

Latinas with Latino partners may have less support for working outside the home because of traditional gender role beliefs (Amaro et al., 1987). Researchers have suggested that traditional gender role beliefs and cultural expectations may increase the role burdens of Latina women (e.g., Amaro et al.; Hondagneu-Sotelo & Avila, 1997). Cultural norms for age at first marriage, number of children, and age of childbirth differ for cultural groups within the US (South, 1993). Latinas more commonly marry and have children at a younger age and have more children than Whites, and this pattern is socially sanctioned (South). The trend for White women is to delay marriage and children to pursue an education and/or financial stability (McCauley & Salter, 1995).

Researchers also have found that certain factors are associated with higher risk for psychological distress and depression among Latina women. In general, perceived spousal support, help with the housework, having a prestigious occupation, and fluency with the English language are associated with lower levels of depression and psychological distress and an overall higher self-reported health status (e.g., Amaro et al., 1987; Krause & Markides, 1985; Rivera, Torres, & Carre, 1997). In contrast, having a high-stress job, a low income, and experiencing discrimination in the workplace are related to depression and psychological distress (e.g., Amaro et al.).

Socioeconomic Status (SES) Differences
in Work-Family Balance

It is undoubtedly the case that the family socioeconomic status is increased when a mother is employed outside of the home. A mother's employment status affects important aspects of her family life, career, and psychological well-being. Advantages of maternal employment include greater financial security, a sense of contributing to society, and personal fulfillment (Ferree, 1984; Hodson, 1996; Moen, 1992; Perry-Jenkins, Repetti, & Crouter, 2000). Disadvantages of maternal employment are role strain (Kossek & Ozeki, 1998), taking on more housework and child care responsibilities than one's partner (Hewlett, 2002; Hochschild, 1989; LeMaster et al., 2004), and spending less time with one's children (Sanders & Bullen, 2005).

Family SES is generally considered an important factor in work-family balance issues, such as children's psychological well-being (Louis & Zhao, 2002), happiness (Peiro, 2005), parental life satisfaction (Hintsa et al., 2006), job strain (Hintsa et al., 2006), and relationship satisfaction (Menninger, 2006). Hintsa and colleagues (2006) examined family SES and parental life satisfaction as predictors of job strain in adulthood. Using structural equation modeling, they found that both family SES and parental life satisfaction predicted job strain for adults. In addition, lower family SES predicted lower educational achievement, which then predicted higher job strain.

However, Kahneman, Krueger, Schkade, Schwarz, and Stone (2006) demonstrated that the belief that people of higher SES have more positive moods is partially an illusory correlation. When participants were asked to predict the percentage of time they are in a bad mood for both higher SES (greater than $100,000) and lower SES (lower than $20,000) groups, the differences were quite large (25.7 percent and 57.7 percent respectively). However, when participants of higher and lower SES provided estimates of the time they are in a bad mood in minutes and hours instead of as a percentage of total time, the differences were much smaller (19.8 percent and 32 percent respectively). People with higher SES indicated greater satisfaction with their lives, but to a lesser degree than people assumed. Further, Louis and Zhao (2002) examined the influences of family SES during childhood on life satisfaction in adulthood and found that, controlling for such variables as age, gender, race, and education, family SES was predictive of more positive adult life satisfaction but accounted for only a small percentage of the variance.

Machismo

Another factor that affects work-life experiences is machismo. Although the definition of machismo is inconsistent in the literature (Ferrari, 2001), it is usually interpreted as the traditional and patriarchal male sex role found in Latin based cultures (Hondagneu-Sotelo, 1993). Torres (1998) argues that much of the research misrepresents machismo by exploiting its negative characteristics (e.g., aggression, dominance, oppression of women) and ignoring its positive characteristics (e.g., self-respect, desire to provide and protect one's family, responsibility). Deyoung and Zigler (1994) suggest that machismo ideology may be viewed as beneficial to women in that it encourages their husbands to provide for and protect them and their children. Further, by subordinating their needs to those of their family, women earn a lifetime of support from their husbands and children and in this way gain some control in the family. Torres (1998) also argues that machismo may be more complex than traditional sex roles, particularly in the context of the family, by interacting with other values such as familismo, dignidad, respeto, and personalismo (Torres, 1998). Despite complications defining the exact meaning of machismo, there remains a fundamental concept of traditional gender role beliefs at the core of all the definitions.

There is little research exploring the role of machismo in employed women's work-life experiences. Research exploring machismo in the family often focuses on child rearing practices. Ferrari (2001) found that machismo predicted punitive measures for punishment among fathers but not among mothers. Deyoung and Zigler (1994) found similar results among Guyanese, whose race is not of Latin origin but whose culture embraces machismo ideology in that machismo values positively correlated with punitive child rearing practices.

One's social values are likely to influence interpretations of the traditional sex role beliefs of machismo. Some research suggests that there may be an acculturation factor involved in how women perceive their responsibilities toward their families and how they behave to meet those responsibilities (Guendelman, Malin, Herr-Harthoron, & Vargas, 2001). These researchers found that women in rural Mexican sites felt more obligated to their husbands and therefore dedicated themselves to domestic duties. In these households, it was up to the husband to decide whether their wives could or should work outside of the home. Among Mexican immigrant women in California, the immigration process requires more flexibility on the part of the family. Although there is usually an agreement that the wife will need to work to help support the family, it is understood that the husband is still the head of the household. Finally, Mexican American women who were born in the US, but whose parents or grandparents were born in Mexico, asserted more independence. These women are more likely to make the choice to work or not work of their own accord, without their husbands' approval (Guendelman et al., 2001). Guendelman and colleagues assert that the women in rural Mexican sites live in a collectivist society where the "concept of the self is weak" (p. 1808) whereas Mexican American women live in an individualistic society.

Religiosity

A final factor that may play a role in mother's work-life experiences is religiosity. Studies have shown that religiosity and religious coping are associated with better psychological adjustment and increases in life satisfaction (Park, Cohen, & Herb, 1990; Tix & Frazier, 1998). Tix and Frazier (1998) examined religious coping among patients and their significant others after kidney transplant surgery. Religious coping was not mediated by other measured variables such as social support and perceived control, but rather had a direct influence on participants' life satisfaction and psychological adjustment. Religious coping may be beneficial for less severe stressful events than transplant surgery as well. Park et al. (1990) surveyed college students several times during a semester and found that religious coping was associated with better psychological adjustment. Although religion may be beneficial when facing life stress, Tix and Frazier suggest that religion is more effective in promoting positive feelings, such as increased life satisfaction, than preventing negative feelings, such as distress.

Although research does not specifically show that religion may help buffer work and family stress for mothers, it does suggest that religion may have a positive influence in the family. Reviewing four articles, Snarey and Dollahite (2001) found evidence that religiosity strengthened family relationships. Brody, Stoneman, and Flor (1996) also found a positive correlation between religiosity and family relations among African Americans from the rural South such that greater formal religiosity was associated with more cohesive family relationships.

Religion also influences sex role beliefs and life style choices (Hare-Mustin, Bennett, & Broderick, 1983). Mahalik and Lagan (2001) found that gender role conflict and gender role stress were associated with religiosity for men. Further, results suggested that gender role stress not only may be influenced by one's religion, but also may be influenced differently depending on one's religion. For example, those who identify as Catholic may be more likely to adhere to traditional sex roles in and out of the family as well as make decisions about work and family based on traditional values (Hare-Mustin et al., 1983). This is unsurprising because religions have different beliefs and place emphasis on different values.

Culture may interact with religion to influence gender role beliefs. For example, Catholic women in Mexico view the Virgin Mary as a symbol for motherhood (Guendelman et al., 2001). This perspective of motherhood is related to the sex role marianismo, which is the female sex role that is associated with the male sex role machismo. Using the Virgin Mary as an example and consistent with Catholicism's value of self-sacrifice, marianismo suggests that women are "morally and spiritually superior to men" (Torres, 1998, p. 18), but yet women still are expected to yield to male authority and self-sacrifice for their children and husbands (Torres, 1998).

The Present Study

To examine the relationships among race (Latina, White), machismo (higher, lower), religiosity (higher, lower), socioeconomic status (higher, lower), and psychological well-being in the work-family domain (overall satisfaction, job satisfaction, and work stress), mothers employed outside of the home were surveyed and interviewed. Based on existing literature (e.g., Hintsa et al., 2006; Kahneman et al., 2006), mothers with lower SES were predicted to have less overall satisfaction, less job satisfaction, and greater work stress than higher SES mothers. This same pattern was predicted for Latina mothers as compared to White mothers (Amaro et al., 1987). Due to the limited research on the relationships among machismo, religiosity, and work-life balance outcomes, the predicted interactions were exploratory. However, machismo and religiosity were predicted to affect the outcome variables differentially. Greater endorsement of machismo was predicted to impact works stress, job satisfaction, and overall life satisfaction for mothers employed outside of the home more negatively because despite research that suggests there is excessive focus on the negative characteristics of machismo (e.g., Deyoung & Zigler, 1994; Torres, 1998), other evidence indicates there are significant burdens associated with traditional gender role beliefs (e.g., Guendelman et al., 2001; Marcus-Newhall, LeMaster et al., 2007; Russo, 1976). Conversely, greater endorsement of religiosity was predicted to lead to more positive outcomes because it would serve as a buffer for the pressures of lower SES mothers and the discrimination faced by Latinas (e.g., Park et al., 1990; Snarey & Dollahite, 2001; Tix & Frazier, 1998). To contextualize the predicted effects for race, SES, machismo, and religiosity, the effects of the interaction between each psychological factor (machismo and religiosity) with race and SES on work-life outcomes were explored.

Method

Participants

We used a multi-phase mixed sampling approach in which we implemented criterion, convenience, opportunistic, random, and snowball sampling. Participants only were selected if they: (1) were employed full time (35+ hours) outside the home; (2) had at least one child under age 6 living in the home; (3) were married; (4) were age 18 or older; and (5) were Latina or White. Mothers employed outside of the home were recruited from: (1) a local shopping center; (2) advertisements published in the *Los Angeles Times*, the *Local Community Values* newspaper, and two college newspapers; (3) flyers distributed at several daycare centers in Los Angeles County; (4) flyers posted at local businesses; and (5) phone lists of selected family households in Los Angeles County. In addition, we used opportunistic sampling by following leads provided by our participants such as mailing flyers to suggested organizations and through snowball sampling of previous participants' referrals. The total sample size was 55, with 24 Latina and 31 White mothers employed outside of the home. The lowest household income range (employed mothers' and fathers' joint income) was between $10,000 and $15,000 and the highest household income was $125,000 or more. The average household income was between $75,000 and $100,000.

Materials

Participants completed a mail survey assessing variables relevant to work-life experiences. The predictor variables were race, SES, religiosity, and machismo. The criterion variables were overall satisfaction, job satisfaction, and work stress.

Race of participant was assessed by self-identification. Participants were excluded if they did not identify as Latina or White. Socioeconomic status was assessed by the annual income (prior to taxes) of both the employed mother and father. A proxy measure of SES used for mostly descriptive purposes was the mothers' job prestige. Job prestige was assessed by ranking the mothers' self-reported job type according to a prestige index (Davis, Smith, Hodge, Nakao, & Treas, 1991), with higher rankings indicating higher prestige. Religiosity was measured with items such as "I take my religion very seriously" and "It is important to do what my religion says is right," measured on a four item 7-point Likert scale ranging from 1 (*strongly disagree*) to 7 (*strongly agree*) with 4 as a neutral midpoint (*neither agree nor disagree*; adapted from Scott, 1965). Participants also provided their religious affiliation, if any, and their frequency of attending religious services. A scale measuring adherence to the Latino cultural values of machismo adapted from Cuellar, Arnold, and Gonzalez (1995) was used. Machismo was measured with nine items on a 7-point Likert scale ranging from 1 (*strongly disagree*) to 7 (*strongly agree*) with 4 as a neutral midpoint (*neither agree nor disagree*). An example question was "Boys should not be allowed to play with dolls."

We measured several outcome variables including overall life satisfaction, job satisfaction, and work stress. Overall life satisfaction was assessed with a two item 7-point Likert scale ranging from 1 (*very dissatisfied*) to 7 (*very satisfied*) with 4 as a neutral midpoint (*neither agree nor disagree*; adapted from Pavot & Diener, 1993). The two items were, "Living your life close to your ideal" and "Getting the important things you want in life." Job satisfaction was measured by two items on a 7-point Likert scale ranging from 1 (*very dissatisfied*) to 7 (*very satisfied*) with 4 as a neutral midpoint (*neither agree nor disagree*; adapted from Gooler, 1996). The items were "I am satisfied with my overall career," and "In general, I don't like my job." Work stress was assessed on a three item 7-point Likert scale ranging from 1 (*strongly disagree*) to 7 (*strongly agree*) with 4 as a neutral midpoint (*neither agree nor disagree*; adapted from Gooler, 1996). The questions were, "I feel pressured at work," "I experience recurring frustration in my job," and "I have a very stressful job."

Motivation for employment was included to help describe mothers' work experiences. Four different motivations for employment were assessed on a scale from 1 (*strongly disagree*) to 7 (*strongly agree*) with 4 as a neutral midpoint (*neither agree nor disagree*), including passion, personal fulfillment, financial need, and pressure from spouse. A complete report of all measures used in the study can be found in Marcus-Newhall, Casad, LeMaster, & Silverman (2007).

To assess similarities and differences in Latina and White mothers' needs for resources, in the interview we asked "When you need help juggling your responsibilities as a mother, what kinds of things help you?" This question was followed by the probe "What kinds of things are not available to you that you feel would help you juggle your life as a mother?" There were several other questions in the interview, results of which are reported elsewhere (LeMaster, Casad, & Marcus-Newhall, 2007; Marcus-Newhall, LeMaster et al., 2007).

Design and Procedure

A correlational design was used to examine the relationships among the predictor variables (race, SES, religiosity, and machismo) and the criterion variables (overall satisfaction, job satisfaction, and work stress).

Participants were prescreened to ensure that they fit the criteria for participating in the study. They were mailed a survey and when the completed survey was received, participants were contacted by phone to complete a tape-recorded telephone interview. Participants were assured that their responses would be kept private and their name would not be linked to their responses. After receiving verbal consent to record the interview, the interviewer proceeded with the interview protocol. Upon completion, participants were sent $20 as compensation and thanked for their time.

Results

Before testing the hypotheses, several demographic analyses were computed to eliminate alternative explanations for the results. There were no differences between Latina and White participants on SES, $t(51) = 1.24$, $p = .22$, with an average household income between $75,000 to $100,000 for both groups. Nor were there differences in religiosity, $t(53) = 1.39$, $p = .17$ ($M_{White} = 4.48$, $SD_{White} = 1.45$, $M_{Latina} = 5.0$, $SD_{Latina} = 1.33$). However, Latinas did report greater endorsement of machismo ($M = 2.91$, $SD = 1.06$) than did the White participants ($M = 1.89$, $SD = .95$), $t(54) = 3.80$, $p = .001$.

To test the hypothesis that cultural factors, including race, SES, machismo, and religiosity are interrelated and predict experiences of stress and satisfaction, several multiple hierarchical regression analyses were computed. All continuous predictor variables were centered to reduce multicollinearity (Aiken & West, 1991). The dichotomous independent variable (race) was dummy coded as zeros and ones. All main effects were entered into step 1, all possible 2-way interactions were entered in step 2, and the 3-way interactions of interest were entered in step 3. If the 3-way interactions were significant, simple effects tests were calculated by recoding the continuous variables as higher or lower (1 *SD* above or below the mean) to test the relationship with the outcome variables and different levels of the predictor variables.

Work Stress

Two separate hierarchical multiple regression analyses were computed. The 3-way interaction for machismo, race, and SES approached significance, $\Delta R^2 = .062$, $F(1, 44) = 5.60$, $p = .064$, $\beta = .525$, $t(44) = 1.90$, $p = .064$. The 3-way interaction of religion, race, and SES was not significant, $\Delta R^2 = .02$, $F(1, 45) = .983$, $p = .327$, nor were any lower order effects.

Simple Effects Tests for Higher Machismo
Among participants with greater endorsement of machismo, Whites with lower SES had higher work stress ($M = 6.86$) than Latinas ($M = 5.24$), $\beta = .64$, $t(44) = 1.94$, $p = .059$ (see Figure 5.1). In contrast, Whites with higher SES had lower work stress ($M = 1.54$) than Latinas ($M = 2.84$), $\beta = -.472$, $t(44) = 1.94$, $p = .059$.

An examination of the questions assessing the reasons the mothers work full time showed a negative correlation between SES and financial need, $r(24) = -.487$, $p = .012$, and a negative correlation between SES and pressure from spouse, $r(24) = -.465$, $p = .017$. Further examination of these correlations by race showed that both Whites and Latinas have a negative relationship pattern between SES and financial need, $r(6) = -.667$, $p = .071$ and $r(16) = -.431$, $p = .074$, respectively. However, only Latinas showed a significant negative correlation between SES and pressure from spouse, $r(16) = -.678$, $p = .002$, (Whites: $r(6) = .298$, $p = .473$).

Simple effects tests for lower machismo
Among participants with less endorsement of machismo, Whites with higher SES had higher work stress ($M = 5.91$) than Latinas ($M = 4.77$), $\beta = .651$, $t(44) = 1.94$, $p = .059$ (see Figure 1). In contrast, Whites with lower SES had lower work stress ($M = 1.95$) than Latinas ($M = 3.00$), $\beta = -.651$, $t(44) = 1.94$, $p = .059$.

An examination of the careers of higher SES White and Latina mothers showed a positive correlation between job prestige and SES, $r(24) = .417$, $p = .033$, supporting the claim that higher SES mothers likely have more demanding careers. Further support for this explanation was found in two marginal positive correlations between job prestige and role conflict, $r(25) = .344$, $p = .079$, and job prestige and work stress, $r(25) = .309$, $p = .117$.

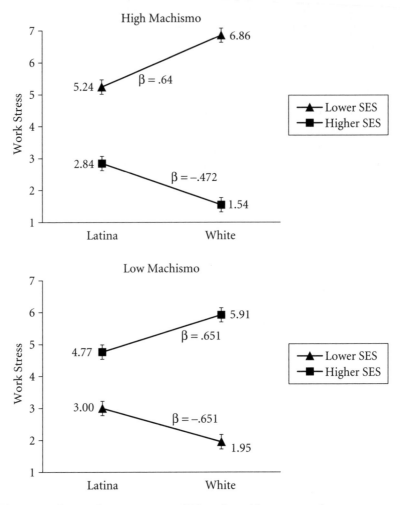

Figure 5.1   Interaction among race, SES, and machismo on work stress.

Job Satisfaction

Two hierarchical multiple regression analyses were computed. The 3-way interaction of machismo, race, and SES was significant, $\Delta R^2 = .098$, $F(1, 36) = 4.38$, $p = .043$, $\beta = .715$, $t(36) = 2.09$, $p = .043$. The 3-way interaction of religion, race, and SES was not found to be significant, $\Delta R^2 = .042$, $F(1, 37) = 1.98$, $p = .168$, nor were any other lower order effects.

Simple Effects Tests for Higher Machismo
Among participants with greater endorsement of machismo, Latinas with lower SES had higher job satisfaction ($M = 6.52$) than Whites ($M = 5.72$), $\beta = -.210$, $t(35) = 1.98$, $p = .056$ (see Figure 5.2). In contrast, Whites with higher SES had higher job satisfaction ($M = 6.40$) than Latinas ($M = 4.93$), $\beta = .468$, $t(35) = 1.98$, $p = .056$.

One explanation for why mothers with lower SES may have high job satisfaction is that their jobs tend to be less demanding and stressful than those for mothers from higher SES categories. For mothers with lower SES, there was a negative correlation between work stress and job satisfaction, $r(13) = -.537$, $p = .039$. Overall, mothers' job prestige showed a marginal trend with work stress, $r(52) = .506$, $p = .135$. The data for work stress showed that lower SES Latinas had lower work stress than Whites. This pattern is consistent with the present finding that lower SES Latinas have greater job satisfaction than lower SES Whites.

Whites with higher SES had higher job satisfaction than Latinas. It is interesting to note that among women with higher machismo beliefs, SES and job satisfaction were positively correlated, but only for Whites, $r(5) = .758$, $p = .048$. Although mothers high in machismo beliefs likely resent being employed full time, White mothers with higher SES may enjoy the benefits of higher financial stability, which is related to job satisfaction.

Simple Effects Tests for Lower Machismo
Among participants with less endorsement of machismo, Whites with lower SES had higher job satisfaction ($M = 6.44$) than Latinas ($M = 5.34$), $\beta = .247$, $t(35) = 1.98$, $p = .056$ (see Figure 5.2). In contrast, Whites with higher SES had lower job satisfaction ($M = 2.61$) than Latinas ($M = 5.11$), $\beta = -.662$, $t(35) = 1.98$, $p = .056$.

The finding that lower SES mothers have relatively high job satisfaction is consistent with the interpretation that lower prestige jobs may be less stressful because they are less demanding. White mothers with higher SES had less job satisfaction than Latinas. This is likely related to job prestige and the demands that accompany higher prestige jobs. There is a positive correlation between job prestige and SES for White mothers, $r(28) = .488$, $p = .011$, but not for Latinas.

Interestingly, the finding that higher SES White mothers who endorse traditional sex roles had a positive correlation between job satisfaction and SES does not hold for their less traditional counterparts. That is, higher SES White mothers who have less endorsement of traditional sex roles do

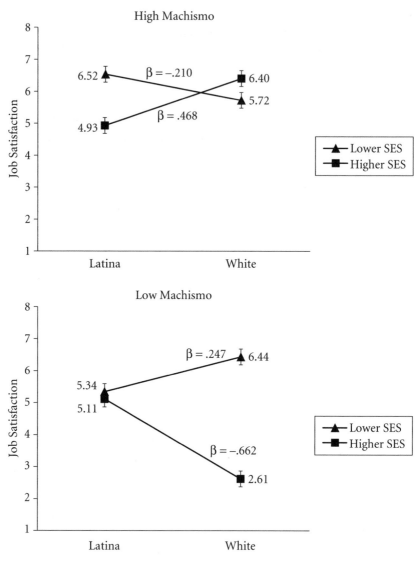

Figure 5.2   Interaction among race, SES, and machismo on job satisfaction.

not report a relationship between job satisfaction and SES, $r(15) = -.254$, $p = .325$. This lends support to the conclusion that higher SES mothers with less traditional sex role beliefs are likely employed for reasons of personal fulfillment. Indeed mothers with higher prestige jobs report working because they are passionate about their jobs, $r(25) = .502$, $p = .008$, and for personal fulfillment, $r(24) = .546$, $p = .004$. Therefore, their lower job satisfaction is likely due to the demanding nature of higher prestige jobs. The finding that higher SES White mothers have less job satisfaction than higher SES Latinas further supports the high-stress prestigious job interpretation because White mothers tend to have more prestigious jobs than Latinas, $t(53) = 2.055$, $p = .045$ (Whites: $M = 55.37$, $SD = 12.22$; Latinas: $M = 48.72$, $SD = 11.48$) but do not differ on household income, $t(51) = 1.24$, $p = .22$.

Overall Satisfaction

Two hierarchical multiple regression analyses were computed. Counter to the prior results, the 3-way interaction of machismo, race, and SES was not found to be significant, $\Delta R^2 = .005$, $F(1, 47) = .312$, $p = .579$, nor was there a significant two-way interaction. There was a trend toward a main effect of SES, $R^2 = .13$, $F(3, 51) = 2.55$, $p = .066$ such that participants with higher SES had higher life satisfaction, $r(53) = .323$, $p = .008$. However partially consistent with prediction, the hierarchical multiple regression analysis computed for religiosity, SES, and race was significant, $\Delta R^2 = .07$, $F(1, 45) = 4.27$, $p = .045$, $\beta = .384$, $t(45) = 2.065$, $p = .045$.

Simple Effects Tests for Latinas

Among Latina participants with higher SES, mothers with higher religiosity had somewhat higher overall life satisfaction ($M = 5.48$) than mothers with lower religiosity ($M = 5.08$), $\beta = -.302$, $t(45) = 1.749$, $p = .087$ (see Figure 5.3). Among Latina participants with lower SES, mothers with higher religiosity had higher overall life satisfaction ($M = 4.10$) than mothers with lower religiosity ($M = 2.75$), $\beta = -.587$, $t(45) = 2.706$, $p = .01$. Mothers with higher SES tended to have high overall life satisfaction regardless of religiosity. However, Latinas lower in SES had higher overall life satisfaction if they also were higher in religiosity.

Simple Effects Tests for Whites

Among White participants with higher SES, mothers with higher religiosity showed a trend toward higher overall life satisfaction ($M = 5.98$) than mothers with lower religiosity ($M = 3.45$), $\beta = -.322$, $t(45) = 1.848$, $p = .071$ (see Figure 5.3). Among White participants with lower SES, mothers with higher religiosity had similar overall life satisfaction ($M = 4.46$) as mothers with lower religiosity ($M = 4.13$), $\beta = -.223$, $t(45) = .942$, $p = .351$. In contrast to the findings for Latina mothers, the satisfaction of White mothers with lower SES was not related to religiosity.

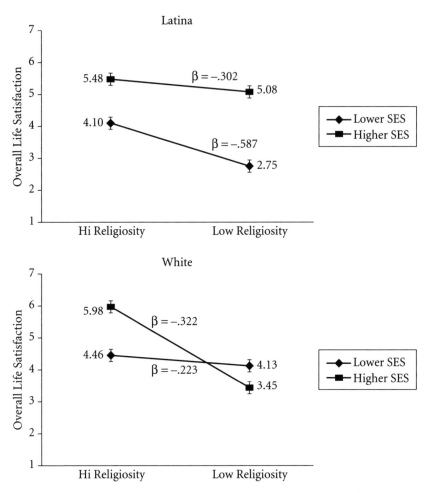

Figure 5.3   Interaction among race, SES, and religiosity on overall life satisfaction.

Resources to Integrate Work and Family

During the interview, participants were asked "When you need help juggling your responsibilities as a mother, what kinds of things help you?" This question was followed by the probe "What kinds of things are not available to you that you feel would help you juggle your life as a mother?" The results indicated that Latina and White mothers desire similar resources, but the resources were mentioned with different frequencies among participants (see Table 5.1).

Table 5.1   Frequencies of resources needed mentioned by Latina and
White mothers.

Rank	Latina mothers	Rank	White mothers
1	Help from spouse (24)	1	Help from other family members (27)
1	Help from other family members (24)	2	Access to affordable high quality daycare (24)
1	Access to affordable high quality daycare (24)	3	More time (21)
2	Help from friends (19)	4	Help from friends (19)
3	Job resources (e.g., flextime) (14)	5	Help from spouse (15)
3	More time (14)	5	Having family close by (15)
3	Support from other mothers (14)	5	More money (15)

Note: Parenthetic values represent the percentage of mothers who mentioned this resource.

A chi-square analysis was conducted to determine whether the frequency with which Latina and White mothers mentioned each resource was significantly different. None of the chi-square analyses were significant. In conclusion, the top three resources indicated by mothers included help from their family (26 percent), access to daycare (24 percent), and help from their spouse (19 percent) and friends (19 percent). Job resources were mentioned by 13 percent of mothers as a resource needed or desired to help integrate work and family life.

Discussion

One of the main purposes of the present study was to elucidate similarities and differences among employed mothers based on race, SES, machismo, and religiosity; partial support for the main effect hypotheses provides evidence of the importance of these variables. For those who held more traditional sex-role beliefs (higher machismo), there was greater work stress and less job satisfaction. Counter to our hypothesis, machismo did not negatively impact overall life satisfaction. It is possible that variables such as perceived spousal support and prestige of occupation were of more importance than machismo in this population (Amaro et al., 1987; Krause & Markides, 1985; Rivera et al., 1997). The hypothesis that religiosity would lead to more positive outcomes was found only for overall life satisfaction (e.g., Park et al., 1990; Snarey & Dollahite, 2001). Interestingly, religiosity did not differentially affect either work stress or job satisfaction. It may be that our measure of religiosity needs to be refined in that we used level of religiosity rather than type of religion, which has been shown to be an important predictive variable (Park et al., 1990; Hare-Mustin et al., 1983).

Findings related to the hypotheses that employed mothers with lower SES and Latina employed mothers would have more negative outcomes were less clear; SES, race, machismo, and religiosity interacted and differentially affected the three outcome variables. One such difference found was that lower SES White mothers who have more traditional attitudes regarding sex roles had higher work stress. Perhaps they resent, or dislike, the fact that they need to work full time to meet the family's financial needs. Latinas with higher machismo and lower SES may not resent the need to work as it is more congruent with their cultural values (e.g., Amaro et al., 1987). However, higher SES White mothers with more traditional sex role beliefs report less work stress, indicating they may be employed for other reasons such as personal fulfillment. In this case, higher SES Latinas with more traditional sex roles may resent having to work because there is less financial need.

Another difference was that lower SES mothers who have less traditional attitudes regarding sex roles reported lower work stress which may be because they experience less conflict with working full time, especially White mothers. Interestingly, higher SES mothers with less traditional sex roles report the most work stress. One explanation for this is that these mothers have higher prestige careers, which also are likely to be demanding and stressful (Schieman, Whitestone, & Van Gundy, 2006).

The data indicated that lower SES Whites and Latinas work for financial need, which likely leads to greater work stress, especially among Whites. Interestingly, even though Latinas with lower SES report greater pressure from their spouse to work than Whites, they still have significantly lower work stress than Whites. Although there were no significant relationships between higher SES and working for personal fulfillment, mothers higher in machismo beliefs and SES report the lowest work stress, especially Whites, indicating they may be working for some other reason that may buffer work stress.

Although the hypotheses were exploratory and there was differential support depending on the outcome variable, it is the case that Latina and White employed mothers of lower and higher socioeconomic status are not experiencing the same demands of work-family balance and that researchers must not use White upper and middle class mothers as the norm by which all others should be judged (e.g., LeMaster et al., 2004). The pattern of results tells a complicated story that suggests further exploration of the moderating variables included in this study and substantiates the need for inclusion of additional moderating variables in future research.

Moreover, the results from this study provide implications for how families manage the work-family interface and how employers support their employees and their families. For example, although differences were detected between Latina and White mothers employed outside of the home, there were few differences in the types of resources they desired to help them better juggle the demands of home and work. As indicated in much of the literature on work and family balance (Barnett & Gareis, this volume; Elman & Gilbert, 1984; Gottfried & Gottfried, this volume; LeMaster et al., 2004, 2007; Saxbe & Repetti, this volume; Scarr, Phillips, & McCartney, 1989), working mothers need greater support from their family, spouse, and friends and access to high quality daycare for their children. Regardless of race, SES, or other moderating variables, these sources of support are necessary.

There are important limitations of this study that must be considered. First, our population was recruited using convenience sampling and therefore we cannot be confident that it is a representative sample. Mothers employed outside of the home who self-selected to participate may be different from those who chose not to participate. Second, the sample size was small, thus statistical power was not great enough to reach conventional statistical significance with a few of the findings and caution should be used when interpreting these results. Third, machismo is one means of assessing traditional gender role stereotypes but it may be too narrow. Broader and multidimensional measures of gender role ideologies are needed to increase the validity of this construct. Fourth, our operationalization of SES was based solely on parental family income before taxes. However, as indicated by our post-hoc analyses, a more general construct of SES might include type of profession, prestige of profession, and perceived financial need of family. Finally, the idea of racial identity versus acculturation or cultural identity needs to be considered. For example, Flores, Tschann, Vanoss Marin, and Pantoja (2004) studied Mexican American husbands and wives and found that those who were more acculturated were less likely to avoid conflict during an argument, supporting the importance of acculturation. For the purposes of this research, a third generation Latina mother may have different experiences and beliefs than a first generation Latina mother and we did not gather this data.

Future research should continue the exploration of work and family balance issues for populations that have tended to be neglected (i.e., anyone other than White middle and upper class). It is imperative that we not assume that research on a homogeneous population is generalizable to a more heterogeneous community. Continued study will allow researchers to determine where there are differences between and similarities among populations so that policy and work place environments will be conducive for all. To understand the stressors and benefits for mothers employed outside of the home and the impact on their families as well as the workplace, moderating variables must be further examined to determine how best to implement policy and provide resources.

Acknowledgment

The research was supported by grants from The John Randolph Haynes and Dora Haynes Foundation and from Scripps College.

References

Aiken, L. S., & West, S. G. (1991). *Multiple regression: Testing and interpreting interactions.* Thousand Oaks, CA: Sage.

Amaro, H., Russo, N., & Johnson, J. (1987). Family and work predictors of psychological well-being among Hispanic women professionals. *Psychology of Women Quarterly, 11*, 505–521.

Barnett, R. C. (1994). Home-to-work spillover revisited: A study of full-time employed women in dual-earner couples. *Journal of Marriage and the Family, 56*, 647–656.

Bridges, J. S., & Orza, A. M. (1993). Effects of maternal employment-childrearing pattern on college students' perceptions of a mother and her child. *Psychology of Women Quarterly, 17*, 103–117.

Brody, G. H., Stoneman, Z., & Flor, D. (1996). Parental religiosity, family processes, and youth competence in rural, two-parent African American families. *Developmental Psychology, 32*, 696–706.

Cuellar, I., Arnold, B., & Gonzalez, G. (1995). Cognitive referents of acculturation: Assessment of cultural constructs in Mexican Americans. *Journal of Community Psychology, 23*, 339–356.

Davis, J. A., Smith, T. W., Hodge, R. W., Nakao, K., & Treas, J. (1991). *Occupational prestige ratings from the 1989 General Social Survey* [Computer file]. Chicago, IL: National Opinion Research Center. Ann Arbor, MI: Interuniversity Consortium for Political and Social Research.

Deyoung, Y., & Zigler, E. (1994). Machismo in two cultures: Relation to punitive child-rearing practices. *American Journal of Orthopsychiatry, 64,* 386–395.

Doherty, K. T. (1998). A mind of her own: Effects of need for closure and gender on reactions to nonconformity. *Sex Roles, 38,* 801–819.

Eagly, A. H., & Steffen, V. J. (1984). Gender stereotypes stem from the distribution of women and men into social roles. *Journal of Personality and Social Psychology, 46,* 735–754.

Eagly, A. H., Wood, W., & Diekman, A. (2000). Social role theory of sex differences and similarities. In T. Eckes & H. M. Trautner (Eds.), *The developmental social psychology of gender* (pp. 123–174). Mahwah, NJ: Erlbaum.

Elman, M., & Gilbert, L. (1984). Coping strategies for role conflict in married professional women with children. *Family Relations, 33,* 317–327.

Ferrari, A. (2001). The impact of culture upon child rearing practices and definitions of maltreatment. *Child Abuse and Neglect, 26,* 793–813.

Ferree, M. M. (1984). The view from below: Women's employment and gender equality in working class families. In B. B. Hess & M. B. Sussman (Eds.), *Women and the family: Two decades of change* (pp. 57–75). New York: Haworth.

Flores, W., Tschann, J. M., Vanoss Marin, B., & Pantoja, P. (2004). Marital conflict and acculturation among Mexican American husbands and wives. *Cultural Diversity and Ethnic Minority Psychology, 10,* 39–52.

Friedman, S. D., & Greenhaus, J. H. (2000). *Work and family – Allies or enemies? What happens when business professionals confront life choices.* New York: Oxford University Press.

Ganong, L. H., & Coleman, M. (1995). The content of mother stereotypes. *Sex Roles, 32,* 495–512.

Gooler, L. E. (1996). Coping with work-family conflict: The role of organizational support. Unpublished doctoral dissertation, City University of New York, New York.

Greenhaus, J. H., Parasuraman, S., Granrose, C. S., Rabinowitz, S., & Beutell, N. J. (1989). Sources of work-family conflict among two-career couples. *Journal of Vocational Behavior, 34,* 133–153.

Guendelman, S., Malin, C., Herr-Harthoron, B., & Vargas, P. N. (2001). Orientations to motherhood and male partner support among women in Mexico and Mexican-origin women in the United States. *Social Science & Medicine, 52,* 1805–1813.

Halpern, D. F., & Murphy, S. E. (2005). From balance to interaction: Why the metaphor is important. In D. F. Halpern, & S. E. Murphy (Eds.), *Changing the metaphor: Work-family balance to work-family integration* (pp. 3–9). Mahwah, NJ: Erlbaum.

Halpern, D. F., & Riggio, H. R. (2006). *Changes at the intersection of work and family, Vol. 1: Family perspectives.* Thousand Oaks, CA: Sage Publications.

Hare-Mustin, R. T., Bennett, S. K., & Broderick, P. C. (1983). Attitude toward motherhood: Gender, generational, and religious comparisons. *Sex Roles, 9,* 643–661.

Herrera, R., & Del Campo, R. (1995). Beyond the superwoman syndrome: Work satisfaction and family functioning among working-class, Mexican American women. *Hispanic Journal of Behavioral Sciences, 17,* 49–60.

Hewlett, S. A. (2002). *Creating a life: Professional women and the question for children.* New York: Talk Miramax Books.

Hintsa, T., Kivimaki, M., Elovainio, M., Keskivaara, P., Hintsanen, M., Pulkki-Raback, L., et al. (2006). Parental socioeconomic position and parental life satisfaction as predictors of job strain in adulthood: 18-year follow-up of the Cardiovascular Risk in Young Finns Study. *Journal of Psychosomatic Research, 61,* 243–249.

Hochshild, A. R. (1989). *The second shift: Working parents and the revolution at home.* New York: Basic Books.

Hodson, R. (1996). Women and job satisfaction. In P. Dubeck & K. Borman (Eds.), *Women and work: A handbook* (pp. 292–293). New York: Garland.

Hondagneu-Sotelo, P. (1993). New perspectives on Latina women. *Feminist Studies, 19,* 193–205.

Hondagneu-Sotelo, P., & Avila, E. (1997). "I'm here, but I'm there:" The meanings of transnational motherhood. *Gender and Society, 11,* 548–571.

Kahneman, D., Krueger, A. B., Schkade, D., Schwarz, N., & Stone, A. A. (2006). Would you be happier if you were richer? A focusing illusion. *Science, 312,* 1908–1910.

Kanter, R. M. (1977). *Work and family in the United States: A critical review and agenda for research and policy.* New York: Sage.

Kossek, E. E., & Ozeki, C. (1998). Work-family conflict, policies, and the job-life satisfaction relationship: A review and directions for organizational behavior-human resources. *Journal of Applied Psychology, 83,* 2, 139–149.

Krause, N., & Markides, K. (1985). Employment and psychological well-being in Mexican American women. *Journal of Health and Social Behavior, 26,* 15–26.

LeMaster, J., Casad, B. J., & Marcus-Newhall, A. (2007). In their own words: Experiences and attitudes of employed and stay-at-home young mothers. Manuscript submitted for publication.

LeMaster, J., Marcus-Newhall, A., Casad, B. J., & Silverman, N. (2004). Life experiences of working and stay-at-home mothers. In J. L. Chin (Ed.), *The psychology of prejudice and discrimination: Gender and sexual orientation* (Vol. 3, pp. 61–91). Westport, CT: Greenwood Press.

Louis, V. V., & Zhao, S. Y. (2002). Effects of family structure, family SES, and adulthood experiences on life satisfaction. *Journal of Family Issues, 23,* 986–1005.

Mahalik, J. R., & Lagan, H. D. (2001). Examining masculine gender role conflict and stress in relation to religious orientation and spiritual well-being. *Psychology of Men and Masculinity, 2,* 24–33.

Marcus-Newhall, A., Casad, B. J., LeMaster, J., & Silverman, N. (2007). Perceptions of working mothers and fathers: Interacting effects of passion, job prestige, and gender. Manuscript in preparation.

Marcus-Newhall, A., LeMaster, J., Casad, B. J., & Shaked, N. (2007). Between a rock and a hard place: Attitudes toward working and stay-at-home mothers. Manuscript submitted for publication.

McCauley, A. P., & Salter, C. (1995). Meeting the needs of young adults. *Population Reports, 41*. Baltimore, Johns Hopkins School of Public Health, Population Information Program.

Menninger, S. W. (2006). The impact of rising women's salaries on marital and relationship satisfaction. *Dissertation Abstracts, 66*, 39–40.

Moen, P. (1992). *Women's two roles*. New York: Auburn House.

Park, C., Cohen, L. H., & Herb, L. (1990). Intrinsic religiousness and religious coping as life stress moderators for Catholics versus Protestants. *Journal of Personality and Social Psychology, 59*, 562–574.

Pavot, W., & Diener, E. (1993). Review of the Satisfaction with Life scale. *Psychological Assessment, 5*, 164–172.

Peiro, A. (2005). Happiness, satisfaction and socio-economic conditions: Some international evidence. *Journal of Socio-Economics, 35*, 348–365.

Perry-Jenkins, M., Repetti, R. L., & Crouter, A. C. (2000). Work and family in the 1990s. *J ournal of Marriage and the Family, 62*, 981–998.

Riggio, H. R., & Halpern, D. F. (2006). *Changes at the intersection of work and family, Vol. 2: O rganizational and worker perspectives*. Thousand Oaks, CA: Sage.

Rivera, R., Torres, M., & Carre, F. (1997). Role burdens: The impact of employment and family responsibilities on the health status of Latino women. *Journal of Health Care for the Poor and Underserved, 8*, 99–113.

Russo, N. F. (1976). The motherhood mandate. *Journal of Social Issues, 5*, 143–153.

Sanders, D., & Bullen, M. M. (2005). *Staying home: From full-time professional to full-time parent*. Boulder, CO: Spencer and Waters.

Scarr, S., Phillips, D., & McCartney, K. (1989). Working mothers and their families. *American Psychologist, 44*, 1402–1409.

Schieman, S., Whitestone, Y. K., & Van Gundy, K. (2006). The nature of work and the stress of higher status. *Journal of Health and Social Behavior, 47*, 242–257.

Scott, W. A. (1965). *Values and organizations: A study of fraternities and sororities*. Chicago, IL: Rand McNally.

Snarey, J. R., & Dollahite, D. C. (2001). Varieties of religion-family linkages. *Journal of Family Psychology, 15*, 646–651.

South, S. J. (1993). Racial and ethnic differences in the desire to marry. *Journal of Marriage and the Family, 55*, 357–370.

Tix, A. P., & Frazier, P. A. (1998). The use of religious coping during stressful life events: Main effects, moderation, and mediation. *Journal of Counseling and Clinical Psychology, 66*, 411–422.

Torres, J. B. (1998). Masculinity and gender roles among Puerto Rican men: Machismo on the U.S. mainland. *American Journal of Orthopsychiatry, 68*, 16–26.

White, L., & Rogers, S. J. (2000). Economic circumstances and family outcomes: A review of the 1990s. *Journal of Marriage and the Family, 62*, 1035–1051.

6

Age, Work, and Family: Balancing Unique Challenges for the Twenty-First Century

Jeanette N. Cleveland

The U.S. family size is smaller and we are living longer. This combination results in population aging (Alley & Crimmins, in press). Not only is the *proportion* of the population over 65 increasing but the population over age 80 is the fastest growing segment of the U.S. population (Alley & Crimmins, in press). Further, population aging contributes to the aging of the workforce. The rapid aging or graying of the U.S. workforce during the twenty-first century and across most of the developed countries brings with it many personal, work, and family issues (Shultz & Adams, in press). In addition, the aging workforce is more diverse in terms of gender, including larger numbers of women, ethnic and racial groups and immigrants (Fullerton, 1997). Thus, non-Whites will comprise a significant proportion of the older workers in the labor force in the future.

Work provides one context for aging challenges. Work issues center on how aging changes our functioning and performance at work or our attitudes towards work, in addition to the effects of organizational climate and supervisory support on older workers. Further, aging occurs within and influences the characteristics, interrelationships, and outcomes within a family. The independence and support needed and provided by an aging person within a family often is significantly influenced by the characteristics and relationships within the family earlier in life. The health of the family member as well as marital status, presence of children, siblings, and relatives are important family characteristics early in life and increasingly so later in life (Connidis, 2001). Finally, although there has been extensive research on work–family conflict, less research has focused on the relationship between age and the reciprocal linkages between work and family. These work–family linkages are embedded within the larger multi-layered context of changing work and family domains.

In this chapter, I will describe how age is related to important work and family issues. However, in order to appreciate the multidisciplinary approaches to the work–family interface, I begin the chapter by describing briefly three key considerations: (1) two dominant approaches to investigating work and family issues: work-oriented approach and family-oriented approach; (2) the ages or points at which one becomes "old" at work and within families; and (3) the stereotypes associated with older people and older workers. Further, drawing from the gerontology literature, actual changes associated with increasing age will be described. In the next sections, I discuss how both actual and perceived individual level age changes may differentially translate into shifts in behaviors, roles and attitudes within the work domain followed by a discussion of age within the family domain. Following this, I describe how age appears to and is likely to influence the linkages between work and family. In the final section, I will identify areas for future research.

Multiple Perspectives in Research on Age and Work–Family Issues

Work and family issues have been examined through two distinct "lenses" (Crouter & McHale, 2005). One lens, common in the industrial/organizational psychology and management literatures, approaches such issues from largely a work perspective. The work perspective emphasizes individual level employee perceptions of work–family conflicts and links to work attitudes, work performance, turnover intentions, and possibly stress and health. The contribution of the work-focused approach is that employees identify possible sources or causes of conflict and possible areas for intervention to eliminate conflict. Further, using a work approach, we are able to assess work characteristics using a number of measures reflecting a range of micro to macro level job and organizational constructs. Organizational representatives including first line supervisors, and Human Resources personnel can utilize this information to design programs to assist employees or identify and then redesign stressful tasks or jobs. However, one limitation of the work-oriented approach is that work–family conflict is assessed primarily from the individual level perspective often using one source: the employee. Even such macro level work constructs as organizational climate are often assessed only through the eyes (or perspective) of the individual employee.

On the other hand, a second approach to understanding the work–family interface is to examine such issues from a family perspective.

Within this perspective, a multi-source perspective of work–family conflict and its outcomes often is used. For example, information about general work characteristics are collected and then related to employee, spouse, and possibly children's perceptions of family satisfaction, conflict, parenting, health and well being. However, one limitation is that fewer work variables are included thereby limiting information on which to base or make decisions about organizational interventions. Both perspectives are essential yet a challenge to integrate. In the current chapter, I attempt to examine age and the work–family interface from both perspectives.

What is "Old," "Older" at Work and within Family?

Before a discussion of age and work–family can begin, one needs to be aware that there is little consensus on what is considered "old" or "older' or "elderly" across the work/management, family or gerontological research literatures (Cleveland & Landy, 1983; Cleveland & Lim, in press). Chronological age is the most frequently used measure of age and aging but there is also subjective age, social age and so forth. Further, "old" age may vary depending upon whether we are referring to the individual within the work setting, at home or in relation to a specific activity such as community service or leisure activities. For example, at work, the age of legal protection begins at 40 years (Weiss & Maurer, 2004). However, for many occupations, age-related perceptions of old may be linked to typical age of job incumbents or typical age for retirement which often is between 60 and 65 years (Cleveland & Lim, in press). The "very old" employees may be those who are over 65 to 70 years.

However, within the family context, old age may not begin until well after retirement or may be more closely linked to the individual's health status and family roles rather than to career stage or work status. Few parents aged 40–50 years would be viewed as old. Even when children leave home, parents are free to pursue greater involvement in leisure or work activities. With increasing roles such as "grandparent," individuals may be viewed as older. However, this is often not associated with perceptions of physical or mental decline as it more likely would be within many work settings. "Old" within the family context then may be linked with personal independence and daily functioning while "old" or "older" within the workplace is associated with changes (often declines) in maximal or optimal performance. Therefore, the age at which an individual becomes "old" at *work* is often at a younger chronological age than the chronological age at which one becomes old within *a family* context.

Therefore, it is important to keep in mind that what we mean by "old" at work may be considerably different than what we mean by "old" or elderly within the family.

Age Stereotypes and Bias

Increasing age is associated with a number of largely negative myths or stereotypes – both concerning "the old person" generally and the "older worker" more specifically. These stereotypes can and do have important yet potentially differential influences on our perceptions of aging family members and workers as well as upon our self-perceptions of aging. A recent meta-analysis of attitudes toward younger and older adults shows a bias against older adults across a number of outcomes (Kite, Stockdale, Whitley, & Johnson, 2005). Bias was largest when assessing stereotypic beliefs and perceptions of attractiveness and was smallest when behaviors, behavioral intentions, or affective evaluations were measured. Competence ratings fell roughly between these two extremes (Kite et al., 2005). The results reinforce the position that perceptions of older adults are complex and multidimensional, not unitary stereotypes.

Research shows that people believe there are a larger proportion of expected losses and fewer expected gains associated with increasingly older ages. Undesirable attributes are expected to increase in older adulthood and these aging-related increases in undesirable attributes become less controllable (Heckhausen & Baltes, 1991). For example, people believe with increasing age, there is a decline in memory abilities (cf. Dixon, 1989; Ryan & See, 1993). Older people are thought to be forgetful, absentminded, or slower (MacNeil, Ramos, & Magafas, 1996), less creative (Rosen & Jerdee, 1976), and less physically capable (Netz & Ben-Sira, 1993; Rosen & Jerdee, 1976; Slotterback & Saarnio, 1996).

Research using the stereotype content model has found evidence that we may automatically categorize older individuals as warm but not competent (Cuddy & Fiske, 2002), and thus likely not associate older people with the role of effective worker. Older employees are perceived as lower in physical capability, lower in ability to learn new skills and tasks, rigid, inflexible, and resistant to supervision, have poor/declining health, unable to cope with job stress, little motivation and lower performance and productivity than younger workers (Parkinson, 2000). Yet older employees receive higher ratings than younger employees on academic skill levels, attendance, ability to get along with coworkers, work ethics, salary expectations, and supervisory skills (Forte & Hansvick, 1999).

People, in part, believe older workers are less capable of development or keeping up-to-date because the dimensions on which older workers are rated lower are those closely related to learning and development. Employers frequently are reluctant to retain older workers for employment because they perceive them as unwilling to adapt to technological changes, lack flexibility, and are unwilling to take on new tasks or adapt to changes (AARP, 1995). Consistent with this, Finkelstein, Burke, and Raju (1995) conducted a meta–analysis of the research literature and found lower ratings for older workers than younger ones on dimensions related to having potential for development.

What Are Documented Changes that Accompany Increasing Age?

Although stereotypes of older persons are complex, some misconceptions may rest, in part, upon actual changes that occur with increasing age. A brief review of key physical and mental changes with age at the individual level is provided.

Drawing from gerontological and industrial gerontological literature, there is evidence of age-related changes in a number of areas for both men and women. However, at least five issues should be emphasized: (1) some changes with increase age are negative reflecting decrements; other changes are positive; (2) there are greater individual differences or variability among older individuals in knowledge, skill, ability and experience than observed between older and younger groups; (3) much less is known about comparisons between aging men and women. Therefore much of the research reported here (except where noted) is based on comparisons of older and younger men; (4) much of the research reported in this section refers to older adults as individual over 70 or 75 years of age; and (5) the type of task used to compare older and younger people is often very narrow and lacks generalizability to either daily family or work activities. It is critical to point out that there is less research that translates or interprets these documented changes to changes in either work or family activities (Hardy, 2006; Salthouse, 1997).

Changes in Visual, Auditory, Motor and Physical Abilities

A number of vision-related changes occur with increasing age. For example, there are increasing rates of loss of contrast sensitivity, reduction in colors sensitivity, greater sensitivity to glare, and declines in dark adaptation (Fozard & Gordon-Salant, 2001). In terms of hearing, older adults experience losses including difficulty understanding speech and increased sensitivity to loudness (Scheiber, 2003). Aging is linked *consistently* to slower response time, disruptions in coordination, loss of flexibility, and other such motor skill declines such as reductions in strength, endurance and dexterity (Fiske & Rogers, 2000). Finally, although there are large individual differences, there are patterns of cardio and musculoskeletal system changes. Oxygen intake declines with age although this can be enhanced through regular exercise and maintained through a schedule of routine cardiorespiratory exercise. Regular physical exercise can keep physical capacity nearly unchanged between the age of 45 to 65 years (Hardy, 2006).

Cognitive Changes

Changes in cognitive functions show both improvements and declines with increasing age. Cognitive functions such as language use or processing complex problems in uncertain situations improve with age. Also motivation, experience, and wisdom of older workers can compensate effectively for the speed and precision that is more characteristic of younger individuals (Baltes & Staudinger, 2000; Czaja & Sharit, 1998; Hardy, 2006). On the other hand, in experimental situations, working memory, problem solving and reasoning, inference formation, encoding and retrieval in memory, and information processing slow with age although not uniformly (Hardy, 2006; Salthouse, 1997). Changes in cognitive processing make it more difficult for older individuals to shift their attention between displays, to multitask, and to maintain a rapid pace of information processing. However, the declines in cognitive functions with age are largely found in lab settings rather than in actual job situations.

Translating Age Changes into the Work Context

The previous two sections suggest that there are both real changes and even greater perceived changes, specifically declines associated with becoming older. However, although change does occur, it may: (a) not transfer to work or family settings; (b) may transfer to work and family settings differentially; or (c) transfer at very different ages to one versus the other. In order to understand the role of age in the work place, it is important to assess how age is correlated with important work outcomes such as performance appraisal ratings, turnover intentions, accidents, work attitudes, and skill-development opportunities.

Job Performance

There is extensive research on the effects of employee chronological age on supervisory ratings of task performance. Meta-analytic studies have shown weak support for age performance rating relationships (Avolio, Waldman, & McDaniel, 1990; McEvoy & Cascio, 1989; Salthouse & Maurer, 1996; Shore & Goldberg, 2005). Further, contextual performance or organizational citizenship behaviors (OCB) include behaviors such as volunteering for tasks not formally part of the job, demonstrating effort, helping and cooperating with others, following organizational rules and supporting organizational objectives (Borman & Motowidlo, 1993). Although much less research has been conducted, there is some evidence that age may be related to predictors or correlates of OCBs. For example, older individuals have higher average scores on measures of agreeableness and conscientiousness that are key correlates of OCBs (Farr & Ringseis, 2002). Even though there may be few differences between younger and older employees in terms of the frequency of OCBs, the reasons that older and younger employees engage in such behavior may vary.

Effect of Experience and Expertise

One thing that we know that typically occurs as people age is that they gain experience and often have higher levels of task-related expertise. Although experience is typically associated with higher levels of work performance, it may be that the relationship between experience and performance is non-linear (McDaniel, Schmidt, & Hunter, 1988). Specifically, the greatest experience-related difference in performance is between an employee who has no experience and one that has one year of experience. Each subsequent year of experience tends to have less impact on performance although this may depend on the task.

While it has been shown that older workers do have more difficulty on some tasks in laboratory settings that require retention of large amounts of information or that require rapid cognitive processing (Salthouse, 1993), there also have been studies showing no age-related difference in the performance of such tasks (Hartley & Little, 1999). The reason that age-related differences in such tasks are inconsistent is two-fold. First, as was pointed out earlier, older employees typically have higher levels of task-related expertise. Second, older workers may exert greater effort on the task than younger individuals (Bunce & Sisa, 2002). This implies that older employees may be able to compensate for cognitive changes in a manner that does not result in impaired task performance.

Work Attitudes, Absences, and Accidents

A number of studies have provided evidence of a positive relationship between worker age and overall job satisfaction (cf. Barnes-Farrell, Lewis, & Matthews, 2006; Cunningham & MacGregor, 2000; Kirkman & Shapiro, 2001). Similar positive age–job satisfaction relationships have been observed in a variety of cultural settings including China (Siu, Spector, Cooper, & Donald, 2001), Japan (Kalleberg & Loscocco, 1983), and Turkey (Nichols, Sugur, & Tasiran, 2003). Job satisfaction is a particularly important work attitude because it is consistently associated with employee withdrawal behaviors (e.g., absenteeism) and intentions to leave an organization.

Warr (1994) cites meta-analytic research (e.g., Hackett, 1990; Martocchio, 1989) indicating that voluntary absenteeism is negatively associated with male employee age; the meta-analytic research did not find any relationship for female employees. For unavoidable absences, the correlation with age is positive. Finally, research suggests there is a negative correlation between age and turnover in the range of −.20 to −.25 (Beehr & Bowling, 2002).

Related to absences, older adults usually experience more serious accident consequences and disability, and recovery is much slower. Although the incidence of injuries is actually lower for older workers (Sterns, Barrett, & Alexander, 1985), older employees once injured take longer to recover and return to work (Warr, 1994).

Training and Development

Research findings suggest that older workers may face discriminatory obstacles in pursuing developmental experiences in at least two ways (Maurer, Andrews, & Weiss, 2003; Maurer & Rafuse, 2001). First, an individual may be denied access to training and development experiences. This is perhaps the most overt and obvious way. Second, an individual may not receive support and/or encouragement (and possibly is even discouraged) in the pursuit of these activities from an organizational or psychological perspective, and incorporate negative age stereotypes into their self-view. They may believe that workers' learning skills decline with age or that they are not motivated to learn new tasks and technologies. This is perhaps a less overt or obvious way. Either way this kind of effect can be harmful to the development of older workers.

Differences in Access

Maurer (2001) reviewed literature reflecting the idea that older workers in organizations may become susceptible to "lost opportunities" for development just as minorities might (Ilgen & Youtz, 1986). Difficult job assignments can be a very valuable source of employee development (McCauley, Ruderman, Ohlott, & Morrow, 1994). Further, challenging work can actually help facilitate participation in skill development activities (cf. Kozlowski & Farr, 1988). However, older workers are sometimes given more routine (rather than complex and challenging) job assignments (Salthouse & Maurer, 1996).

Another area where developmental resources or opportunities may be experienced with lower frequency is in relation to social relationships that enhance development and learning. Tsui and O'Reilly (1989) studied comparative ages in supervisor-subordinate dyads and found that older workers were rated lower, were liked less, and experienced more role ambiguity compared to younger workers. Relatedly, the frequency of communication between an older worker and younger coworkers is likely to be lower than communication among the younger workers (Zenger & Lawrence, 1989).

In addition, older employees may lack opportunities to form special, intimate peer relationships at work that provide high psychosocial support (Kram & Isabella, 1985). Social networks may decay with time which can result in older employees being confronted with the loss of emotional support and increasing isolation (Schabracq, 1994). Older employees may have fewer opportunities to receive support from coworkers, supervisors, and other people. This combined with stereotypes and changes in the older workers themselves might lead to decreased tendency to develop. Consistent with this, beliefs about older workers' motivation to develop were significantly more negative than were beliefs about older workers' ability to develop (Wrenn & Maurer, 2004).

Self-Perceptions of Decline

Workers' concepts of appropriate aging behavior might be influenced by stereotypes when they look for cues and role definitions provided by others regarding what is appropriate for people of their age (Greller &

Stroh,1995; Maurer et al., 2003). For example, employees who believed that various abilities declined after age 50 also held more negative beliefs about older workers' ability to learn and develop (Wrenn & Maurer, 2004). Therefore, an important determinant of people's negative perceptions of older workers development capability is their belief about the decline of abilities with age in general. Other research suggests that older workers felt less cognitively able and had lower perceptions of themselves as possessing learning qualities compared to younger workers (Maurer et al., 2003). Workers who perceived themselves to be older relative to their coworkers tended to perceive their own intelligence as lower and their own minds as declining more in recent years than employees who perceived themselves to be younger relative to their coworkers. However, the differences on these variables were small. Further, there were no actual differences in participation rates for development activities between these groups.

Direct and Indirect Age Effects

Age has direct effects on work behaviors and attitudes, but also functions as a *moderator* variable. The direct effects of age on outcomes are due to the health-related changes that occur over time and are independent of the workplace. In that sense, age is simply a proxy for those changes. A moderator variable is any variable that changes the strength or form of the relationship between two or more other variables (Baron & Kenny, 1986). Older employees may react differently to certain job and organizational conditions compared to their younger counterparts, specifically job characteristics and organizational climate.

Jobs differ considerably on a number of dimensions. In addition, some jobs have higher levels of stressors than others including placing greater physical and sensory demands on workers than other jobs. These jobs might require high levels of sustained physical exertion (e.g., fire fighting), heavy lifting (e.g., baggage handing), or working in harsh or inhospitable environments (e.g., work on oil rigs). Other jobs may require the ability to hear at very high or low frequencies, or that require very high visual acuity. Finally, other jobs may involve long hours of activity or concentration. Although the average performance of older and younger employees may not differ, older workers may show increasing declines in maximal or sustained peak performance under more taxing or stressful work conditions (Maurer, in press).

Organizational climates likely differ in the regard or the value they display toward older employees (Maurer, in press). Although this aspect of climate has not received a great deal of attention, such differences may influence the behavior of older employees. For example, when organizational climate toward older employees is negative, older employees may develop low performance expectations, more negative work attitudes, and low motivation. It is possible, for example, that such climate differences influence what Pierce, Gardner, Dunham, and Cummings (1989) termed Organization-Based Self-Esteem (OBSE) or "the self-perceived value that individuals have of themselves as organizational members acting within an organizational context" (p. 625). This is important because OBSE was found to be negatively related to both depression and physical health symptoms (Jex & Elacqua, 1999).

Translation of Age Changes into the Family Context

Intergenerational bonds are perceived as strong by most families in today's society. Intergenerational solidarity reflects closeness in affect, interaction, and help exchange between generations. However, one predominant and persistent myth about family life is that the elderly are neglected or abandoned by their families, especially their children. This myth is based on three assumptions: (1) three generation households were dominate in the past, (2) three generation households reflect better family relationships, and (3) the respect accorded older persons in the past equates with affection (Nydegger, 1983). However, with much higher mortality rates and lower life expectancy in the past, the likelihood of multiple generations living together was in fact a rarity. It is only recently that larger numbers of households include multiple generations. When three generations did live together, it was often either a function of inheritance laws and the control by older parents of property or when one parent died, leaving the other alone. Further, because publicly funded assistance for older people was either limited or nonexistent, making a three generation household was in many ways a forced choice for family members who could no longer live alone (Connidis, 2001).

However, living longer does mean there is greater likelihood that multiple generation families in the US will increase. Further, longer life expectancy implies that individuals will spend more time in particular familial relationship (Farkas & Hogan, 1995). Parents will know their children into their middle age and grandparents are living longer to see their grandchildren achieve adulthood and become parents. This longevity also increases the potential for conflict in families not necessarily because there is less family love but because the demands and expectations are greater for inter-generation care and interactions (Connidis, 2001).

Independence and Support: A Delicate Balance

Two general themes appear to characterize growing older and growing elderly within the family context: independence and support. Although these may seem like polar opposites of a continuum, we attempt to maintain a balance between these two facets as we age. However, the relationship between independence and support is complex and depends on a number of other factors. First, it is important to keep in mind what span of age to which we are referring. As indicated previously, "older" within the work context begins in the 40s and extends into one's 60s and perhaps 70s. In the family, "older" may begin shortly before retirement age and continue well into one's 80s or 90s. Therefore, it is perhaps important within the family context to makes a distinction between "younger old" and "older old." A second consideration when discussing independence and support is the physical, cognitive, and emotional health of the individual. Health is considered a direct age effect. Third, less direct yet still critical factors to consider are marital status of the aging person(s), number and availability of children, siblings, and grandchildren. The number and quality of the roles that the older family member occupies can enhance or inhibit the increasing balance between independent and support. Finally, it is important to consider the financial and economic resources of the aging person.

Independence with Increasing Age

The availability of a marital partner and kin (whether it be children, siblings, etc.) are key parameters in both support and independence. Married men and women are more likely to live independently and separately from children than are widowed or single older individuals. The majority of individuals aged 25 to 74 years are married. This continues to be true for men between 75 and 84 years where 75 percent of men are married while less than one-third of women continue to be married. These gender differences are largely due to differences in widowhood rates. Further there are differences by race for persons 75 to 84 years with White persons (76 percent) most likely to be married, followed by Hispanics (62 percent), and by Blacks (55 percent). The presence of a spouse then clearly has different implications for both intimate relationships and independence among older men and older women. Older women are more likely in later ages not to have a spouse. Therefore, it is critical to identify when discussing age and the work–family interface, to make a distinction between older men and older women.

One indicator of independence is living arrangement. The majority of people aged 65 years or more live with a family member, predominately a spouse (Kinsella, 1995). Men are much more likely to be in this situation than women (80 percent vs. 56 percent). Again this is primarily due to higher widowhood rates among women, greater life expectancy of women, and higher remarriage rates of men. However, since the 1960s, a growing proportion of both men and women live alone or independently (Kinsella, 1995). Widowed women are more likely to live on their own if they did so for at least 3 months before the age of 60 (Bess, 1999). In addition, there are racial variations in independent and solo living circumstances. White persons aged 60 and over are far more likely to live with a spouse only, while Asian, Black, Hispanic and Native American persons are more likely to be living with other kin only (Himes, Hogan, & Eggebeen, 1996).

Older people prefer to live independently for as long as possible (Mack, Salmoni, Viverais-Dressler, Porter, & Garg, 1997). Older persons especially in Western cultures prefer to receive help from formal service agencies rather than from their children. This is especially true if the assistance needed is for a lengthy time period (Wielink, Huijsman, & McDonnell, 1997). Older persons prefer that their independence is maintained by service from the community rather than from children. However, there are other considerations as well including economic resources to sustain independent living, how healthy one is to live solo, and the availability of kin especially children and spouse. The likelihood of living alone when older decreases as the number of children and siblings increase (Wolf, 1990). Yet the preference for living independently is realized especially by older women through greater financial security (Kinsella, 1995).

Only 5 percent of all individuals aged 65 and over currently live in institutional settings. Institutionalization is more likely among women than men, those with fewer children, the nonmarried, Whites and older seniors (Belgrave & Bradsher, 1994; Carriere & Pelletier, 1995). The presence of at least one daughter or sibling minimizes the chances of being placed in a nursing home (Freedman, 1996). Family members provide at least 60–80 percent of long-term care for dependent elderly members. Formal or institutional care occurs only after family care-giving resources are depleted Living with a child, single or married, was the major solution if aging parents were too frail to live alone (Zachritz & Gutmann, 1996). Whenever possible, parents preferred to live with an unmarried child or other relatives.

Importance of Relationships: Spousal and Kin Support

Retirement has the potential to alter the relationship between spouses. Among men, aging is associated with greater sensitivity, familial affiliation, passivity and introspection. Among women, aging is associated with increased aggression, dominance, and assertiveness (Zube, 1988). Therefore, retirement has the potential to change the division of household labor between partners perhaps leading to less gender differentiation and more similarity in definition of masculinity and femininity (Brubaker, 1985). However, even with the increase of women's participation in the labor force, in practice, women of all ages take on more of the responsibilities of housekeeping, kinship and child care whether or not they work outside of the home. Further, the pattern of activities that couples shared prior to retirement are critical determinants of the effects of retirement on the marriage (Szinovacz, 1996).

The majority of older persons have children. Nearly 90 percent of mothers age 80 had a surviving son while nearly 90 percent of mothers age 90 had a surviving daughter. Further, most older parents have one child living close by which may reflect a preference of parents and children not to live far from one another. Factors associated with greater proximity to the nearest child are family size (the more children a parent and a child has, the closer the nearest child lives), health of the parent (healthier parents are more geographically distant), age of parent (parents over 80 live nearer by), parents socioeconomic status (high SES means great distance), and parent martial status (married parents live nearer to the most proximate child than do divorced or separated parent) (Lin & Rogerson, 1995). Older parents (over 80) live nearer to their children, reflecting the expectation that with age the older parents will move closer to adult children if they need support (Silverstein & Angelleli, 1998).

Family gatherings or arrangements to get together in person are more frequently organized by older parents (Eisenhandler, 1992). Older men often act as family head while older women play the roles of kinkeeper and comforter (Rosenthal, 1985, 1987). The kinkeeper function serves to keep family members in touch with each other while the comforter role provides emotional support and advice. Older parents then serve a cohesive function in the family. They draw members across generations together as part of an extended family network.

Yet again, the theme of independence is reflected in the nature of parenting during older age. The two most common aspirations among middle aged parents for their early adult children are their: (1) happiness and educational success; followed by (2) career success, a happy family, personal fulfillment and being good and healthy people (Ryff, Lee, Essex, & Schmutte, 1994). That is, the outcome of successful parenting results in the independence of adult children. The value of independence grows and transforms with old age. It is reflected in parental appreciation of their children's maturity and parental concern for having their own independence respected by their children (Eisenhandler, 1992). Being a parent in old age is not necessarily central to one's identity for either mothers or fathers.

Much research indicates that older parent–adult child helping relationships are typically characterized by reciprocity except when the parent is in very poor health. Increasing numbers of family elders are involved in kinship role beyond that of the traditional grandparent or great-grandparent roles. Many are "surrogate parents" providing primary care to their grandchildren following divorce or incapacitation of the middle generation. Approximately 2.3 million people over age 60 have grandchildren living with them and 30 percent are responsible for the care of their grandchildren (Giarrusso, Silverstein, Gasn, & Bengtson, 2005). In a variety of support areas, older parents are more likely to give than to receive help (Spitze & Logan, 1992). Therefore, adult children may be caring for both children and parents yet there may be tangible benefits in doing so (Vierck & Hodges, 2005).

Linkages Among Work and Family as We Age

Managing the conflict or achieving a balance between work and family has been a reoccurring challenge for employees and organizations (Greenhaus & Beutell, 1985). However, this challenge has increased as greater numbers of households evolve from single-earner to dual-earner. Work–family conflict models propose that conflict arises when the demands of one domain are incompatible with demands of the other domain (Adams, King, & King, 1996). The conflict that occurs between work and nonwork roles can be a source of stress, with physical and psychological outcomes for the individual. These outcomes have been shown to impact the work organization (e.g., burnout, reduced job satisfaction) as well as family relationships (e.g., marital and life satisfaction, child and adolescent adjustment) of the individual (e.g., Allen, Herst, Bruck, & Sutton, 2000; Frone, Russell, & Cooper, 1992). In sum, work–family conflict can have a significant impact on the quality of both work and family life.

One of the largest potential causes of work–family conflict is the presence of children, especially young ones (Baltes & Young, in press). However, the increase in the number of elderly individuals in the industrialized societies and the need for families to care for them has created a new potential set of stressors that may redefine the content and causes of work–family conflict, especially as we age. Yet both researchers and practitioners know little about the specific issues associated with aging and work–nonwork interfaces or how to address them.

Older Employees and Work–Family Issues

Though there is little research on the topic, it is important to investigate whether there are differences between older and younger workers in their experiences and reactions to the balance between work and family. With respect to work–family conflict, a consistent finding is that conflict between work and family increases as one enters into marriage and/or has children (Higgins, Duxbury, & Lee, 1994). However, research also suggests that as the age of the youngest child increases, the amount of work–family conflict experienced will decrease. Job strain models such as Karasek (1979) predict that stress will be the greatest in situations where employees have little or no control of the stressor. Because parents with younger children experience heavy and often unpredictable demands on their time (e.g., Hochschild, 2003), it is consistent that they generally report the highest level of work–family conflict.

Using the life-stage approach, Higgins et al. (1994) found that an individual's life-stage was related to both work interfering with family and family interfering with work conflict. Specifically, for both men and women, levels of both types of work–family conflict were lower in the later life-stages. Importantly, gender differences were found. While men reported lower levels of conflict in each successive life stage, women reported similar levels of work–family conflict in the early stages and then reported a large drop off in work–family conflict in later life-stages (Baltes & Young, in press).

In sum, based upon child-centered life stage theory, there is evidence that work–family conflict will increase during the first few life stages and then decrease as individuals move through the later life-stages. However, eldercare is not considered in the categorization of an individual's life-stage. Eldercare presents individuals and working families with unique challenges to balance work and family responsibilities. Older workers as well as younger workers bear this responsibility. Eldercare may add another potential stressor to later stages of working individuals. Experts on work–family conflict across the lifespan may have neglected to assess a potential critical stressor in later stages (Baltes & Young, in press). Future research must include eldercare in the life stages model. Further, although reports of work–family conflict may decrease with age, balancing work and family may continue to be or increase in importance to older workers (Baltes & Young, in press).

Varying Importance of Work versus Family

Research has demonstrated that there does seem to be a shift in the importance individuals attribute to their career versus their family across the lifespan. Specifically, it appears as though younger employees focus more on their career than older employees (Evans & Bartolomé, 1984; Staudinger, 1996). Furthermore, younger workers focus more on the problems and challenges with their children than on their relationships with their significant others (Staines & O'Connor, 1980). Older employees, in contrast, report paying more attention to private life in general and to their marriages in particular. Not only does the importance given to work versus family seem to change over the life course, but it appears that the importance given to balancing the two does as well (Baltes & Young, in press). One caveat here however; much of this research is based on data collected on male employees. It is critical to determine whether or not these relationships hold for female employees as well.

There is evidence that balancing work and family life increases in importance for older employees (Evans & Bartolomé, 1979, 1981, 1984). Furthermore, older employees, unlike younger employees, do not see work–family conflict as inevitable and engage in more coping strategies. Although there are large individual differences, older employees show much "more sensitivity to the problems and opportunities present in their leisure and family lives" (Evans & Bartolomé, 1984, p. 19).

In sum, the research suggests that there is a shift in focus among older people from work to family. Although this shift suggests lower levels of work–family conflict, one reason may be that work–family balance takes on greater importance for older individuals. Therefore, it would appear as though organizations will still need to concern themselves with helping their employees balance work and family.

Eldercare

Given the steady increase in the proportion of elderly, it is likely that the number of working adults attempting to balance careers, childcare, and eldercare responsibilities has also increased. This trend is expected to continue to grow rapidly over the next decades (Bond, Galinsky, & Swanberg, 1998). Research investigating the impact of working and providing eldercare has in fact indicated that participation in both domains leads to numerous negative consequences. Individual negative consequences include increased stress (e.g., Neal, Chapman, Ingersoll-Dayton, & Emen, 1993), increased work/family conflict (e.g., Hepburn & Barling, 1996), and other physical aliments such as anxiety, sleeping problems and headaches (e.g., Wagner, Creedon, Salso, & Neal, 1989).

A great deal of research has focused on investigating organizational consequences. For example, eldercare negatively affects the amount of time that an individual spends at work (e.g., Dantzenberg, Diederiks, Philipsen, Stevens, Tan, & Vernooij-Dassen, 2000; Enright & Friss, 1987; Gibeau & Anastas, 1989; Scharlach & Boyd, 1989; Singleton, 2000). Fifty-five percent of working caregivers reported missing work, with the average absenteeism among these employees being 9 hours per month (Enright & Friss, 1987). Employees who provide eldercare lose approximately 4.8 million dollars in unpaid work, missed wages, and lost opportunities (Singleton, 2000). Even when caregivers were at work, they felt that they sometimes worked more slowly because of worries brought on by the care-giving role (Enright & Friss, 1987). Further, care giving employees reported higher accident rates, lower productivity, and more use of work time for personal phone calls (Dellmann-Jenkins, Bennett, & Brahce, 1994).

According to Baltes and Young (in press), rearranging one's work schedule in order to accommodate eldercare responsibilities is a significant predictor of stress for the caregiver employee (Orodenker, 1990). Employees may be forced to abandon their jobs completely to pursue full-time care (Stone, Cafferata, & Sangl, 1987). Such career sidetracks may contribute to individuals feeling stressed, frustrated, and regretful, Such feelings may translate to animosity toward their caregiver role or the care recipient (e.g. Harris, Long, & Fujii, 1998).

Age and Work–Family: Comparisons between Childcare and Eldercare

There are many factors that likely contribute to the extent to which individuals experience negative consequences resulting from their participation in both work and eldercare roles that distinguish it from childcare challenges. These include gender, occupation, distance from elderly parent, coordination of care among living siblings/relatives, and movement toward greater dependence until death.

Gender

Women typically assume the eldercare role to a greater extent than men (Stone et al., 1987). Working men reduce the amount of eldercare that they engage in while working women do not (Stoller, 1983). Thus, working women may be affected differently by eldercare responsibilities than their working male counterparts. In addition to the amount of care, the type of care given to elders varies by gender. Women tend to provide more domestic and personal care services, while such tasks as financial management are more evenly distributed between men and women caregivers (Horowitz, 1985). Further, while men engage in instrumental care activities such as lawn mowing, women tend to help with the activities of daily life (e.g., feeding, bathing, and clothing) (Singleton, 2000). Thus, the care that women provide is not only more extensive, but also more time-consuming and more likely to interfere with their own daily activities (including work).

Consistent with this, women tend to experience negative consequences to a greater degree as a result of their care giving role. For example, women caregivers report more absenteeism from work and more general stress then their working and care giving male counterparts (Buffardi, Smith, O'Brien, & Edwins, 1999). Further, while working men are more likely to reduce their caregiver role, working women are more likely to distance themselves from the organization by taking time off without pay, reducing their hours, and rearranging their work schedules. Thus, the differences in how men and women cope with competing demands of eldercare and work likely put women at a disadvantage in the workplace (e.g., Gignac, Kelloway, & Gottlieb, 1996).

Occupation

Higher status jobs are often characterized by more flexibility and greater control and thus allow more opportunity to attend to eldercare responsibilities (Archbold, 1983). The instability of the situation makes juggling work and eldercare difficult (Guberman & Maheu, 1999). This instability can result from the needs of recipient of care, from the instability of the family situation, and also from the instability of an individual's working environment. Although higher status jobs may have greater control, they also may be more demanding, and therefore more stressful.

Distance from Family

Unlike childcare, the target of care may not live within the same household as the caregiver. The actual distance between the caregiver and the care recipient is a critical factor in eldercare. Approximately 8–13 percent of employed caregivers live with the elder they care for (Wagner et al. 1989). The stress of caring for multiple households and commuting/traveling is reduced by reducing the distance between the caregiver and the care receiver. However, living with the care recipient may also cause stress because it may be more difficult to control the extent to which one is involved in eldercare and more difficult to limit the time spent in caregiving activities.

Research on the physical distance between caregiver and care suggests that caregivers and care recipients living together experience more negative consequences. Specifically, sharing a household was associated with more demands on the caregiver's time, and greater likelihood of work–caregiving conflict (Horowitz, 1985). Yet, a recent study indicates that the length of travel time to the elder significantly increased work interfering with family conflict (Joseph & Hallman, 1996). More specifically, respondents living with an elder reported lower work–family conflict scores than those respondents whose elderly relatives lived 31–120 miles away. Therefore, research on the role of distance in eldercare is mixed. It is necessary that future research determine under what circumstances it is beneficial for the care recipient to live with the caregiver, and under what circumstances more distance would be appropriate.

Sharing Eldercare Decisions with Other Family Members

Another factor that is unique to eldercare is shared decision making among family members regarding the care of the elderly. This factor operates both when siblings are either in close geographic proximity to each other and the elderly parent and when they are located at a distance from each other and/or the parent. With childcare, the in-resident parents are responsible for the manner in which the child is raised and cared for. Decisions about child rearing are jointly made. However, this is often not the case with the care of an aging family member. Adult children may significantly disagree about the type and the extent of care needed for an aging parent. One reason for this is that siblings may vary in terms of direct or first-hand interactions with the elderly parent. Therefore they may disagree on the parent's capability to function independently on a day to day basis. Adult children may disagree about the interpretations of aged parent's wishes or preferences for care. Finally, rather than a movement toward growth and independence as is typical in childrearing, the outcome of eldercare is toward an ending. This outcome is one of the more difficult and stressful of life events. It is likely one that will challenge and be regarded by siblings or grandchildren as extremely stressful.

Moving towards Greater Dependence

The nature of the care needed by the care recipient is a factor that influences one's ability to balance work and care giving. Certain kinds of elder disabilities and care requirements are more time consuming and more stressful than others. In particular, caring for an elder's daily functioning needs (e.g., bathing, dressing, and transportation) is particularly challenging and potentially more stressful (Montgomery, Gonyea, & Hooyman, 1985). Further, caring for elders with cognitive deficits as opposed to physical disabilities is particularly difficult (e.g., Scharlach, 1989).

The number and extensiveness of care responsibilities increase as the elder's ailments become more serious. More care giving tasks performed are associated with individual's greater perceptions of work–family conflict (Gibeau & Anastas, 1989). More specifically, the degree of an elder's limitations in daily activity, memory impairment, emotional health, and poor judgment were found to be significant predictors of work–family conflict for caregivers (Gibeau & Anastas, 1989). Recent research has continued to indicate that feelings of interference for an employed caregiver increase as an elder's health decreases and time spent in care increases (e.g., Dautzenberg et al., 2000).

Research on eldercare issues demonstrate that: 1) balancing work and eldercare is a difficult process and can cause large amounts of work–family conflict; 2) individuals belonging to certain groups may endure more of the strain of eldercare because of societal norms (e.g., gender) or socioeconomic status; and 3) organizations have been slow to respond to eldercare issues (Baltes & Young, in press). Points one and three suggest that eldercare is a large challenge, and that this challenge can negatively affect individuals' family and work lives. And unfortunately, employees are not receiving much help from their employers in dealing with this issue. Given the fact that the amount of employees having to deal with eldercare will continue to increase over the next decades, this problem will only grow in magnitude and, thus, future research on organizational (and governmental) level policies and programs that would help employees meet this eldercare challenge is sorely needed.

A Caveat: The Sandwich Generation

A growing body of research has begun to explore what is typically referred to as "the sandwich generation" or those individuals who are caring for both children and elders at the same time (Miller, 1981). Multiple caregiver roles likely contribute to greater role conflict as individuals are struggling to identify themselves as parent, employee, son/daughter, homemaker, etc., all at the same time., Recently, the importance of investigating the "sandwich generation" has been realized (Neal & Hammer, 2007).

Generally, individuals are more likely to be sandwiched between work, childcare, and eldercare between the ages of 40 and 64, with a greater likelihood of being sandwiched occurring at the lower bound of this age range (Matthews & Rosenthal, 1993). In a discussion of the sandwich generation, Dellmann-Jenkins et al. (1994) suggest that the sandwich generation experiences more stress, greater emotional strain, tardiness, unscheduled days off, depression, anxiety, and sleeplessness than those individuals who are not sandwiched (i.e., working and caring for both children and elders). Aside from individual consequences, research shows that dual caregiving roles affect organizational functioning. For example, recent research has found "sandwiched" caregiving responsibilities to impact organizational productivity as well as organizational climate (Neal & Hammer, 2007; Robinson, Barbee, Martin, Singer, & Yegidis, 2003).

Conclusion and Recommendations

With increasing life expectancies, increasing proportions of work families in the workforce, and the potential for longer working lives, future research regarding work–family conflict needs to focus on a number of individual level work issues as well as individual level nonwork issues. It is critical to understand the meaning of age within both the work and the family domain. Further, it is important to know what is meant by successful performance or functioning within each domain. The physical and mental process of aging translates differently into relationships and performance at work and within family. However, the precise translation often depends on the reciprocal linkages and influences of each of the domains upon the other. There is consistent evidence that there are greater individual differences among older people than among younger people on a number of skills, abilities, and functioning levels. It is also clear that with increasing age, work and family circumstances are more varied than are younger people.

Therefore, understanding the linkages between work and family will be increasingly important for organizations to understand as we age if they want to maintain their competitive advantage.

While it seems older employees report lower levels of work–family conflict, achieving work–family balance is important to them. In fact, older workers may value the balance between work and family life to a greater extent than younger workers (due to increased focus upon family and personal relationships) and are more willing to engage in coping behaviors to achieve this goal (Baltes & Young, in press). Second, the responsibility to care for older relatives will continue to increase, which may increase stressors that can lead to work–family conflict for both younger and older workers.

There are several research and practical implications of the aging population and workforce as it relates to the balance between work and family. First, both men and women are living longer and healthier lives. Therefore, we will have a greater number of generations living at the same time; depending upon a number of external factors (including government retirement benefits or incentives), we may also have more generations working side by side within organizations. It is important then to more fully understand the effects of aging on both women and men under realistic task situations. Currently much of the gerontology literature shows significant age declines mostly when very narrowly constructed experimental tasks are used. These tasks have little generalizability to work or family settings. Further, organizations often construct job tasks so that incumbents' skills, abilities and knowledge are best utilized for an extended period of time. If workers are consistently required to work at maximal performance levels, they would be strained to do this within a short timeframe. Therefore, jobs often are constructed to avoid taxing the incumbent excessively and repeatedly. We need to incorporate the strengths and limitations associated with aging into this job design and human factors perspective. There are complex relationships among work experience, work performance and age (McEvoy & Cascio, 1989; Salthouse & Maurer, 1996). Some research indicates that older workers are as productive as younger workers in both skill-demanding and speed-demanding jobs (Spirduso, Francis, & MacRae, 2005). Harma and Ilmarinen (1999) state that workers become physically weaker with age but mentally stronger and these changes should be reflected in work responsibilities that are less physically demanding but include more of the mental characteristics that improve with age. The concepts of work ability and employability address the connection between the capabilities of the worker (ability) and the structure of job tasks, and design of the work environment (Ilmarinen, 1999).

In addition, Baltes and Young (in press) and others have urged a life-span perspective on understanding work and family conflict. It is critical that research documents within-person and within-family changes across time in addition to shorter-term cross-sectional research comparing older and younger people. Related to this, the issues directly surrounding eldercare are increasingly important. Future research needs to address the conflicting evidence regarding the differential impact eldercare has on women and men as well as ethnic variations in eldercare. Research results are mixed on the role that distance plays between the caregiver and the care recipient. Related to this, shared caregiver decision-making is another potential stressor for eldercare providers. Finally, researchers need to investigate more thoroughly the role of social support and of the organization in providing individuals with additional eldercare responsibilities.

References

AARP (1995). *American business and older workers: A road map to the 21st century.* Washington, DC: DYG, Inc.

Adams, G. A., King, L. A., & King, D. W. (1996). Relationship of job and family involvement, family social support, and work/family conflict with job and life satisfaction. *Journal of Applied Psychology, 81*(4), 411–420.

Allen, T. D., Herst, D. E. L., Bruck, C. S., & Sutton (2000). Consequences associated with work-to-family conflict: A review and agenda for future research. *Journal of Occupational Health Psychology, 5,* 278–308.

Alley, D., & Crimmins, E. (in press). Demography of aging and work. In K. S. Shultz & G. A. Adams (Eds.), *Aging and work in the 21st century.* Mahwah, NJ: Lawrence Erlbaum and Associates.

Archbold, P. G. (1983). Impact of parent-caring on women. *Family Relations, 32,* 39–45.

Avolio, B. J., Waldman, D. A., & McDaniel, M. A. (1990). Age and work performance in nonmanagerial jobs: The effects of experience and occupational type. *Academy of Management Journal, 33,* 407–422.

Baltes, P. B., & Staudinger, U. M. (2000). Wisdom: A metaheuristic (pragmatic) to orchestrate mind and virtue toward excellence. *American Psychologist, 55,* 122–136.

Baltes, P. B., & Young, L. M. (in press). Aging and work/family issues. In K. S. Shultz & G. A. Adams (Eds.), *Aging and work in the 21st century.* Mahwah, NJ: Lawrence Erlbaum and Associates.

Barnes-Farrell, J., Lewis, W. R., & Matthews, R. (2006, March). Anticipating retirement: The roles of health, perceived control and optimism in important life domains. In G. Fisher, *Using archival data: Research examples studying issues among older workers.* Symposium presented at *Work, Stress, & Health 2006,* Miami, FL.

Baron, R., & Kenny, D. A. (1986). The moderator-mediator distinction in social-psychological research: Conceptual, strategic, and statistical considerations. *Journal of Personality and Social Psychology, 51,* 1173–1182.

Beehr, T. A., & Bowling, N. A. (2002). Career issues facing older workers. In D. Feldman (Ed.), *Work careers: A developmental perspective* (pp. 214–241). San Francisco: Jossey-Bass.

Belgrave, L. L., & Bradsher, J. E. (1994). Health as a factor in institutionalization: Disparities between African Americans and Whites. *Research on Aging, 16,* 115–141.

Bess, I. (1999). Widows living alone. *Canadian Social Trends, Summer,* 2–5.

Bond, J. T., Galinsky, E., & Swanberg, J. E. (1998). *The 1997 national study of the changing workforce.* New York: Families and Work Institute.

Borman, W., & Motowidlo, S. (1993). Expanding the criterion domain to include elements of contextual performance. In N. Schmitt & W. C. Borman (Eds.), *Personnel selection in organizations* (pp. 71–98). San Francisco: Jossey-Bass.

Brubaker, T. H. (1985). Responsibility for household tasks: A look at golden anniversary couples aged 75 years and older. In W. A. Perterson & J. Quadagno (Eds.), *Social bonds in later life* (pp. 27–36). Beverly Hills: Sage Publications.

Buffardi, L. C., Smith, J. L., O'Brien, A. S., & Edwins, C. J. (1999). The impact of dependent-care responsibility and gender on work attitudes. *Journal of Occupational Health Psychology, 4,* 356–367.

Bunce, D., & Sisa, L. (2002). Age differences in perceived workload across a short vigil. *Ergonomics, 45,* 949–960.

Carriere, Y., & Pelletier, L. (1995). Factors underlying the institutionalization of elderly persons in Canada. *Journal of Gerontological Sciences, 50,* S164–S172.

Cleveland, J. N., & Landy, F. J. (1983). The effects of person and job stereotypes on two personnel decisions. *Journal of Applied Psychology, 68,* 609–619.

Cleveland, J. N., & Lim, A. S. (in press). Employee age and performance in organizations. In K. S. Shultz & G. A. Adams (Eds.), *Aging and work in the 21st century.* Mahwah, NJ: Lawrence Erlbaum and Associates.

Connidis, I. A. (2001). *Family ties and aging.* Thousand Oaks, CA: Sage Publications.

Crouter, A., & McHale, S. (2005). The long arm of the job revisited: Parenting in dual-earner families. In T. Luster & L. Okagaki (Eds.), *Parenting: An ecological perspective: Monographs in parenting,* (2nd ed., p. 442). Mahwah, NJ: Lawrence Erlbaum Associates Publishers.

Cuddy, A. J. C., & Fiske, S. T. (2002). Doddering but dear: Process, content, and function in stereotyping of older persons. In T. D. Nelson (Ed.), *Ageism.* (pp. 4–26). Cambridge, MA: MIT Press.

Cunningham, J. B., & MacGregor, J. (2000). Trust and the design of work: Complementary constructs in satisfaction and performance. *Human Relations, 53,* 1575–1591.

Czaja, S. J., & Sharit, J. (1998). Ability-performance relationships as a function of age and task experience for a data entry task. *Journal of Experimental Psychology: Applied, 4,* 332–351.

Dautzenberg, M. G., Diederiks, J. P., Philipsen, H., Stevens, F. C., Tan, F. E., & Vernooij-Dassen, M. J. (2000). The competing demands of paid work and parent care: Middle-aged daughter providing assistance to elderly parents. *Research on Aging, 22,* 165–187.

Dellmann-Jenkins, M., Bennett, J. M., & Brahce, C. I. (1994). Shaping the corporate response to workers with elder care commitments: Considerations for gerontologists. *Educational Gerontology, 20,* 395–405.

Dixon, R. (1989). Questionnaire research on metamemory and aging: Issues of structure and function. In L. Poon, D. Rubin, & B. Wilson (Eds.), *Everyday cognition in adulthood and late life* (pp. 395–415). Cambridge: Cambridge University Press.

Eisenhandler, S. A. (1992). Lifelong roles and cameo appearances: Elderly parents and relationships with adult children. *Journal of Aging Studies, 6,* 243–257.

Enright, R. B., & Friss, L. (1987). *Employed caregivers of brain-impaired adults: An assessment of the dual role.* Final report submitted to the Geronotological Society of America. San Francisco: Family Survival Project.

Evans, P., & Bartolomé, F. (1979). Professional lives versus private lives: Shifting patterns of managerial commitment. *Organizational Dynamics, 7,* 2–29.

Evans, P., & Bartolomé, F. (1981). *Must success cost so much?* New York: Basic Books.

Evans, P., & Bartolomé, F. (1984). The changing pictures of the relationship between career and family. *Journal of Occupational Behavior, 5,* 9–21.

Farkas, J. I., & Hogan, D. P. (1995). The demography of changing intergenerational relationships. In V. L. Bengtson, K. W. Schaire, & L. M. Burton (Eds.), *Adult intergenerational relationships: Effects of societal change* (pp. 1–25). New York: Springer.

Farr, J. L., & Ringseis, E. L. (2002). The older worker in organizational context: Beyond the individual. In C. L. Cooper & I. T. Robertson (Eds.), *International review of industrial and organizational psychology* (Vol. 17, pp. 31–76). Chichester, England: John Wiley.

Finkelstein, L. M., Burke, M. J., & Raju, M. S. (1995). Age discrimination in simulated employment contexts: An integrative analysis. *Journal of Applied Psychology, 80,* 652–663.

Finkelstein, L. M., & Farrell, S. K. (in press). An expanded view of age bias in the workplace. In K. S. Shultz & G. A. Adams (Eds.), *Aging and work in the 21st century.* Mahwah, NJ: Lawrence Erlbaum and Associates.

Fiske, A. D., & Rogers, W. A. (2000). Influence of training and experience on skill acquisition and maintenance in older adults. *Journal of Aging and Physical Activity, 8,* 373–378.

Forte, C. S., & Hansvick, C. L. (1999). Applicant age as a subjective employability factor: A study of workers over and under age fifty. *Journal of Employment Counseling, 36,* 24–34.

Fozard, J. L., & Gordon-Salant, S. (2001). Changes in vision and hearing with aging. In J. E. Birren & K. W. Schaie (Eds.), *Handbook of psychology of aging* (pp. 241–266). San Diego: Academic Press.

Freedman, V. A. (1996). Family structure and the risk of nursing home admission. *Journal of Gerontology Series B: Psychological Sciences and Social Sciences, 51*, S61–S69.

Frone, M. R., Russell, M., & Cooper, M. L. (1992). Antecedents and outcomes of work-family conflict: Testing a model of the work-family interface. *Journal of Applied Psychology, 77*, 65–78.

Fullerton, N. H. (1997). Labor Force 2006: Slowing down and changing composition. *Monthly Labor Review, 120*, 23–28.

Giarrusso, R., Silverstein, M., Gasn, D., & Bengtson, V. L. (2005). Aging parents and adult children: New perspectives on intergenerational relationships. In H. L. Johnson (Ed.), *The Cambridge handbook of age and aging* (pp. 413–421). Cambridge: Cambridge University Press.

Gibeau, J. L., & Anastas, J. W. (1989). Breadwinners and caregivers: Interviews with working women. *Journal of Gerontological Social Work, 14*, 19–40.

Gignac, M. A., Kelloway, E. K., & Gottlieb, B. H. (1996). The impact of care giving on employment: A mediational model of work-family conflict. *Canadian Journal on Aging, 15*, 525–542.

Greenhaus, J. H., & Beutell, N. J. (1985). Sources of conflict between work and family roles. *Academy of Management Review, 10*, 76–88.

Greller, M. M., & Stroh, L. K. (1995). Careers in midlife and beyond: A fallow field in need of sustenance. *Journal of Vocational Behavior, 47*, 232–247.

Guberman, N. M., & Maheu, P. (1999). Combining employment and care giving: An intricate juggling act. *Canadian Journal of Aging, 18*, 84–106.

Hardy, M. (2006). Older workers. In R. H. Binstock & L. K. George (Eds.), *The handbook of aging and the social sciences* (6th ed., pp. 201–218). Burlington, MA: Academic Press.

Hackett, R. D. (1990). Age, tenure, and employee absenteeism. *Human Relations, 43*, 601–619.

Harma, M., & Ilmarinen, J. E. (1999). Towards the 24 hour society – new approaches for aging shift workers? *Scandinavian Journal of Work Environment & Health, 25*, 610–615.

Harris, P. B., Long, S.O., & Fujii, M. (1998). Men and elder care in Japan: A ripple of change? *Journal of Cross-Cultural Gerontology, 13*, 177–198.

Hartley, A. A., & Little, D. M. (1999). Age-related differences and similarities in dual-task interference. *Journal of Experimental Psychology: General, 128*, 416–449.

Heckhausen, J., & Baltes, P. B. (1991). Perceived controllability of expected psychological change across adulthood and old age. *Journal of Gerontology, 46*, 165–173.

Hepburn, C. G., & Barling, J. (1996). Eldercare responsibilities, interrole conflict, and employee absence: A daily study. *Journal of Occupational Health Psychology, 1*, 311–318.

Higgins, C., Duxbury, L., & Lee, C. (1994). Impact of life-cycle stage and gender on the ability to balance work and family responsibilities. *Family Relations, 43*, 144–150.

Himes, C. L., Hogan, D. P., & Eggebeen, D. J. (1996). Living arrangements of minority elders. *Journal of Gerontology Series B: Psychological Sciences and Social Sciences, 15*, S42–S48.

Hochschild, A. (2003). Marriage, family, and economics: The time bind: When work becomes home and home becomes work. In J. M. Henslin (Ed.), *Down to earth sociology: Introductory readings* (pp. 379–389). New York: Free Press.

Horowitz, A. (1985). Family and care giving to the frail elderly. In M. P. Lawton & C. Maddox (Eds.), *Annual review of gerontology and geriatrics.* (Vol. 5, pp. 194–246). New York: Springer.

Ilgen, D. R., & Youtz, M. A. (1986). Factors affecting the evaluation and development of minorities in organizations. In K. Rowland & G. Ferris (Eds.), *Research in personnel and human resource management* (pp. 307–337). Greenwich: JAI Press.

Ilmarinen, J. E. (1999). *Aging workers in the European Union: Status and promotion of work ability, employability, and employment.* Helsinki: Finnish Institute of Occupational Health, Ministry of Social Affairs and Health, Ministry of Labor.

Jex, S. M., & Elacqua, T. C. (1999). Time management as a moderator of relations between stressors and employee strain. *Work & Stress, 13*, 182–191.

Joseph, A. E., & Hallman, B. C. (1996). Caught in the triangle: The influence of home, work, and elder location in work-family balance. *Canadian Journal on Aging, 15*, 393–412.

Kalleberg, A. L., & Loscocco, K. A. (1983). Aging, values, and rewards: Explaining age differences in job satisfaction. *American Sociological Review, 48*, 78–90.

Karasek, R. (1979). Job demands, job decision latitude and mental strain: Implications for job redesign. *Administrative Science Quarterly, 24*, 285–307.

Kinsella, K. (1995). Aging and the family: Present and future demographic issues. In R. Blieszner & V. H. Bedfore (Eds.), *Handbook of aging and the family* (pp. 32–36). Westport, CT: Greenwood.

Kite, M. E., Stockdale, G. D., Whitley, B. E., & Johnson, B. (2005). Attitudes toward younger and older adults: An updated meta-analytic review. *Journal of Social Issues, 61*, 241–266.

Kirkman, B. L., & Shapiro, D. L. (2001). The impact of cultural values on job satisfaction and organizational commitment in self-managing work teams: The mediating role of employee resistance. *Academy of Management Journal, 44*, 557–569.

Kozlowski, S., & Farr, J. (1988). An integrative model of updating and performance. *Human Performance, 1*, 5–29.

Kram, K., & Isabella, L. (1985). Mentoring alternatives: The role of peer relationships in career development. *Academy of Management Journal, 28*, 110–132.

Lin, G., & Rogerson, P. A. (1995). Elderly parents and the geographic availability of their adult children. *Research on Aging, 17,* 303–331.

Mack, R., Salmoni, A., Viverais-Dressler, G., Porter, E., & Garg, R. (1997). Perceived risks to independent living: The views of older, community-dwelling adults. *The Gerontologist, 37,* 729–736.

MacNeil, R. D., Ramos, C. I., & Magafas, A. M. (1996). Age stereotyping among college students: A replication and expansion. *Educational Gerontology, 22,* 229–243.

Martocchio, J. J. (1989). Age-related differences in employee absenteeism: A meta-analysis. *Psychology and Aging, 4,* 409–414.

Matthews, A. M., & Rosenthal, C. J. (1993). Balancing work and family in an aging society: The Canadian experience. In G. L. Maddox & M. P. Lawton (Eds.), *Focus on kinship, aging and social change.* New York: Using Co.

Maurer, T. J. (2001). Career-relevant learning and development, worker age, and beliefs about self-efficacy for development. *Journal of Management, 27,* 123–140.

Maurer, T. J. (in press). Employee development and training issues related to the aging workforce. In K. S. Shultz & G. A. Adams (Eds.), *Aging and work in the 21st century.* Mahwah, NJ: Lawrence Erlbaum and Associates.

Maurer, T., Andrews, K., & Weiss, E. (2003). Toward understanding and managing stereotypical beliefs about older workers' ability and desire for learning and development. *Research in Personnel and Human Resources Management, 22,* 253–285.

Maurer, T. J., & Rafuse, N. E. (2001). Learning, not litigating: Managing employee development and avoiding claims of age discrimination. *Academy of Management Executive, 15,* 110–121.

McCauley, C. D., Ruderman, M. N., Ohlott, P. J., & Morrow, J. E. (1994). Assessing the developmental components of managerial jobs. *Journal of Applied Psychology, 79,* 544–560.

McDaniel, M. A., Schmidt, F. L., & Hunter, J. E. (1988). Job experience correlates of job performance. *Journal of Applied Psychology, 73,* 327–330.

McEvoy, G. M., & Cascio, W. F. (1989). Cumulative evidence of the relationship between age and job performance. *Journal of Applied Psychology, 74,* 11–17.

Miller, D. A. (1981). The "sandwich" generation: Adult children of the aging. *Social Work, 26,* 419–423.

Montgomery, R. J. V., Gonyea, J. G. M., & Hooyman, N. R. (1985). Care giving and the experience of subjective and objective burden. *Family Relations, 34,* 19–26.

Neal, M. B., Chapman, N. J., Ingersoll-Dayton, B., & Emen, A. C. (1993). *Balancing work and care giving for children, adults, and elders.* Newbury Park: Sage Publications.

Neal, M. B., & Hammer, L. B. (2007). *Working couples caring for children and aging parents: Effects on work and well-being.* Mahwah, NJ: Lawrence Erlbaum and Associates.

Netz, Y., & Ben-Sira, D. (1993). Attitudes of young people, adults, and older adults from three-generation families toward the concepts "ideal person," "youth," and "old person." *Educational Gerontology, 19,* 607–621.

Nichols, T., Sugur, N., & Tasiran, A. C. (2003). Signs of change in Turkey's working class: Workers' age-related perceptions in the modern manufacturing sector. *British Journal of Sociology, 54,* 527–545.

Nydegger, C. N. (1983). Family ties of the aged in cross-cultural perspective. *The Gerontologist, 23,* 26–32.

Orodenker, S. Z. (1990). Family and care giving in a changing society: The effects of employment on caregiver stress. *Family and Community Health, 12,* 58–70.

Parkinson, L. (2000). Mediating with high-conflict couples. *Family and Conciliation Courts Review, 38,* 69–76.

Pierce, L., Gardner, D. G., Dunham, R. B., & Cummings, L. L. (1989). Moderation by organization-based self-esteem of role condition employee response relationships. *Academy of Management Journal, 36,* 271–288.

Robinson, M. M., Barbee, A. P., Martin, M., Singer, T. L., & Yegidis, B. (2003). The organizational costs of caregiving: A call to action. *Administration in Social Work, 27,* 83–102.

Rosen, B., & Jerdee, T. H. (1976). The nature of job-related age stereotypes. *Journal of Applied Psychology, 62,* 180–183.

Rosenthal, C. J. (1985). Kinkeeping in the familial division of labor. *Journal of Marriage and the Family, 47*(4), 965–974.

Rosenthal, C. J. (1987). Generational succession: The passing on of family headship. *Journal of Comparative Family Studies, 18*(1), 61–77.

Ryan, E., & See, S. (1993). Age-based beliefs about memory changes for self and others across adulthood. *Journal of Gerontology, 48,* 199–201.

Ryff, C. D., Lee, U. H., Essex, M. J., & Schmutte, P. S. (1994). My children and me: Midlife evaluations of grown children and self. *Psychology and Aging, 9*(2), 195–205.

Salthouse, T. A. (1993). Speed mediation of adult age differences in cognition. *Developmental Psychology, 29,* 722–738.

Salthouse, T. A., & Maurer, T. J. (1996). Aging, job performance, and career development. In J. E. Birren & I. K. W. Schaie (Eds.), *Handbook of the psychology of aging.* (4th ed., pp. 353–364).

Schabracq, M. (1994). Motivational and cultural factors underlying dysfunctioning of older employees. In J. Snel & R. Cremer (Eds.), *Work and aging: A European perspective* (pp. 235–249). London: Taylor & Francis Ltd.

Scharlach, A. E. (1989). A comparison of employed caregivers of cognitively impaired and physically impaired elderly persons. *Research on Aging, 11,* 225–243.

Scharlach, A. E., & Boyd, S. L. (1989). Care giving and employment: Results of an employee survey, *The Gerontologist, 31,* 778–787.

Scheiber, F. (2003). Human factors and aging: Identifying and compensating for age relationship deficits in sensory and cognitive function. In N. Charness & K. W. Schaie (Eds.), *Impact of technology on successful aging* (pp. 42–84). New York: Springer.

Shore, L. M., & Goldberg, C. B. (2005). Age discrimination in the workplace. In R. L. Dipboye & A. Colella (Eds.), *Discrimination at work: The psychological and organizational bases* (pp. 203–226). Mahwah, NJ: Erlbaum.

Shultz, K. S., & Adams, G. A. (Eds.) (in press). *Aging and work in the 21st century*, Mahwah, NJ: Lawrence Erlbaum and Associates.

Silverstein, M., & Angelleli, J. J. (1998). Older parents' expectations of moving closer to their children. *Journal of Gerontology: Social Sciences, 53B*(3), S153–S163.

Singleton, J. (2000). Women caring for elderly family members: Shaping non-traditional work and family initiatives. *Journal of Comparative Family Studies*, 367–375.

Siu, O., Spector, P. E., Cooper, C. L., & Donald, I. (2001). Age differences in coping and locus of control: A study of managerial stress in Hong Kong. *Journal of Applied Psychology, 16*, 707–710.

Slotterback, C. S., & Saarnio, D. A. (1996). Attitudes toward older adults reported by young adults: Variation based on attitudinal task and attribute categories. *Psychology and Aging, 11*, 563–571.

Spirduso, W. W., Francis, K. L., & MacRae, P. G. (2005). *Physical dimensions of aging* (2nd ed.), Champaign, IL: Human Kinetics.

Spitze, G., & Logan, J. R. (1992). Helping as a component of parent-adult child relations. *Research on Aging, 14*(3), 291–312.

Staines, G. L., & O'Connor, P. (1980). Conflicts among work, leisure, and family roles. *Monthly Labor Review*, August, 35–39.

Staudinger, U. M. (1996). Wisdom and the social-interactive foundation of the mind. In P. B. Baltes & U. M. Staudinger (Eds.), *Interactive minds: Life-span perspectives on the social foundation of cognition* (pp. 276–315). New York: Cambridge University Press.

Sterns, H. L., Barrett, G. V., & Alexander, R. A. (1985). Accidents and the aging individual. In J. E. Birren & K. W. Schaie (Eds.), *Handbook of the psychology of aging* (2nd ed., pp. 703–724). New York: Van Nostrand Rinehold.

Stoller, E. P. (1983). Parental care giving by adult children. *Journal of Marriage and the Family, 45*, 851–858.

Stone, R., Cafferata, G. L., & Sangl, J. (1987). Caregivers of the frail elderly: A national profile. *The Gerontologist, 27*, 616–626.

Szinovacz, M. (1996). Couples' employment/retirement patterns and perception of marital quality. *Research on Aging, 18*, 243–268.

Tsui, A., & O'Reilly, C. (1989). Beyond simple demographic effects: The importance of relational demography in superior-subordinate dyads. *Academy of Management Journal, 32*, 402–423.

Vierck, E., & Hodges, K. (2005). *Aging: Lifestyles, work and money*. Westport, CT: Greenwood Press.

Wagner, D. L. (1987). Corporate eldercare project: Findings. In M. A. Creedon (Ed.), *Issues for an aging America: Employees and eldercare: A briefing book* (pp. 25–29). Bridgeport: University of Bridgeport, Center for the Study of Aging.

Wagner, D. L., Creedon, M. A., Sasala, J. M., & Neal, M. B. (1989). *Employees and eldercare: Designing effective responses for the workplace*. Bridgeport: University of Bridgeport: Center for the Study of Aging.

Warr, P. B. (1994). Age and employment. In H. Triandis, M. Dunnette, & L. Hough (Eds.), *Handbook of industrial and organizational psychology* (Vol. 4, 2nd ed., pp. 485–550). Palo Alto, CA: Consulting Psychologists Press.

Weiss, E. M., & Maurer, T. J. (2004). Age discrimination in personnel decisions: A re-examination. *Journal of Applied Social Psychology, 34*, 1551–1562.

Wielink, G., Huijsman, R., & McDonnell, J. (1997). Preferences for care: A study of the elders living independently in the Netherlands. *Research on Aging, 19*(2), 174–198.

Wolf, D. A. (1990). Household patterns of older women. *Research on Aging, 12*(4), 463–486.

Wrenn, K., & Maurer, T. (2004). Beliefs about older workers' learning and development behavior in relation to beliefs about malleability of skills, age-related decline and control. *Journal of Applied Social Psychology, 34*, 223–242.

Zachrtiz, J., & Gutmann, M. P. (1996). Residence and family support systems for widows in nineteenth and early twentieth century Texas. In T. Hareven (Ed.), *Aging and generational relation in historical and cross-cultural perspective* (pp. 225–253). Berlin: Walter de Gruyter & Co.

Zenger, T., & Lawrence, B. (1989). Organizational demography: The differential effects of age and tenure distributions on technical communication. *Academy of Management Journal, 32*, 353–376.

Zube, M. (1988). Changing behavior and outlook of aging men and women; Implications for marriage in the middle and later years. *Family Relations, 31*, 147–156.

7

Bringing All Families to Work Today: Equality for Gay and Lesbian Workers and Families

M. V. Lee Badgett

One of the hottest family-related debates going on in the US today concerns whether gay and lesbian couples should have the right to marry. What is now in the headlines has been brewing under the radar screen in workplaces across the country for almost two decades, however. Gay, lesbian, and bisexual (GLB) people are seeking recognition and equal treatment for their families in courts and legislatures now, but recent policy successes parallel and build on gains made in the American workplace since the 1990s. In this chapter, I want to reconnect those two strands of change to demonstrate the continuing need for employers to take action. By reframing gay and lesbian family issues as work–family issues, I also hope to connect two sometimes disparate forces for change, with GLB employees joining forces with others in their workplace to make workplaces friendlier to all families.

Certainly the discussion about gay families has come a long way from the days in which "gay" implied isolated individuals, not families, and "heterosexual" meant at least the likelihood of families, especially for female workers. Thanks to the highly charged public debates about marriage, Americans' awareness of the existence of gay families and the perceived family needs of GLB people has increased substantially over the past two decades. Now many realize that GLB workers may be wage-earning providers for their families and have the same challenges in balancing family and work responsibilities that heterosexual workers experience. Less awareness exists of the flipside of that reality, however: GLB workers experience these "normal" challenges in a context of sexual orientation discrimination, creating more subtle dynamics that employers, policy-makers, and researchers also need to understand and remedy.

Below I first lay out what we know about GLB families and workers. Next, I discuss how their workplace positions have improved substantially yet remain far from equality. The policy climate, in particular, remains hostile to recognizing the needs of GLB families, but employers also have a long way to go. Finally, I outline how we can reframe GLB issues as work–family issues and develop the beginnings of a business case for change.

New Understandings of Gay, Lesbian, and Bisexual Families

Although counts on surveys vary, most surveys of random samples of the U.S. population find somewhere between 2 and 6 percent of the population identifies as gay, lesbian, or bisexual. The National Survey of Family Growth in 2002, for instance, found that 4.1 percent of 18–44-year-old men and women identify as homosexual or bisexual (Mosher, Chandra, & Jones, 2005). Recent research suggests that 30–45 percent of gay men have partners and 50–60 percent of lesbians have partners, which is a bit below the U.S. average of 62 percent of adults in couples (married and unmarried) in 2000 (Carpenter & Gates, 2006). Census 2000 counted 1.2 million men and women who reported a same-sex unmarried partner, or roughly 1 percent of all couples (U.S. Bureau of the Census, 2003). While that figure is undoubtedly an undercount (Badgett & Rogers, 2003), it represents a fourfold increase from the number of same-sex couples counted in 1990 and has led to an increase in the visibility of gay couples nationwide. We know less about other kinds of gay family formations, such as the broader kinship networks anthropologist Kath Weston (1991) refers to as "families we choose," but GLB people are likely to have ties to other relatives for whom they may have some financial or caregiving responsibilities.

These most visible gay and lesbian families challenge the stereotypes of gay couples in other ways. One in five male couples and a third of female same-sex couples are raising children under 18 in their homes (U.S. Bureau of the Census, 2003). Single gay men and lesbians are also raising children, and some work suggests that a higher percentage of gay singles than couples has children (Carpenter & Gates, 2006).

Not surprisingly, GLB adults who have families also participate in the paid labor force. People with same-sex partners are more likely to be employed in the labor force (71 percent) than are people in married couples (65 percent; Sears, Gates, & Rubenstein, 2005). And while same-sex couples do not appear to use gender roles to divvy up who does what within families, we see some differences in labor market outcomes within same-sex couples that may reflect strategies for managing work and family responsibilities. In the 1990 Census, members of same-sex couples were more likely to have both partners working than were different sex couples, but the number of weeks worked in the year was quite different for almost half of same-sex couples (Klawitter, 1995). Same-sex couples are less likely to be in single-wage earner relationships than married different-sex couples, but still 20 percent of childless couples and 34 percent of couples with children have a single wage earner in the 2000 Census (Sears et al., 2005). Whatever these patterns mean about the time allocation decision-making process within same-sex couples, the outcomes are further evidence that gay couples are grappling with the same kind of work–family challenges as heterosexual families.

Although the work–family challenges are the same, the workplace context is quite different for GLB employees in ways that add some gay-specific challenges. First, the threat of employment discrimination, such as the loss of a job or promotion, is ever-present in most parts of the US and puts GLB workers and their families in a precarious position. Recent studies find that employment discrimination remains common against GLB people around the world (e.g., Badgett, 2001; Badgett & Frank, 2007). Only 17 states and the District of Columbia forbid anti-gay job discrimination, leaving many millions of GLB employees vulnerable to an arbitrary loss of job or promotion. A decade of research suggests that gay men earn as much as one-third less than similarly qualified heterosexual men, suggesting that discrimination hurts workers in their paychecks (Badgett, 2006).

Second, a more complicated disadvantage involves decisions about disclosure of a stigmatized sexual orientation, which can make GLB workers more vulnerable to discrimination. The fear of discrimination remains a barrier to employees' openness about their sexual orientation to supervisors and coworkers (Badgett, 2001). Families matter here, too. Even putting pictures of a partner or children on a desk – a common workplace practice for heterosexual employees – can constitute coming out for gay workers. Having families to support also may raise the stakes for GLB workers who are considering being more open. But remaining "closeted" does not necessarily rule out differential treatment, especially when workplace sociability is important for teamwork or moving up career ladders (Badgett, 2001), and as I discuss later, the closet can take a psychological toll on workers that might well have effects on families, too.

Third, compensation discrimination against GLB people is the norm in most workplaces because GLB workers' domestic partners and children are rarely included in health care or survivor benefits. Family ties are especially crucial for health care benefits, since most non-elderly get health insurance through their employer or a family member's employer (U.S. Bureau of the Census, 2002). At least partly because of employer practices, GLB people who have partners are almost twice as likely to be uninsured as married people; one in five people in a same-sex relationship lack insurance coverage of any kind (Ash & Badgett, 2006). Overall, social stigma, as well as feared and actual discrimination, put GLB workers and their families in a very different context from heterosexual workers and families.

An Incomplete Revolution

In the 1990s, GLB employees and their heterosexual allies increasingly challenged the discriminatory treatment described previously. GLB workers formed groups or lobbied individually at their workplaces for equal treatment and freedom from discrimination (Badgett, 2001; Raeburn, 2004). Corporations have been much more responsive to requests from GLB people than legislators. By 2006, 86 percent of Fortune 500 companies had added sexual orientation to their company nondiscrimination policies (Luther, 2006). As of this writing, half of the Fortune 500 provide domestic partner health benefits to employees' same-sex partners (and usually to different-sex unmarried partners, as well).

Some of these changes came about because of innovative public policies. In 1997, the City and County of San Francisco implemented an "Equal Benefit Ordinance" requiring city contractors to offer equal benefits to spouses and domestic partners. That law began a wave of change among small and large firms alike, which was especially powerful for large companies with operations in many locations (Rogers & Dunham, 2003). Several other cities followed with similar policies, as did the State of California.

The revolution remains incomplete, however. Taking all employers into account, including those not in the Fortune 500, shows that a small minority of employees work for a firm offering benefits to the families of the GLB employee. A 2004 survey by the Kaiser Family Foundation and Health Research Trust found that only 14 percent of firms offer such coverage (Kaiser Family Foundation, 2004).

More recently, the call for workplace equality has shifted to the debate about marriage equality for same-sex couples. Employers' provision of benefits shows up prominently in the list of reasons that same-sex couples need access to marriage. Health care benefits are not the only reason that some gay couples want to marry, but court decisions and legislators prominently allude to those benefits in the course of their deliberations. Massachusetts remains the only state to give full marriage rights to couples, and even that situation is under attack from opponents of marriage equality. Vermont, Connecticut, New Jersey, and California offer almost all of the rights of marriage as "civil unions" or enhanced domestic partnerships. Hawaii, New Jersey, Maine, and the District of Columbia offer a status with a more limited set of rights and responsibilities to same-sex couples (and sometimes to unmarried different-sex couples).

Oddly enough, it is not clear how much of a difference marriage and civil unions have made for employment benefits. A 2005 Hewitt Associates survey of large employers operating in Massachusetts found that only 20–25 percent of them offered spousal benefits to same-sex spouses (Hewitt Associate, 2005). Far more employers continued to recognize domestic partnerships of their GLB employees, with only a few dropping partner coverage completely. Although advocates argue that state insurance codes require equal treatment of same-sex and different-sex spouses (including civil union partners) for employers with insured plans, employers with self-insured plans have more leeway to define spouse so as to exclude legally married same-sex spouses (Gay & Lesbian Advocates & Defenders, no date). ERISA, the federal law governing most private employers' health and retirement plans, offers no protection for same-sex spouses who are treated differently from different-sex spouses (Hewitt Associates, 2005).

State-level action cannot completely equalize the rights of same-sex couples. The 1996 federal Defense of Marriage Act defines marriage as being limited to different-sex couples and leaves over a thousand federal benefits off-limits to gay couples. In addition to exclusion from those federal benefits, the IRS considers domestic partner benefits as taxable income to the employee under most circumstances, generating extra tax bills of hundreds or even thousands of dollars for families.

Although progress toward marriage has been slow, with recent court setbacks in New York and Washington State, the progress toward some granting of rights to gay couples has been positive, and in 2006, 20 percent of U.S. residents live in a state that recognizes registered gay relationships (calculated from Human Rights Campaign, 2006b; U.S. Census Bureau, 2003). These victories have come at some cost, though. The most obvious cost is the political backlash that has led 19 states (and counting) to pass constitutional amendments limiting marriage to different-sex couples, even though 38 states had already put such laws on the books since the mid-1990s (see

Human Rights Campaign, 2006a). Referendum campaigns, in particular, are known to generate enormous psychological stress for GLB people, their allies, and their families (Russell, 2000). Employers might already see spillover stress from these issues in the workplace. Employers have also experienced more direct resistance related to political backlash, as when the American Family Association fought with Ford Motor Co. over its support for GLB employees.

Another worry is that the campaign for legal recognition for gay couples has led to a sense of complacency or a diversion of resources away from employer-centered efforts. For instance, from 2000 to 2003, 75 Fortune 500 companies added partner coverage; over the next three years only 50 companies added coverage (Luther, 2006). The apparent slowdown could be the result of the most progressive employers being picked off first, or of double-digit health care inflation scaring off employers rather than a turning away from pressure on employers. But clearly employers still have a long way to go before gay employees and their families will be treated equally everywhere, and if judicial and legislative efforts to gain legal recognition fail to achieve gains right away, more attention might once again be focused on employers. Employers, at least, will not be able to hand off responsibility for equal treatment to policymakers for quite a while, it would seem.

Reframing Gay Workplace Issues

Perhaps in the lull between phases of the marriage debate, those organizations and individual actors concerned about fairness and work–family balance might consider reframing gay family issues. Now most of the debate in and outside of workplaces sees sexual orientation inequality as a *civil rights issue* that is "solved" by granting marriage rights and is limited to same-sex couples. Instead of relying on a civil rights framework for gay family issues, I would argue that placing gay family issues inside the *work–family* rubric would expand the potential for change.

These two ways of framing gay issues are not mutually exclusive, but the contrast might help GLB activists tap into new sources of energy and allies who could lead to greater short- to medium-run progress. Domestic partnership benefits and other ways of promoting equal employment rights for GLB people can be pitched to employers as part of a package of work–family initiatives that will improve employees' lives and will benefit employers. Pulling away from the civil rights paradigm also could serve to convince employers that family diversity is a reality so that other kinds of non-gay family structures, such as the families of employees with different-sex partners, also are treated equally. Finally, GLB workplace activists have become skilled in direct education and organizing, which could help work–family activists expand support for other seemingly non-gay-related issues, such as family leave policies or child care subsidies. Many large companies have GLB employee resource groups that could provide experienced leaders and allies on many work–family issues.

The efforts to win domestic partner benefits provide many concrete examples of the crossover benefit of working with GLB groups. These efforts have largely been led by GLB employees (Badgett, 2001; Scully & Creed, 1999). In many cases, GLB employees have argued that employers should provide equal benefits for all people with unmarried partners, whether a different-sex or same-sex partner. Employers have sometimes resisted covering different-sex unmarried partners since they have the option of marriage, and indeed, they are far more numerous than are employees with same-sex partners (Ash & Badgett, 2006; Badgett, 2001). Nevertheless, the fact that 14 percent of employers offer partner coverage to same-sex partners, and 12 percent offer partner coverage to different-sex partners, suggests that the fate of the two groups of partners are closely tied (Kaiser Family Foundation, 2004). There are even examples of situations in which discussions of benefits for partners led employers to allow employees to choose which individuals to cover through job-related health insurance, including family members who were not partners or children (Rogers & Dunham, 2003; Scully & Creed, 1999).

GLB employees are also likely to share many other work–family issues with heterosexual employees but might first prioritize equal recognition of partners and children. The diversity of GLB families mean that policies like paid family leave or subsidized child care also will be important for GLB families, but only if their family relationships are recognized. For instance, only California and Rhode Island recognize same-sex domestic partners for purposes of state-mandated family leave policies.

A Business Case for GLB Equality

Like many other work–family issues, offering equal treatment to GLB employees involves a cost to employers. Rapidly rising health insurance costs heighten the concerns about equal benefits for same-sex partners (not to mention the larger group of different-sex partners). Other kinds of

family-related benefits, such as pension benefits or family leaves, have gar-
nered less attention, perhaps because those benefits involve less cost.

Even health care costs will rise less than employers might expect. Two
issues have dominated the discussion (see Badgett, 2000). First, employers
worry about adverse selection, in which employees sign up a partner who
has higher-than-average health care costs. This concern arose primarily
in the context of the early stages of the HIV epidemic, and some insurance
companies imposed a temporary surcharge on employers to take that possibility into account. However, employer experience has not born out this
concern (Badgett, 2000; Badgett, 2001), and the health status of people with
partners has proven to be quite similar to that of married people (Ash &
Badgett, 2006).

The second big cost issue is that of enrollment. More people enrolling
for health insurance means higher premium payments for employers.
Again, expectations have exceeded reality. Both employer reports and a recent
study using Current Population Survey data show that on average 0.1–0.3
percent of employees will want to sign up a domestic partner for health
care benefits (Ash & Badgett, 2006). Take-up of the benefit is low primarily because GLB employees' partners are more likely to be employed and to
have their own employer-provided coverage than are married employees'
spouses. Also, the value of the domestic partner benefits is considered to
be taxable income, unlike the payments for spouses. Those two factors reduce
take-up by GLB employees with partners to only 20–30 percent.

Altogether then, the expected cost increase for employers would be
roughly in line with the enrollment increase, or generally well under 1 percent of total health care expenditures (Ash & Badgett, 2006; Luther, 2006).
At a time when health care costs are rapidly rising, GLB employees can
argue (or at least hope) that a small increase of this magnitude might not
have a noticeable impact on the bottom line. But it is instructive to note
that the boom in partner benefit offerings occurred in the 1990s when health
care cost inflation temporarily moderated (Badgett, 2001). In the current
climate, it seems likely that employers will want to know more about the
bottom line impact of offering partner coverage.

The financial gains from partner coverage are more difficult to estimate
than the costs. However, the benefits are likely to be real, including lower
employee turnover that reduces recruitment, hiring, and training costs, along
with the possibility of improving access to a potentially lucrative market
niche.

Understanding these positive impacts requires thinking from the perspective of the unique situation faced by GLB workers discussed earlier:

the disclosure dilemma. On one hand, sexual orientation is not a visible characteristic, and hiding one's GLB status (i.e., remaining in the closet) might provide some protection against the threat of discrimination. Several studies have found that past experiences with discrimination reduced the likelihood that a GLB person would come out (Hall, 1989; Schneider, 1986). Similarly, the perceived level of discriminatory treatment of GLB people in a workplace increases the likelihood that gay men and lesbians will use avoidance or counterfeiting strategies (i.e., staying closeted) and make it less likely that they will use integrative strategies (i.e., coming out; Button, 2001). Similarly, Ragins and Cornwell (2001) showed that people who had experienced or observed sexual orientation discrimination in the workplace were less likely to come out. Interviews by Woods (1993) and Seidman, Meeks, and Traschen (1999) revealed that GLB respondents' fears of discrimination clearly impact their decisions to conceal their sexual orientation.

On the other hand, being closeted can have other costs to GLB people, including psychological harm and indirect discrimination from limiting social interactions with coworkers (see a longer discussion in Badgett, 2001). When workers come out (the flipside of being closeted), they gain in several important ways. Using different measures of general anxiety or anxiety in particular contexts, several studies found that people who were more out reported lower levels of anxiety and conflict between work and personal life (Day & Schoenrade, 1997; Griffith & Hebl, 2002; Hall, 1989; Jordan & Deluty, 1998). Several studies found that being out tended to increase GLB workers' job satisfaction (Day & Schoenrade, 1997; Driscoll, Kelley, & Fassinger, 1996; Griffith & Hebl, 2002). In addition, Day and Schoenrade's survey participants who were more out also reported sharing their employer's values and goals more than workers who were more closeted (Day & Schoenrade, 1997). However, some studies looked for but did not find this link (Ellis & Riggle, 1995; Ragins & Cornwell, 2001). A study by Ellis and Riggle (1995) shows that more out workers report higher levels of satisfaction with their coworkers.

Given the crucial mediating factor in GLB workplace life – the closet – employers have an interest in encouraging more openness among GLB workers. Indirect benefits include improving mental health, work–family balance, and coworker relationships among GLB employees. Direct benefits include the possibility of lower employee turnover if workers are more satisfied with their jobs and are more aligned with employer objectives. Employers can encourage openness and loyalty among GLB workers through supportive policies and practices.

A growing body of research finds a clear correlation between employer support and disclosure, suggesting that a causal link is at least plausible:

- *Supportive workplace policies*: Several studies have found higher levels of disclosure in workplaces with non-discrimination policies that include sexual orientation (Badgett, 2001; Griffith & Hebl, 2002; Ragins & Cornwell, 2001; Rostosky & Riggle, 2002). The influence may be large: Badgett's study (2001) suggested that an employer nondiscrimination policy increased the probability of a worker being completely out by 21 percent. Ragins and Cornwell (2001) found that the single most encouraging employer practice was welcoming a same-sex partner to social events. Gay support groups in the workplace also appeared to encourage workers to come out, but including sexual orientation in diversity training did not. Rostosky and Riggle (2002) found that coming out is also more likely when the respondent's partner works in a place with a sexual orientation nondiscrimination law.
- *Perceptions that a workplace is gay-supportive*: Griffith and Hebl (2002) found that perceptions of a workplace's gay-friendliness are more important in encouraging disclosure than actual workplace policies for gay and lesbian workers in Houston. Day and Schoenrade (1997) reported that more out employees perceive a higher level of support for the principle of nondiscrimination based on sexual orientation. Driscoll and colleagues (1996) found that more supportive workplace climates increase disclosure among the lesbians they studied.
- *Good reactions by coworkers*: Several studies found that the expectation of positive coworkers' reactions increases disclosure among GLB workers (Badgett, 2001; Griffith & Hebl, 2002). Badgett (2001) found that seeing other out gay workers being treated fairly in the workplace increases the probability of coming out by 18 percent. Griffith and Hebl's study (2002) revealed that coworkers' positive attitudes and comfort level with GLB people also improve job satisfaction and lower anxiety for GLB workers.
- *Presence of gay co-workers*: Ragins and Cornwell (2001) found that workers with gay coworkers were more likely to be out. However, Badgett (2001) saw no direct connection with gay coworkers, finding instead (as noted above) that the impact of gay workers on other workers' disclosure decisions depends on perceptions of how out co-workers are treated. (Ragins & Cornwell did not ask whether the coworkers were out.)

Workplace equality for GLB people can also make an employer more attractive to heterosexual workers who prefer to work in a diverse and tolerant environment (e.g. Florida, 2002). Some recent opinion surveys show that heterosexual workers value equal treatment of GLB workers and believe that partner benefits give firms a recruiting advantage (see Badgett & Gates, 2006).

Finally, the spread of domestic partner benefits has tended to be across industries, suggesting that employers respond to equity policies of their labor market competitors (Badgett, 2001; Raeburn, 2004). As competitors begin to offer partner benefits, firms that do not might find themselves having a harder time recruiting workers. This source of pressure reinforces the other impetus for change mentioned earlier: to find ways to reduce turnover and to be an attractive option for job-searchers.

An additional "carrot" for employers to develop policies that ensure equal treatment for GLB workers is sometimes said to be improving access to the gay market. While the talk about the size and distinctiveness of the gay market is surely overstated (see longer discussion in Badgett, 2001), there might be situations in which companies can strategically align their products with the ethos and concerns of the gay community to improve the profit bottom line by increasing revenues instead of reducing costs (the business impact suggested above). GLB consumers might be more likely to buy from companies that treat GLB employees equally (Witeck & Combs, 2006), and sometimes companies advertising in gay magazines or newspapers will tout their employment policies to attract new customers.

Although it is not possible at this stage in the research on gay issues to add up both costs and benefits to firms in dollar terms, the clear message is that any cost calculations will overstate – and perhaps dramatically overstate – the net cost to employers of equal treatment of GLB workers because the uptake of these benefits is likely to be lower than most estimates and potential gains from these actions are likely to be ignored.

Conclusions

One work–family scholar once suggested to me that a potential downside to pursuing GLB issues as work–family issues would be giving up the powerful tool of civil rights enforcement in the courts. But there is no reason why both strategies could not operate at once. GLB legal organizations have had some limited success in gaining access to partner benefits through litigation in the minority of states where protective legislation has been enacted, and there is no obvious reason why such efforts could not continue. The successful work in corporations has used the promise of a better competitive position in the labor market and the carrot of city contracts to encourage voluntary change. The voluntary efforts have relied both on equity arguments and business-based arguments, both of which are compatible with work–family arguments, as this chapter shows.

Both the similarities of GLB families and heterosexual families and their differences – the context of inequality for GLB employees – create a moral and political imperative for work–family advocates to incorporate gay and lesbian family issues into their agendas. A search of websites of a non-random selection of national work-family organizations failed to uncover examples of organizations that have taken on GLB issues in any meaningful way. Legislative advocacy, workplace advocacy, and research should pay greater attention to the diversity of families, and adding GLB family issues will be an important first step in that direction.

Acknowledgements

The author thanks Lynn Comella for her assistance in gathering and analyzing some of the studies cited in the business case section of the paper, and to Deborah Ho for her assistance in preparing the manuscript. Some of that discussion also draws on work more fully presented in Badgett and Gates (2006).

References

Ash, M., & Badgett, M. V. L. (2006). Separate and unequal: The effect of unequal access to employment-based health insurance on same-sex and unmarried different-sex couples. *Contemporary Economic Policy, 24*(4), 582–599.

Badgett, M. V. L. (2000). Calculating costs with credibility: Health care benefits for domestic partners. *Angles: The Policy Journal of the Institute for Gay and Lesbian Strategic Studies, 5*(1), 1–8.

Badgett, M. V. L. (2001). *Money, myths, and change: The economic lives of lesbians and gay men.* Chicago: University of Chicago Press.

Badgett, M. V. L. (2006). Discrimination based on sexual orientation: A review of the economics literature and beyond. In W. M. Rodgers III (Ed.), *The handbook of the economics of discrimination* (pp. 161–186). Northampton, MA: Edward Elgar Publishing.

Badgett, M. V. L., & Frank, J. (2007). *Sexual orientation discrimination: An international perspective. Routledge IAFFE Advances in Feminist Economics.* New York: Routledge.

Badgett, M. V. L., & Gates, G. J. (2006, October). *The effect of marriage equality and domestic partnership for business and the economy.* Los Angeles: Williams Institute, UCLA School of Law.

Badgett, M. V. L., & Rogers, M. A. (2003). *Left out of the count: Missing same-sex couples in census 2000.* Amherst, MA: Institute for Gay and Lesbian Strategic Studies.

Button, S. B. (2001). Organizational efforts to affirm sexual diversity: A cross-level examination. *Journal of Applied Psychology, 86,* 17–28.

Carpenter, C., & Gates, G. (2006, December). *Gay and lesbian partnerships: Evidence from multiple surveys* (CCPR-058-06). Los Angeles, CA: University of California, Los Angeles, California Center for Population Research.

Day, N., & Schoenrade, P. (1997). Staying in the closet versus coming out: Relationships between communication about sexual orientation and work attitudes. *Personnel Psychology, 50,* 147–163.

Driscoll, J. M., Kelley, F. A., & Fassinger, R. E. (1996). Lesbian identity and disclosure in the workplace: Relation to occupational stress and satisfaction. *Journal of Vocational Behavior, 48,* 229–242.

Ellis, A. L., & Riggle, E. D. B. (1995). The relation of job satisfaction and degree of openness about one's sexual orientation for lesbians and gay men. *Journal of Homosexuality, 30*(2), 75–85.

Florida, R. (2002). *The rise of the creative class: And how it's transforming work, leisure, community, and everyday life.* New York, NY: Basic Books.

Gay & Lesbian Advocates & Defenders (no date). *Same-sex spousal health benefits in Massachusetts after Goodridge.* Retrieved September 18, 2006, from http://www.glad.org/rights/HealthBenefitsAfterGoodridge.html

Griffith, K. H., & Hebl, M. R. (2002). The disclosure dilemma for gay men and lesbians: "Coming out" at work. *Journal of Applied Psychology, 87*(6), 1191–1199.

Hall, M. (1989). Private experiences in the public domain: Lesbians in organizations. In J. R. Hearn, D. L. Sheppard, P. Tancred, & G. Burrel (Eds.), *The sexuality of organization* (pp. 125–138). Thousand Oaks, CA: Sage.

Hewitt Associates (2005, September). *State of the (same-sex) union.* Study presented at the annual summit for Out & Equal, Denver, CO.

Human Rights Campaign (2006a). *State prohibitions on marriage for same-sex couples.* Retrieved September 29, 2006, from http://www.hrc.org/Template.cfm?Section=Center&CONTENTID=28225&TEMPLATE=/ContentManagemet/ContentDisplay.cfm

Human Rights Campaign (2006b). *Relationship recognition in the U.S.* Retrieved October 9, 2006, from http://www.hrc.org/Template.cfm?Section=Your_Community&Template=/ContentManagement/ContentDisplay.cfm&ContentID=16305

Jordan, K. M., & Deluty, R. H. (1998). Coming out for lesbian women: Its relation to anxiety, positive affectivity, self-esteem, and social support. *Journal of Homosexuality, 35*(2), 41–63.

Kaiser Family Foundation & Health Research and Educational Trust (2004). *Employer health benefits, 2004 annual survey.* Retrieved November 1, 2005, from http://www.kff.org/insurance/7148/upload/2004-Employer-Health-Benefits-Survey-Full-Report.pdf

Klawitter, M. (1995, April). *Did they find each other or create each other?: Labor market linkages between partners in same-sex and different-sex couples.* Study presented at the annual conference for Population Assoc. of America, San Francisco, CA.

Luther, S. (2006). *The state of the workplace for gay, lesbian, bisexual and transgender Americans: 2005–2006.* Washington, DC: The Human Rights Campaign Foundation.

Mosher, W. D., Chandra, A., & Jones J. (2005, September). Sexual behavior and selected health measures: Men and women 15–44 years of age, United States, 2002. *Advance Data from Vital and Health Statistics, 362,* 1–56.

Raeburn, N. (2004). *Changing corporate America from inside-out: Lesbian and gay workplace rights.* Minneapolis: University of Minnesota Press.

Ragins, B. R., & Cornwell, J. M. (2001). Pink triangles: Antecedents and consequences of perceived workplace discrimination against gay and lesbian employees. *Journal of Applied Psychology, 86*(6), 1244–1261.

Rogers, M. A., & Dunham, D. (2003). *Contracts with equality: An evaluation of the San Francisco Equal Benefits Ordinance.* Amherst, MA: Institute for Gay and Lesbian Strategic Studies.

Rostosky, S. S., & Riggle, E. D. B. (2002). "Out" at work: The relation of actor and partner workplace policy and internalized homophobia to disclosure status. *Journal of Counseling Psychology, 49*(4), 411–419.

Russell, G. M. (2000). *Voted out: The psychological consequences of anti-gay politics.* New York: New York University Press.

Scully, M., & Creed, W. E. D. (1999). Restructured families: Issues of equality and need. *The Annals of the American Academy of Political and Social Science, 562*(1), 47–65.

Schneider, B. (1986). Coming out at work: Bridging the private/public gap. *Work and Occupations, 13*(4), 463–487.

Sears, R. B., Gates, G., & Rubenstein, W. B. (2005). *Same-sex couples and same-sex couples raising children in the United States.* Los Angeles: Williams Institute, UCLA School of Law.

Seidman, S., Meeks, C., & Traschen, F. (1999). Beyond the closet? The changing social meaning of homosexuality in the United States. *Sexualities, 2*(1), 9–34.

U.S. Bureau of the Census (2003, February). *Married-couple and unmarried-partner households: 2000.* Retrieved September 29, 2006, from http://www.census.gov/prod/2003pubs/censr-5.pdf

U.S. Bureau of the Census (2002, September). *Health insurance coverage: 2001.* Retrieved September 29, 2006, from http://www.census.gov/prod/2002pubs/p60-220.pdf

Weston, K. (1991). *Families we choose: Lesbians, gays, kinship.* New York: Columbia University Press.

Witeck, R., & Combs W. (2006). *Business inside out: Capturing millions of brand loyal gay consumers.* Chicago, IL: Kaplan Publishing.

Woods, J. D. (1993). *The corporate closet: The professional lives of gay men in America.* New York: Free Press.

Part III

Work, Stress, and Health Linkages: How Does Working and Caring for Families Affect Health?

Part III

Introduction

Diane F. Halpern

When *Forbes* and other magazines list the best companies to work for, the smiling people on the cover and their quotes in the glossy pages that follow are all about the various options that allow employees to control their work hours and the way they work. Not surprisingly, the best companies to work for also enjoy high levels of returns on their investments. Could at least part of the answer for the success of these businesses be due to giving employees the flexibility to control their own work lives?

The importance of being able to control when and how we work is the central theme in the leading psychological model of work stress, which is known as the "Job Demand Control Model" (Karasek, 1979; Karasek & Theorell, 1990). According to this model, the stress of a job has two primary components: (1) the psychological demands of the job, such as having too much work to complete in the amount of time allotted; and (2) the decision latitude or extent to which a worker has the ability to control stressful work situations, such as deciding on the rate at which work is completed or order in which tasks are done. Thus, the stress of a job depends on both the nature of the job and whether workers believe that they have the ability to control the stressful aspects of the job. When employees can make decisions related to the way they work, they are able to devise coping strategies that can mitigate the effects of stress.

Most of the research by psychologists who address the linkages between work and health has been conducted around a model in which stress intervenes between work and health, and it is stress, in varying amounts and types, that determines health outcomes (Halpern, 2005). This model has at least two causal arrows with stress affecting health and work affecting stress.

The Biology of Stress

A stressor is a threat from the environment that activates a complex chain of events in what is known as the hypothamic-pituitary-adrenal axis (HPA) and the release of hormones that travel through the bloodstream and affect many different organs. Because the travel of hormones is relatively slow, the effects of stress continue to affect organs much longer than the actual stressor (Gazzaniga & Heatherton, 2003). Researchers know the physiological markers of stress, which include increased levels of the hormone cortisol, increased muscle tension, changes in heart rate, and high blood pressure. Behavioral measures include memory impairments, which results from cortisol damage to the neurons in the hippocampus (a primary areas of the brain that underlies memory) and other brain locations (Sapolsky, 1994).

In a study that used random assignment of participants to conditions to establish strong causal links, Cohen and his colleagues (Cohen, Frank, Doyle, Skoner, Rabin, & Gwaltney, 1998) assigned healthy volunteers to different levels of exposure to the virus that causes colds. They found that volunteers who reported the highest levels of chronic or long-term stress had worse cold symptoms and higher viral counts than those volunteers who reported less stress. They also found that interpersonal and work-related stressors (they used the terms under- and over-employment) were mostly responsible for these results. Surprisingly, health practices such as smoking, maintaining a poor diet, and lack of exercise had very small effects on the incidence of colds. The entire field of psychoneuroendocrinology has been growing rapidly as we understand the way the immune system responds to psychological variables such as stress. When the underlying physiological basis of the stress response is activated too often or too intensely the function of the immune system is impaired, increasing the probability and severity of ill health (Herbert & Cohen, 1993; McEwen, 2002).

How Work Stress Affects Health

In Part III, researchers examine the effects on mental and physical health of work–family stress and a related but opposite construct, work–family balance. Halpern, Tan, and Carsten examine caregiver stress and the effect of employment while caring for someone who is unable to provide self-care on the health and well-being of caregivers. This is a particularly timely topic as aging baby-boomers find themselves caring for their own parents, who comprise the oldest living cohort in the history of humankind. The authors relate the caregivers' concerns to California's new paid leave insurance and find that the new legislation is being used by very few caregivers because it does not address their main concerns.

Saxbe and Repetti continue the study of stress and work by showing how physiological measures of stress and its effects need to be related to work-related measures. The "daily grind," with its many hassles coupled with more intensive periods of stress, such as loss of a job or financial hardships cause our bodies to respond in ways that are protective in the short-run. Unfortunately, work-related stress is long-term and its effects on physical health and mental health have been underestimated because most studies do not use both physiological and behavioral measures.

In addition to work-related stress, Grzywacz, Butler, and Almeida examine work–family balance, which they describe as an equal or balanced investment in both work and life outside of work. They found that less than 10 percent of the population is "balanced" in their investments in work and family, by their definition. They examine the physical and mental correlates of both work–family conflict and work–family balance. Their results and conclusions should convince all employers that it is good business to create workplaces that allow their employees to balance both critical aspects of their lives.

References

Cohen, S., Frank, E., Doyle, W. J., Skoner, D. P., Rabin, B. S., & Gwaltney, J. M. Jr., (1998). Types of stressors that increase susceptibility to the common cold in healthy adults. *Health Psychology, 17*, 214–223.

Gazzaniga, M. S., & Heatherton, T. F. (2003). *Psychological science: Mind, brain, and behavior.* New York: W. W. Norton Company.

Halpern, D. F. (2005). How time-flexible work policies can reduce stress, improve health, and save money. *Stress and Health, 21*, 157–168.

Herbert, T. B., & Cohen, S. (1993). Depression and immunity: A meta-analytic review. *Psychological Bulletin, 113*, 472–486.

Karasek, Jr., R. A. (1979). Job demands, job decision latitude and mental strain: Implications for job redesign. *Administrative Science Quarterly, 24*, 285–307.

Karasek, R. A., & Theorell, T. (1990). *Healthy work: Stress, productivity, and the reconstruction of working life.* New York: Basic Books.

McEwen, B. (2002). *The end of stress as we know it.* Washington, DC: The DANA Press (Joseph Henry Press).

Sapolsky, R. M. (1994). *Why zebras don't get ulcers.* New York: Freeman.

8

California Paid Family Leave: Is It Working for Caregivers?

Diane F. Halpern, Sherylle J. Tan, and Melissa Carsten

How can working families take care of sick or frail relatives while also meeting the demands of their jobs? For the estimated 28,872,766 caregivers in the United States, 3,419,481 of whom reside in California, this is not a rhetorical question (Family Caregiver Alliance, 2006). Far too many parents face the painful choice between staying at home to care for a sick child or losing their job, and along with it the money needed to buy groceries and pay the rent. The number of working adults with significant caregiving responsibilities is expected to rise dramatically. Over the next ten years, it is estimated that almost one in ten Americans will need to take time off work to care for an elderly family member, thus the need for paid family leave is not a woman's problem or a child care problem – it is a universal problem (National Alliance on Caregiving, 2005). With almost 50 million baby boomers approaching retirement in the next decade, the responsibilities of American workers who care for their elderly parents will affect every segment of society. Because many informal caregivers are also balancing full- or part-time jobs, it is not surprising that working caregivers often face financial impediments, as well as emotional and physical health problems. What is surprising, however, is the lack of state and federal assistance available to workers who take time off to provide care to a family member.

President George W. Bush proclaimed that November be National Family Caregivers Month, even though when compared to other industrialized nations, the US has not made a commitment to provide government-subsidized aid for families balancing work and caregiving responsibilities (Proclamation 7957, 2005). In fact, the US is among only three major industrialized countries worldwide that fail to offer any kind of paid leave support. Virtually all European counties and many South American countries offer various forms of wage replacement to parents caring for newborns as well as to individuals caring for elderly parents. Until July 2004, financial assistance for new parents or individuals caring for an elderly parent or relative was nonexistent in the US. As a result, many workers either exhausted their vacation days or were forced to suffer lost wages when taking time off. Whereas many of these workers (over 35 million since 1993) have taken advantage of the job security that is offered under the Federal Medical Leave Act (FMLA), there is still concern over whether taking unpaid leave will drive families into a state of financial hardship (Cantor et al., 2001).

The California Paid Family Leave Insurance Program (CPFL) is the first in the nation to offer employees who pay into the State Disability Insurance program (SDI) up to six weeks of partially paid time off when caring for a newborn or sick family member. Specifically, this new program offers a wage replacement of up to 55 percent of the worker's salary, or no more than $850 per week. Wage replacement is designed to reduce the economic hardships on workers with substantial caregiving responsibilities (Lovell, 2006). Californians were eligible to begin receiving the benefit on July 1, 2004. With the program still in its infancy, the national spotlight is on California for evidence that the paid leave program offers financial and emotional relief to informal caregivers.

Evidence for Caregiver Burden

There is a substantial amount of research to show that family caregivers suffer more financial and emotional hardship than non-caregivers. The informal caregiver role is frequently filled by a spouse or relative who does not receive financial compensation for the care they provide. Furthermore, it is evident that informal caregivers invest large amounts of time and financial resources to ensure that their care receiver is comfortable and healthy (Max, Webber, & Fox, 1995; Moss Lawton, Kleban, & Duhamel, 1993). It is estimated that caregivers spend at least $6,000 a year on doctor's bills and prescription medication for their care receiver (Stommel, Colins, & Givens, 1994). The additional cost of lost wages for working caregivers can result in an average expenditure of $33,000 a year (Teri & Truax, 1994). As a result, informal caregivers are said to experience high levels of stress, anger, resentment, and isolation (Vitaliano, Zhang, & Scanlan, 2003). The combination of financial and emotional strain contributes to caregiver burnout and depression. Additionally, caregivers have been shown to be more prone to physical illness due to the chronic stressors generated by providing informal care (Vitaliano, Young, & Zhang, 2004).

The research suggests that the combined stress and emotional strain of caregiving is a significant health factor for caregivers and a factor which non-caregivers are able to avoid. Caregivers who provide care to an elderly family member have a greater risk of health problems and higher mortality rates than non-caregivers (Schulz & Beach, 1999; Vitaliano et al., 2003). With an established link between caregiver strain and health problems, the threat of severe illness and mortality is all too real for those assuming an informal caregiving role.

Taken together, research findings on caregiver strain highlight the financial, emotional, and physical hardships that caregivers experience. These hardships are often intensified when caregivers work full-time. In fact, working caregivers have been shown to miss more workdays and report feeling more drained than workers who do not assume a caregiver role (Lee, 1997). This latter study also supported the notion that working caregivers suffer more physical health problems, such as sporadic weight gain, weight loss, or headaches, than non-caregivers.

Caregivers who work full-time often struggle with the competing demands of work and family. Low-income caregivers spend significantly more time providing care than higher-income families. As a result, low-income caregivers spend more time away from work to address their caregiving responsibilities (Heymann, 2000). Additionally, caregivers who are caring for frail elders are more likely to reduce their work hours or rearrange their work schedule to provide care (Stone & Short, 1990). The burden of reduced work hours and the subsequent reduced income have been shown to impact the well-being of the entire family (Covinsky et al., 2001).

In addition to lost wages, many caregivers who take time off also face the threat of job loss. With little support from their employers, caregivers may find it increasingly difficult to meet their care receivers' physical and emotional needs (Lee, Walker, & Shoup, 2001). Low-income caregivers, especially, have very few or no family-friendly benefits (e.g., paid leave or flexible schedules) to assist them in meeting their care receivers' needs (Heymann, 2000). Furthermore, low-income caregivers are less likely to have access to paid sick leave or paid vacation time.

Thus, caregivers are often forced to choose between a job that offers the financial support they need and the family members they love. Longitudinal research findings suggest that approximately 38 percent of caregivers adjust their work schedules within one month of assuming a caregiver role and

13 percent leave their job completely within two months of assuming a caregiver role (Franklin, Ames, & King, 1994). As informal caregivers continue to struggle with achieving balance between work and caregiving responsibilities, many researchers argue that the strain on caregivers can have negative consequences for their ability to satisfy the demands in both areas of their lives.

Potential Benefits of California Paid Family Leave

In 1992, the federal government passed a bill to allow workers 12 weeks of unpaid leave to care for a sick or injured family member, or to bond with a new child. The Family Medical Leave Act (FMLA) provides workers with job security during their time off work but does not offer any compensation. The passing of FMLA inspired many researchers to look deeper into the potential tradeoffs of taking time off work to care for a family member. On the one hand, employees are able to take time off without the threat of losing their job. On the other, a loss of financial stability and prospective advancement opportunities may add strain to these already overwhelmed caregivers. Whereas FMLA may offer the job stability that caregivers need during their time away from work, it does not offer any financial assistance. Thus caregivers may still find themselves experiencing financial hardship due to lost wages. The prospect of a paid leave program might be especially helpful to these workers. Specifically, programs similar to California's Paid Family Leave Insurance program are likely to reduce the financial strain that caregivers experience when taking time off work to care for a loved one.

California is the first state in the nation to offer Paid Family Leave (CPFL) to individuals caring for a sick family member. This new program allows workers who pay into the State Disability Insurance Program (SDI) to receive 55 percent of their wages or no more than $850 per week to care for a sick or injured family member or to bond with a new child. California workers began paying into the program on January 1, 2004 with benefits available as of July 1, 2004. CPFL allows workers up to six weeks of partially paid leave per 12-month period (see Table 8.1 for further information on California Paid Family Leave). With this new program in place, and with other state governments looking to California for information on how the program is used, we set out to survey caregivers in Southern California about their knowledge, need, and feelings regarding California Paid Family Leave.

Table 8.1 FAQs about California Paid Leave.

Q. What is Paid Family Leave?

A. Paid Family Leave is unemployment compensation disability insurance paid to workers who suffer a wage loss when they take time off work to care for a seriously ill family member or to bond with a new minor child.

Q. Who does Paid Family Leave cover?

A. Employees covered by State Disability Insurance (SDI) are also covered by Paid Family Leave insurance. Self-employed individuals are covered by Paid Family Leave if they participate in the SDI Elective Coverage Program.

Q. For how long may a worker receive Paid Family Leave insurance benefits?

A. Workers may receive up to six (6) weeks of benefits that may be paid over a 12-month period.

Q. Who pays?

A. The Paid Family Leave insurance program is fully funded by employees' contributions, similar to the SDI program. Beginning January 1, 2004, employers are required to deduct the Paid Family Leave contributions from the wages of employees who are covered by the SDI program.

Q. How much will leave-takers receive?

A. Weekly benefit amounts will be approximately 55 percent of the worker's earnings up to the maximum weekly benefit amount. For Paid Family Leave insurance claims beginning January 1, 2005 through December 31, 2005, weekly benefits will range from $50 to $840.

Source: California Employment Development Department website (http://www.edd.ca.gov)

Our Study

A total of 367 respondents from local caregiver support groups and a caregiver support agency located in Los Angeles County completed a paper-and-pencil survey to gauge caregivers' financial, emotional, and physical well-being as well as their knowledge of the CPFL program. The average age of respondents was 60 years old, with females comprising the majority of respondents (77 percent). Approximately 83 percent of respondents were caring for either a spouse or a parent, and 40 percent were working at least part-time. Of those individuals who were working at least part-time,

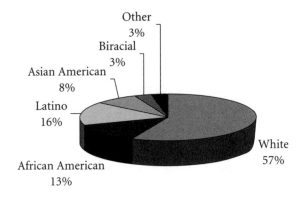

Figure 8.1   Ethnic breakdown of caregivers.

Figure 8.2   Self-reported income level of caregivers.

74 percent indicated working for someone else and 22 percent were self-employed (see Figures 8.1 and 8.2 for further demographic information).

The survey used in this study was designed to assess caregivers' work and leave-taking experiences. Respondents were asked about their employment status and their ability to take both paid and unpaid leave. Additionally, participants were asked questions regarding their physical and mental health, economic hardships, and familiarity with the California Paid Family Leave Insurance Program. The survey included items to assess caregivers' work concerns about lost pay and losing their jobs in relation to taking time off to provide care. Finally, scale items from the "Cornell Retirement and Well-being Survey" and the "Midlife Development Inventory" were used to measure caregiver health and mental well being (See sample items in Table 8.2).

Table 8.2 Means and standard deviations for working caregivers who can and cannot take time off work without the threat of job loss.

Survey question	Mean		t
	Time off	*No time off*	
On a scale from 1 (Not hard at all) to 7 (Very hard), how hard has it been for your family to make ends meet?	3.21 (1.3)	4.28 (1.1)	−3.1
On a scale from 1 (Seriously Ill) to 7 (Best of Health), what number best describes how your health has been lately?	4.92 (1.2)	3.78 (1.3)	−4.3
On a scale from 1 (No Energy) to 7 (Full of Energy), what number best describes how much energy you have had lately?	4.14 (1.4)	2.95 (1.3)	−4.4
It has been difficult for my care receiver to make medical appointments because it is hard for me to miss work. (respond on a scale from 1 (Strongly Disagree) to 7 (Strongly Agree).)	3.03 (2.2)	4.78 (2.1)	−4.1

Note: Standard deviations in parentheses. All t values significant at the $p < .001$ level.

In addition to the scale items, the survey also asked respondents to talk about their caregiving experience in their own words. Specifically, caregivers were asked about the ways in which they made their care receivers feel more comfortable, reasons for missing medical appointments, and why they were not taking advantage of the CPFL program. The open-ended answers were coded into major categories or themes.

Financial Hardships

The results of this study provide further evidence that working caregivers have a difficult time balancing their multiple responsibilities. The data show that working and non-working caregivers are equally unhappy with their financial situation. Working caregivers who responded to the survey indicated that the benefits offered by their employer when taking time off were not sufficient to sustain their caregiving responsibilities:

- 48 percent of the working caregivers reported having no paid time off (i.e., no paid sick leave or vacation);

- 24 percent stated that they could not take unpaid time off without the threat of losing their job; and
- 50 percent of caregivers who could take time off with pay reported receiving all or almost all of their pay on days that they took off work to provide care to a family member.

As a result, many of the working caregivers reported experiencing several forms of financial hardship:

- 16 percent stated that they had to do without "extra things;"
- 10 percent had been late with payments on basic services; and
- 5 percent had been threatened with eviction.

Furthermore, findings show that working caregivers who could not take time off without the threat of losing their job reported more financial hardship than working caregivers who were not threatened with job loss (see Table 8.2).

As for the differences among working caregivers with different work hours, individuals who work more hours per week are more worried about:

- the lack of time they are able to spend with their care receiver ($r = .22$, $p < .01$);
- the loss of wages incurred by taking time off ($r = .12$, $p < .05$); and
- potential job loss due to taking time off to care for a family member ($r = .23$, $p < .01$).

These results suggest that as caregivers work longer hours, they worry more about their own financial well-being, as well as the emotional and physical well-being of their care receiver. The finding that caregivers who work longer hours are more concerned about lost wages and time away from their care receiver suggests that some caregivers feel torn between taking time off to attend to their family's needs and working to achieve financial security. This finding is especially salient in light of the benefits offered by California Paid Family Leave. It is possible that this group of workers might find comfort in receiving more financial assistance for days taken off work to be with their care receiver.

In addition to the findings reported above, comments from caregivers themselves suggest that all caregivers, working and not working, are concerned about the financial well-being of their families. One of the major themes that caregivers stated most often dealt with financial struggles. As one caregiver stated, "I am constantly afraid of not having enough money to take care of my sons and my mother." It seems that many caregivers grapple with competing financial demands. Three categories of reasons were given to explain financial struggles:

1 Work-related concerns:
   - A general lack of organizational/management support for taking time off work.
   - Caregiver had to quit job due to care receiver's condition.
2 Financial difficulties:
   - Caregiver's concerns about the caregiver's own financial well-being, and that of his/her family.
3 Other salient factors:
   - Self-employed caregivers comment on loss of pay, loss of revenue for their business, or lost clients due to taking time off work.
   - Caregiver's comment on needing assistance for state and federal programs.

Emotional and Physical Difficulties

In addition to the financial struggles that caregivers face, the findings also highlight an overall theme of negative affect and physical health problems among caregivers. Among caregivers who work part- or full-time, those individuals who are able to take time off without the threat of losing their job report more positive well-being overall.

Working caregivers who could not take time off without the threat of losing their job reported more emotional strain ($t(49) = 4.2$, $p < .001$; see Figure 8.3) and less overall energy than working caregivers who could take time off without the threat of job loss (see Table 8.2). In addition, working caregivers who could not take time off work without the threat of losing their job reported more physical health problems and a greater incidence of missed medical appointments for their care receiver. This latter finding suggests that caregivers are struggling to maintain not only their own physical health, but also their care receivers' medical regimens.

Taken together, these findings show that those individuals who can take time off without the threat of losing their job suffer less emotional hardship. This finding supports those of previous studies reporting less strain and burnout among caregivers who are able to alter their work schedule or reduce their work hours (Covinsky et al., 2001; Franklin et al., 1994). Caregivers who stated that their job was threatened when they took time

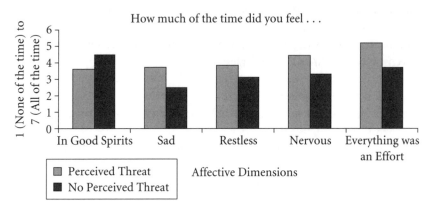

Figure 8.3　Affective responses for those who can and cannot take time off work without the threat of losing their job.

off also reported feeling more emotional strain, more financial insecurity, more physical health problems, and less energy. Moreover, it appears that the threat of job loss also affects the caregiver's ability to provide sufficient assistance to their care receiver. Evidence for this claim is provided by our finding that caregivers who feel threatened with job loss reported more missed medical appointments compared to those who can take time off without the threat of job loss.

The subjective physical and emotional health status of the caregiver was also a salient theme in the respondents' general comments. Comments included:

- caregiver's deteriorating health;
- direct comments on suffering from symptoms of depression;
- direct comments on suffering from extreme stress;
- comments on being burnt-out or feeling emotionally and/or physically drained; and
- comments on needing a break or some form of respite.

Many of the caregivers mentioned that it was difficult to maintain the physical and emotional well-being of their care receiver because of their own deteriorating health conditions. One caregiver put it this way: "Due to my own illness, things I usually can perform are limited. [I] have to have surgery of my own [and I] delayed my own care to get him where he is now."

Work-related reasons were not the only salient factors in missing medical appointments for care receivers. When asked about the reasons that their care receivers missed medical appointments, many caregivers, both working and not working, stated that they simply could not arrange transportation for their care receiver. As one caregiver noted, "We didn't have the transportation or the financial resources to get there." Others mentioned that their care receiver was too ill to attend the doctor's appointment or that they simply forgot the appointment altogether. For example, one caregiver mentioned, "She was not feeling well enough to go out and get in the car and it was too hot outside for her."

Reasons for missed appointments included:

- caregiver could not take time off work for care receiver medical appointments;
- care receiver was too ill to attend medical appointments or care receiver was hospitalized during the scheduled doctor visit;
- caregiver could not arrange transportation for care receiver's medical appointment;
- caregiver and/or care receiver forgot about the medical appointment;
- caregiver had to cancel the appointment due to other obligations;
- care receiver refused to leave the house and/or visit the doctor; and
- caregiver lacked the physical assistance needed to move the care receiver.

Perhaps the most notable finding was the overwhelming number of caregivers who stated that their care receiver would not have lived as long if not for the care they provided. Additionally, our caregivers reported numerous ways in which they helped their care receiver feel better physically and emotionally. For example, when reporting on her care receiver's well-being, one caregiver stated, "I feel she would waste away emotionally and physically without her family's presence." Another caregiver put it this way: "The medical doctors and my fellow nurses say that if we did not give him the care he receives at home, he would have died long ago." Comments such as these suggest that caregivers feel a sense of obligation to maintain the physical and emotional health of their care receivers. For working caregivers, this obligation may only add to the strain they feel when they are unable to take time off work.

Use of California Paid Family Leave

While very few of our respondents were taking advantage of the CPFL program, the data show that the respondents felt very positive about the benefit and the potential relief that it could offer working caregivers. Overall, the results suggest that there is a strong need for Paid Family Leave among informal caregivers living in California.

The findings of this study show that a large percentage of the caregiver population could directly benefit from a program such as California Paid Family Leave. Whereas more than 95 percent of our sample stated that they felt positive or very positive about the program, only 1 percent stated that they were either using or intended on using the program. The low percentage can be attributed to the finding that 52 percent of the working caregivers stated that 55 percent of their salary was not enough money to live on or that they would lose money by taking CPFL. However, only 8 percent stated that they were satisfied with the wages they received when taking paid time off. The remaining 40 percent of working caregivers provided other reasons for not taking advantage of the benefit. These reasons for not using CPFL related to work. Reasons included:

- caregiver reports that their workload would pile up or there is no one to assist them in meeting work requirements;
- caregiver is self-employed and is not qualified for CPFL, or only receives pay for the hours worked; and
- caregiver uses time at work as respite from caregiving or continues to work because it is personally fulfilling.

More specifically, many of the caregivers mentioned that their job provided some relief from their caregiving responsibilities. One respondent said, "I need time away from my wife who I take care of." Comments such as this reveal the extreme stress and hardship that caregivers feel on a daily basis. Even a large number of the non-working caregivers stated that they would enjoy some form of respite and that caregiving is a "24-hour-a-day job" with few opportunities for relief. It is possible that a full- or part-time work schedule offers caregivers the "time off" they need to remain resilient. With so many caregivers longing for some form of respite, it appears that maintaining a full time job is one source of relief from the burdens of caregiving.

Many of our self-employed respondents stated that their time off work had greater ramifications than just reduced hours or pay. For example, those individuals who owned their own business or worked for themselves felt that they would lose clients if they took more time off work. One business owner put it this way, "I am the boss so I would not get paid; being a dentist, I have schedules to be responsible for." Another respondent said, "Being self-employed is hard when you are a caregiver. I live off my savings and I am a writer, but I am too tired to write, plus I have no time off for myself."

In addition to the themes mentioned earlier, caregivers spoke frequently about the lack of support that they received from management when taking time off. For example, one caregiver stated, "My company does not allow us to use [CPFL] because we can only use allotted time and no more." Others spoke about the fact that they would have too much work to catch up on when they returned to their job. As one respondent put it, "There's no one else who knows my job. I can't miss a day. If I do, I have to come in that evening or on the weekend to make it up." These are some of the reasons why caregivers were not taking advantage of the California Paid Family Leave Insurance program.

Conclusions and Implications

The findings of this study suggest that caregivers who are attempting to balance work and family responsibilities could benefit from a program such as California Paid Family Leave, but that at 55 percent of the worker's salary, the rate is too low; caregivers are already stretching their salaries to support their family care receivers and the high medical costs they incur. Although very few of the respondents were taking advantage of the benefit, the data collected on physical, financial, and emotional hardship show that caregivers are struggling to meet their multiple responsibilities. Our finding that a substantial proportion of caregivers believe that going to work provides a respite from the demands of caring for ill family members has been replicated with a national survey conducted in Australia. Bainbridge, Cregan, and Kulik (2006) found that respondents often noted the benefits of working outside of their home, especially when they were caring for relatives with emotional disabilities. Thus, the concern expressed by employers opposed to family leave that employees would take excessive leaves if they were provided with paid leave has not materialized, nor is it likely to occur. Although relatively few of our respondents who needed paid leave actually took it, they reported that the additional strain that is put on caregivers who attempt to balance work and caregiving has been a cause of burnout and physical illness. These findings are corroborated in a study of rural parents with sick children (Grzywacz, Rao, Woods, Preisser, & Gesler, 2005). The researchers found that poorer children's health was associated with decrements in parents' work because of the emotional exhaustion they experienced. This effect could be partially mediated if parents had even a short period for recovery. Findings were the same for the women and men in their study. These findings provide support for the need for and potential benefits of a program such as California Paid Family Leave, but at a higher proportion of reimbursed salary and extension to self-employed individuals so that it can actually achieve its intended goal.

When FMLA, which covers approximately 60 percent of the workforce, and CPFL are utilized together, a worker who needs to take time off to care for a family member will receive both job security and a partial wage replacement. These programs could reduce the strain and anxiety that results when individuals fear that taking time off could result in job loss. Furthermore, using these programs for time off to attend medical appointments could also benefit the health of the care receiver.

Current changes to the program such as an increase in the maximum wage received each week and the option of aid to self-employed workers could increase the likelihood of utilization. With only 0.03 percent of the population in California currently using the benefit, it has been suggested that many Californians are still unaware of the program (California Employment Development Department, 2005). Since the program has only been fully operational for one year, it is possible that more individuals will take advantage of this much-needed benefit as time goes on. Our research suggests that greater awareness will not swell usage for low-wage caregivers.

There are substantial costs to employers when their employees have to struggle to care for sick or frail family members. MetLife (2006) calculated the average cost to employers for every employee with caregiving responsibilities by assuming median weekly salaries and the cost of replacing employees, absenteeism, partial absenteeism, workday interruptions, elder crises, supervision time, unpaid leave, and moving from full-time to part-time employment. With all of these variables accounted for the average cost per employee is $2,441. Enhancement of CPFL so that more caregivers can remain in the workforce will benefit employers, employees, and the general economy. These conclusions are also supported by a study of various types of employers in New Jersey (Appelbaum & Milkman, n.d.). They make a strong case for the return-on-investment for all types of businesses when caregivers are able to take paid leave.

The findings of this study offer further support for the notion that working caregivers could benefit from the financial boost and secure time off provided by a program such as CPFL if it were funded at a higher rate. Caregivers who were able to take leave from work without fearing job loss reported higher satisfaction with their financial situation as well as better overall physical and emotional health.

It is clear that managing this dual – and often conflicting – role of caregiver and employee takes a physical and financial toll on caregivers. Thus, it is essential that programs such as CPFL continue to evolve to provide a greater percentage of workers' salaries, so that caregivers can afford to offer the vital care that their care receivers need. With the growth and improvement of programs like CPFL, the "honor and support" encouraged by President Bush in his Proclamation of National Family Caregivers Month may become a reality (Proclamation 7957, 2005).

Acknowledgment

We gratefully acknowledge the generous support from the California Wellness Foundation who provided funding for this research.

References

Appelbaum, E., & Milkman, R. (n.d.). *Achieving a workable balance: New Jersey's employers' experiences managing employee leaves and turnover*. Retrieved October 2, 2006 from www.cww.rutgers.edu

Bainbridge, H. T. J., Cregan, C., & Kulik, C. T. (2006). The effect of multiple roles on caregiver stress outcomes. *Journal of Applied Psychology, 91*, 490–497.

California Employment Development Department (2005, June). *Paid family leave year in review July 1, 2004 – June 30, 2005*. Retrieved September 21, 2005 from http://www.edd.ca.gov/direp/pflanniv.asp

Cantor, D., Waldfogel, J., Kerwin, J., Wright, M. M., Levin, K., Rauch, T. H., et al. (2001). *Balancing the needs of families and employers: The family and medical leave surveys 2000 update*. Washington, DC: U.S. Department of Labor.

Covinsky, K. E., Eng, C., Lui, L., Sands, L. P., Sehgal, A. R., Walter, L. C., et al. (2001). Reduced employment in caregivers of frail elders: Impact of ethnicity, patient clinical characteristics, and caregiver characteristics. *Journal of Gerontology, 56A*(11), M707–M713.

Franklin, S. T., Ames, B. D., & King, S. (1994). Acquiring the family eldercare role: Influence on female employment adaptation. *Research on Ageing, 16*(1), 27–42.

Grzywacz, J. G., Rao, P., Woods, C. R., Preisser, J. S., & Gesler, W. M. (2005). Children's health and workers' productivity: An examination of family interference with work in rural America. *Journal of Occupational Health Psychology, 10*, 382–392.

Heymann, J. (2000). *The widening gap: Why America's working families are in jeopardy and what can be done about it*. New York, NY: Basic Books.

Lee, J. A. (1997). Balancing elder care responsibilities and work: Two empirical studies. *Journal of Occupational Health Psychology, 2*(3), 220–228.

Lee, J. A., Walker, M., & Shoup, R. (2001). Balancing elder care responsibilities and work: The impact of emotional health. *Journal of Business and Psychology, 16*(2), 277–289.

Lovell, V. (2006, July). *Valuing good health in San Francisco: The costs and benefits of a proposed paid sick days policy.* Institute for Women's Policy Research, No. B 252. Retrieved September 4, 2006 from www.iwpr.org

Max, W., Webber, P. A., & Fox, P. J. (1995). Alzheimer's disease. The unpaid burden of caring. *Journal of Aging and Health, 7*(2), 179–199.

MetLife. (2006, July). *The MetLife caregiving cost study: Productivity losses to U.S. business.* Retrieved August 10, 2006 from www.metlife.org

Moss, M. S., Lawton, M. P., Kleban, M. H., & Duhamel, L. (1993). Time use of caregivers of impaired elders before and after institutionalization. *Journal of Gerontology, Social Sciences, 48*(3), S102–S111.

National Alliance for Caregiving and American Association of Retired Persons (2004). *Caregiving in the U.S.* Bethesda, MD: National Alliance for Caregiving.

National Family Caregivers Association & Family Caregiver Alliance (2006). Prevalence, hours and economic value of family caregiving: Updated state-by-state analysis of 2004 national estimates by Peter S. Arno, Ph.D. Kensington, MD: NFCA & San Francisico, CA: FCA. Retrieved from: http://www.caregiver.org/caregiver/jsp/content/pdfs/State_Caregiving_Data_Arno_20061107.pdf

Proclamation 7957, 70 Fed. Reg. 67637–67638 (November 7, 2005).

Schulz, R., & Beach, S. R. (1999). Caregiving as a risk factor for mortality: The caregiver health effects study. *Journal of the American Medical Association, 282*(23), 2215–2219.

Stone, R. I., & Short, P. F. (1990). The competing demands of employment and informal caregiving to disabled elders. *Medical Care, 28*(6), 513–526.

Strommel, M., Collins, C. E., & Givens, B. A. (1994). The cost of family contributions to the care of persons with dementia, *The Gerontologist, 34,* 199–205.

Teri, L., & Truax, P. (1994). Assessment of depression in dementia patients: Association of caregiver mood with depression ratings. *Gerontologist, 34,* 231–234.

Vitaliano, P. P., Young, H. M., & Zhang, J. (2004). Is caregiving a risk factor for illness? *Current Directions in Psychological Science, 13*(1), 13–16.

Vitaliano, P. P., Zhang, J., & Scanlan, J. M. (2003). Is caregiving hazardous to one's physical health? A meta-analysis. *Psychological Bulletin, 129*(6), 946–972.

9

Taking the Temperature of Family Life: Preliminary Results from an Observational Study

Darby E. Saxbe and Rena L. Repetti

Conducting work–family research is a little like being a meteorologist: the basic principles of climatology are fixed, but the weather is always changing. For millennia, humans have formed families and labored to support them, but the structure of both work and family has changed dramatically over the past century, especially in the industrialized world. Family members once lived within an extended multigenerational network; today, the "typical" (though not universal) family structure is the nuclear unit, with just two adults shouldering household and childcare duties. At the same time, over the past century, the pace of paid work has been accelerated by new technologies and a global economy. Women have entered the workforce *en masse*, and dual-income families with children now comprise the predominant household composition in the United States (Bianchi & Raley, 2005). Technology has also altered the tenor of family life. Some innovations save labor and facilitate contact between family members – microwave ovens, cell phones – while others may distract and isolate family members from each other – video games, TV, and the aforementioned cell phones, when loaded with voicemails from work.

As weakened social, civic, and extended family ties compromise families' support networks, parents devote more time than ever to demanding jobs. The resulting time crunch appears to take a particular toll on women, the traditional keepers of the home front. For today's parents, many of who came of age during the feminist movement of the 1970s, the idealized stay-at-home mother seems as remote and unlikely as the black-and-white sitcoms that depict her. At the same time, despite women's participation in the work force, gender roles still appear to hold some sway over the distribution of labor at home. Data from the National Survey of Families and Households suggests that men typically contribute between one-fourth and one-third of total household labor, and are less likely to participate in childcare and in "core" household tasks (cooking, cleaning) than women (Bianchi, Milkie, Sayer, & Robinson, 2000). Perhaps as a result, more than a third of women report "always feeling rushed" (Mattingly & Bianchi, 2003), and the comically harried mother has become a trope in popular media. According to the sociologist Arlie Hochschild, the difficulty of balancing work and home creates a "time bind," in which parents, particularly women, devote even more hours to their jobs in order to avoid the overwhelming demands of the household, and then must catch up at home (Hochschild, 1997).

Despite these pressures, the family is still popularly seen as a source of refuge and restoration from the demands of the outside world. In popular culture, even dysfunctional clans – like the family at the center of the quirky comedy *Little Miss Sunshine* – often are pictured as providing sanctuary from a chaotic world. "Family values," or at least some families' values, continue to inspire political rhetoric and to draw voters to the ballot box. Realities may be "changing," but the family home, at its best, continues to offer the promise of a physical and emotional haven for its members.

How can researchers chronicle changing work–family realities in all their complexity? Given the ever-shifting nature of both the home and the workplace, it is important for research to remain dynamic as well. Returning to the meteorology metaphor, some research in this area focuses on large-scale surveys and the mapping of demographic trends, much like using global satellites to capture shifts in temperature and precipitation. Other researchers hone in on psychological processes, such as the impact of work-related stress on close relationships, a basic science approach that resembles the study of how wind patterns produce storms. Often missing from both lines of work–family literature is a sense of what the "weather" looks like and feels like on the ground. How are families responding, on a daily basis, to changes in the workplace, the economy, technology, schools, and gender roles? To truly understand the fabric of everyday life, researchers need to start with very basic questions. Where are family members spending time? How and when do they come together after the workday? What activities do they pursue? Does home still feel like a shelter, or are family members experiencing stormy weather?

This chapter will discuss work–family research that speaks to these questions, focusing primarily on an intensive ethnographic study of work–family life conducted by the Center for Everyday Lives of Families (CELF). We will begin by describing the study itself, an exploration of "a week in the life" of 32 dual-earner Los Angeles families. Next, we will outline preliminary findings that reflect the "changing realities" of this volume's title. We will summarize research on how family members greet each other after the workday, when and where family members spend time in the evening after work, how families members feel when together or alone, how families eat dinner, and even how family members' stress hormones appear to fluctuate across the day. Throughout, we will highlight a tension that seems to characterize these families' efforts to come together, the difficulty of negotiating between the pull of outside distractions and the promise of home as a haven. While families in our sample appear to want to spend time together, and to enjoy the time they spend with each other, finding this time and instantiating it as routine appears challenging for many families. This tension appears to be especially acute for women, for whom home functions both as a refuge and a workplace, a place to unwind but also a source of family demands and responsibilities.

Before beginning this discussion, we need to make clear that the findings described in this chapter come from a collaborative study with many researchers working together; by presenting them here, we do not wish to take credit for our colleagues' efforts. These ideas are the collective product of a tremendous amount of work, both in collecting these data, and in making sense of this complicated dataset. The contributions of our participating families are also not to be discounted. They agreed to go under our researchers' microscope, sacrificing time and privacy in order to enrich our understanding of the contemporary work–family climate.

The Everyday Lives of Families Study

Much of the research highlighted in this chapter was conducted by the Center for the Everyday Lives of Families (CELF), an interdisciplinary research group headquartered at the University of California, Los Angeles, and funded generously by the Alfred P. Sloan Foundation. CELF's mission was to capture a "week in the life" of 32 middle-class families residing in the greater Los Angeles area. Most of the CELF data was collected between 2002 and 2004. Families were eligible for the study if they had a mortgage on their home and included two cohabitating adults, both of whom worked full-time (more than 30 hours per week), and at least two children, one of whom was between 8 and 10 years of age at the time of the study. Outside those stipulations, the families studied by CELF ranged widely in social and cultural background. While the majority of families were of Caucasian descent, African-American, Latino, East Asian, and South Asian families were also represented within the sample, as well as two families led by gay males. Parents' ages ranged from 28 to 58 years, with a median age of 41 for both men and women. The couples in the study had been married or partnered for 3–18 (median 13) years. The median annual family income was $100,000, with a range from $51,000 to $196,000. Most of the participating parents reported 40–49 hour workweeks, although almost a third of fathers (and 13 percent of mothers) worked over 50 hours per week.

The study included intensive observation of each family. Before beginning the study, family members were interviewed about daily routines and beliefs about education and physical health, and filled out questionnaires asking about recent life events and personality characteristics. During the week of the family's participation, family members were videotaped and physically tracked by researchers for four days (two weekdays and two weekend days). Tracking typically began when one of the parents returned home from work and continued every ten minutes thereafter, until children went to bed; at each tracking interval, a researcher recorded every family member's activity and location. On three separate weekdays, two of which overlapped with filming days, participating family members completed four diary measures of mood and work events and provided four saliva samples, which were then analyzed for levels of cortisol, a hormone connected with stress and physiological arousal. At a separate session, after completing the study week, family members filled out questionnaires on marital quality and current symptoms of depression.

Analyses of these data are ongoing, as family members' interactions are transcribed and coded by CELF researchers. We present a number of preliminary findings here, culled from coded video data, tracking data, and cortisol data, as well as results from a collaboration with another Sloan-funded study, the University of Chicago's 500 Families Study, which is led by Barbara Schneider and Linda Waite (Schneider & Waite, 2005).

Preliminary Results: Families Coming Together After Work

Greetings and First Contact

When families return home at the close of the work or school day, a busy, transitional time begins; families must shift gears from the day's activities, back into the household social environment, while preparing for the evening's meal and the evening's extracurricular and homework activities. The time can be one of joyful reconnection among family members, but it can also be marked by pressure and stress. This "first hour home" has been of particular interest to CELF researchers. One focus has been on family member's reunions with each other and the greeting sequences connected with these reunions. Anthropologists believe that every culture has some codified system of greeting and acknowledging others, and that greetings provide clues about the nature of the relationship between greeters, as well as each person's relative status and power.

Almost all reunion sequences involving parents – specifically, the greeting that marked a parent's arrival home – were captured on videotape by CELF researchers. Subsequently, a group of anthropologists and psychologists (Ochs, Graesch, Mittman, Bradbury, & Repetti, 2006) coded these greeting sequences, using four general categories reflecting whether the behavior shown by the greeter was characterized by positive affect, negative affect, distraction, or "logistical talk" (e.g., a piece of information or a request to complete a household task). The researchers expected most greetings to be marked by positivity and affection, as family members were reuniting after not seeing each other all day. To their surprise, over almost 100 reunions, greetings were primarily positive less than half of the time. Distraction was almost equally common as positive affect, while negative affect and logistical talk each characterized about 10 percent of reunions.

Ochs and her CELF colleagues also found that the nature of the greeting shown to returning parents appeared to be influenced by gender. Mothers were the first to have contact with their children on three-quarters of the weekdays that were videotaped, with a mean difference of almost two hours between mothers' first contact and fathers' first contact. Perhaps because fathers were, on average, more likely to arrive home later than their wives, fathers' appearance was less likely to be heralded positively by family members, or even heralded at all. Only about a third of family members' reunions with fathers were characterized by positive affect, according to CELF coders. Wives greeting their husbands were almost as likely to show negative as positive affect, and also showed high levels of distracted and logistical behavior. When children greeted their returning father, they were more likely to show distraction than positivity; fully half of reunions between fathers and children were coded as "distracted," while less than a third of father–child reunions were predominantly positive.

What keeps family members from responding positively to returning parents, particularly fathers? The high percentage of "distracted" reunions speaks to the many competing activities and diversions that seem to shift family members' attention away from each other. As CELF researchers have gleaned from activity data (discussed later in this chapter), children spend most of their weekday evening time pursuing "indoor leisure," which includes watching television, playing video games, and surfing the Internet. As a number of our video clips of family reunions attest, it is not rare for returning fathers to find themselves competing for attention with a video game in progress or a favorite television show. At the same time, as discussed later in this chapter, wives appear to spend a large proportion of their evening time at home engaged in chores (Graesch, Broege, Arnold, Owens, & Schneider, 2006). Since the first few hours home might be particularly taxing, given the demands of dinner preparation, it is perhaps no surprise that many wives gave their husbands an apparently lukewarm reception. The long gap (almost two hours, on average) between parents' arrivals home means that, in many families, both children and wives had a chance to become fully ensconced in evening activities by the time fathers returned home from work.

If this pattern of reunions is borne out by future research, it has interesting implications for work–family researchers. In the literature on psychological "unwinding" from work, researchers have examined constructs like negative emotion spillover (that is, the transfer of negative feelings from the workplace into the home) and social withdrawal (a coping strategy observed after higher-workload days) (Story & Repetti, 2006). However, little allowance has been made for the ways that other family members respond to returning workers. If a worker is met with disinterested children at the end of a long workday, withdrawal from family members might be an involuntary default response. Similarly, a critical greeting from an annoyed spouse might trigger another type of "unwinding" response. In either case, a returning spouse's desire to relieve pressure from the workday by having a pleasant conversation or even by venting about the day's events would be quashed. Differences in the reception received by fathers and mothers, and by first-arriving parents and second-arriving parents, might also underlie some of the gender differences found in work–family recovery.

The study of reunions underscores researchers' need to examine the family as a whole, as an interrelated ecosystem rather than a collection of individual members. To that end, naturalistic, observational methods help place family interactions in context. Family members are unlikely to be able to reconstruct or to accurately self-report the nature of their greetings and reunions in the kind of detail that a video record allows.

Physical Togetherness

Just as reunions reflect family members' closeness and involvement with each other, so too does their physical proximity – the degree to which they spend time in each other's presence while at home. Focusing on data from the first 20 families to participate in the study, CELF's tracking database was used to examine the spatial cohesion of family members in the evening after the work or school day (Ochs & Shohet, 2006). Interestingly, these CELF researchers found that family members rarely congregate in a single space in the evening. Across the 20 families, the number of times that all family members were observed together in the same home space accounted for about 15 percent of all weekday evening observations. However, five of the 20 families were *never* together in a shared space in the evening, at least when tracking observations were made.

This finding echoes results from other studies of American family time, which have also found that families devote relatively little time to joint activities. For example, one study (Crouter, Tucker, Head, & McHale, 2004) discovered that dual-income families with adolescent children only devoted about four hours per week to shared family activities, and that most of that time was spent eating dinner together and watching television. However, adolescents who spent more time in family activities tended to have fewer conduct problems and fewer depressive symptoms two years later.

Even though family members were observed gathered all together relatively infrequently in the CELF data, parents were also not often seen alone at home, or exclusively together with no children present. Instead, Ochs and her colleagues found that the most frequently observed configuration on weekday evenings was one parent sharing a home space with one or more children. The fact that individual parents were most often found to be sharing space with children, rather than with each other or with the whole family gathered *en masse*, reflects our observation that mothers and fathers are divvying up childcare responsibilities in the evenings. For example, a father might help one child with homework at the kitchen table while the mother gives another child her bath. While a "divide and conquer" approach to childcare makes sense in the face of evening time demands, and allows each parent a chance to connect with individual children, it also leaves families fairly low on other types of restorative time: time all together to pursue group activities, and alone time for parents to decompress, either individually or with each other.

The relative infrequency of whole-family gatherings was surprising to CELF researchers, and contrasts with qualitative studies of family time in other cultures. For example, in Italy, families appear to spend more time at home together in closer physical proximity, according to preliminary anecdotal results from i-CELF, a study conducted by a satellite group of CELF researchers in Rome, Italy with a small sample of eight families (E. Ochs, personal communication, Spring 2006). This apparent cultural difference – which needs to be borne out by systematic research – may be due to the fact that urban Italians, at least in the i-CELF sample, tend to reside in smaller living spaces and to share a single car, which leads to greater coordination of work-home routines. In contrast to families in many other cultures across the world, middle-class families in the US often own more than one car and are accustomed to generous amounts of private space; the average allocation of living space for each American family member has tripled in square footage since the 1950s (Graesch, 2006; Wilson & Boehland, 2006). Spacious homes offer families more breathing room, but also might lead to greater fragmentation at home, as family members spread out and pursue activities in separate spaces. In a small subsample of CELF families, children in four out of five households had television sets in their bedrooms (Pigeron, 2006), which might offer further inducement for isolation.

Families' Use of Outdoor Spaces

Families' spacious homes, as discussed above, often include outdoor spaces, especially in balmy Southern California. Arnold and Lang (2003) analyzed data from ten CELF families and found that the families invested both financially and emotionally in outdoor home spaces – front and back lawns, garages, and swimming pools. These spaces often became a focal point of home tours that were conducted by individual family members, and were spoken of with pride and a strong sense of ownership. However, surprisingly, family members were observed spending very little actual leisure time in these "leisure spaces." In fact, despite mostly pleasant weather during filming, Arnold and Lang (2003) found that seven of the ten families did not spend *any* leisure time in their back yards. Two families had formal pools, but no family members were seen using these pools during filming. For eight of the ten families, time spent in front yard spaces was almost exclusively confined to coming and going in cars, unloading groceries, and unloading trash. This research indicates that, while families appreciate their outdoor spaces, they do not often take advantage of them. Once again, the pulls of distractions and diversions, from chores to telecommuting to a myriad of enticing indoor leisure activities, seem to conspire to keep family members indoors but often separated.

Families' Use of Indoor Spaces

While the CELF study focused on close observation of a small sample of families, the Sloan-funded 500 Families Study, led by University of Chicago researchers Barbara Schneider and Linda Waite, used Experience Sampling Methodology (ESM) to study a large number of middle-class, dual-income families in the Chicago area (Schneider & Waite, 2005). In an ESM study, participants are signaled or electronically beeped at random intervals within a particular timeframe, such as once every few waking hours, and asked to provide information about their activities, and in this case their location, proximity to other family members, and mood. A group of CELF and 500 Families researchers (Graesch et al., 2006) combined their sources of data in order to get a more complete picture of everyday family life, focusing on weekday afternoons and evenings and merging ESM responses from the Chicago dataset with the CELF tracking observations.

Activities at Home

Graesch and colleagues' analysis of the merged dataset found that the majority of family time at home in the evening (almost a third of total observations) was spent engaged in "indoor leisure" activities including television watching, Internet surfing, reading, and playing games. Household chores and communication (i.e., talking on the phone, using email) were the second and third most frequently pursued activities at home. However, this pattern shifted when activity reports from both studies were examined by individual family members. The authors discovered that leisure was the most frequently pursued activity for fathers and children, but mothers spent more time doing chores than any other activity – about a fourth of their total observations. Mothers also spent a considerable amount of time in the kitchen – about a third of the total time they were home on weekday evenings. Another study (Ahrentzen, Levine, & Michelson, 1989) that examined the activity patterns of dual-income Canadian families over a 24-hour period during the workweek found similar gender differences. While at home, the Canadian mothers spent twice as much time alone in the kitchen and more time with children in bedrooms and bathrooms than did fathers. Men spent more time than women in the living room, engaged in passive leisure, while women spent more time in the kitchen, doing chores and caring for children.

Children in the merged CELF and 500 Families dataset spent the largest proportion of their weekday evening time in leisure (almost 40 percent of children's time was spent engaged in leisure, compared to about a fourth of fathers' time and less than a fifth of mothers' time) (Graesch et al., 2006). Children's second and third most frequently pursued activities were communication and schoolwork, followed by personal care (dressing, bathing); children apparently spent very little time doing chores, at least according to their own reports and to tracking observations. The fact that chores did not appear to be on children's radar screens suggests that parents are not systematically delegating household responsibilities to their children, even though parents themselves – especially mothers – are devoting substantial time to chores.

Feelings about Activities
In the 500 Families Study, family members were also asked to rate their emotions when responding to ESM beeps. Graesch et al. (2006) found that mean scores recorded by both fathers and children reflect an overall emotionally positive experience in the home on weekday evenings when engaged in leisure, their primary activity. On the other hand, Graesch and colleagues reported that, when mothers were engaged in their primary activity, chores, their emotions were mostly negative, with greater feelings of stress and irritation and lower levels of happiness. When family members were together, family members' emotional experiences were more likely to be positive than when alone, a shift that was most notable for fathers. Mothers reported slightly more feelings of stress and irritation when with other family members than alone, but also reported more happiness and enjoyment than at other times – especially when the family was gathered together to participate in the common activity of eating a meal.

These researchers' results indicate that family time together can serve as a restorative activity that positively impacts family members' emotional well-being. Compared to their husbands and their children, mothers are more likely to report negative emotions and feelings of stress and irritation while at home on weekday evenings, particularly when doing chores. This finding is unsurprising, given that women appear to have more responsibilities at home and to spend more time engaged in household labor, a pursuit that is usually regarded as undesirable. However, the researchers found that all family members, including mothers, feel happier when the family is gathered together, especially when they are engaged in a single activity like sitting down to a meal. It is striking that, while all family members report that they enjoy group time, such time appeared to be fairly rare in both the merged and the CELF-only dataset. Just as families cultivate outdoor spaces but rarely use them, so too do family members appear to appreciate group togetherness without always managing to achieve it.

Family Media Use

As discussed above, both the CELF and 500 Family Study found indoor leisure to be the most frequently reported evening activity of family members, particularly children, for whom leisure was the most represented category of both primary *and* secondary activities. More often than not, that leisure includes some form of electronic media, like video games, television, and computer use, so how parents and children relate to media is an important, but little-studied, aspect of contemporary family life. Does media use lead to the spatial and emotional fracturing of family life, or does it give family members more opportunities to come together in a joint activity? In a study of families with young children, researchers found the television to be on about six hours a day, on average (Vandewater, Bickham, Lee, Cummings, Wartella, & Rideout, 2005), and families in about a third of the homes reported that television is on "always" or "most of the time," even if no one is watching. In a study of the television viewing habits of the 500 Families sample, Dempsey (2005) found that parents view over 9 hours of television each week, while adolescents watch about 13 hours. Mihaly Csikszentmihalyi, who pioneered Experience Sampling Methodology, and Robert Kubey found that television watching is one of the few leisure activities that makes people feel worse – less energetic, less able to concentrate, and less relaxed – after they have engaged in it (Kubey & Csikszentmihalyi, 1990). Yet we know little about the effects of television, whether it is on in the background or actively being watched, on family interactions, or the household emotional climate.

The CELF dataset lends itself to intensive exploration of these issues. As a start, Pigeron (2006) examined the media consumption habits of the first five families to participate in the CELF study. Each household included more than one TV set (the median number was three), and, strikingly, in four of the five households, at least one child had a TV set in his or her bedroom. Pigeron (2006) also found that, in four of the five households, at least one television was constantly on, whether or not any family members were watching. Each household also included one or more computers (median two), and one or more cellular telephones. Family members, especially older children and adults, were frequently observed multi-tasking with media; working on the computer while talking on the phone, for example. Media consumption can divert family members from time together, at least occasionally: Shohet, Ochs, Campos, and Beck (in press) found that, in a third of weekday dinners, family members were seen pursuing activities outside the scope of the dinner. Watching television and talking on the phone were among the biggest dinner distractions.

These observations of media use unearthed a surprising finding. While media consumption is often considered an isolating activity that separates family members from each other, in this sample, more often than not, media use was a dyadic or multi-party activity. For example, CELF researchers observed parents and children cuddling in front of the television, or siblings collaborating to play a video game. In one family, a father and son watch a sports game together, and enthusiastically root for their favorite team. Similarly, Dempsey's analysis (2005) of the 500 Families data found that television is not necessarily a solitary diversion. Dempsey found that more than half of family members' television viewing took place in the company of other family members, and was frequently accompanied by chatting and interacting. However, in the same study, Dempsey also found that adolescents who watched the most television spent the least amount of time talking with their parents, suggesting that television does not always facilitate conversation – at least among the heaviest viewers.

Just as with families' space use and meal consumption, this study of media use highlights some interesting contradictions in modern family life. Family members often appear to devote considerable time to electronic media; television, phones, and other devices seem to pull families away from time together, as when encroaching upon dinner, for example. However, families may also use media as a platform for togetherness and developing shared interests. As with a number of the areas outlined in this chapter, media use is an important part of family life that is poorly understood and difficult to measure using conventional methods.

Eating and Meal Preparation

Researchers have noted that children in families that eat dinner together regularly tend to report less anxiety, and do better academically, than children in families without such a routine (reviewed by Fiese, Tomcho, Douglas, Josephs, Poltrock, & Baker, 2002). How often do American families eat dinner together? According to several large studies, a significant percentage of children eat regular family dinners. For example, a study of almost 100,000 preteens and adolescents found that about 45 percent reported eating dinner with their families between five and seven times per week (Fulkerson, Story, Mellin, Leffert, Neumark-Sztainer, & French, 2006). However, it is difficult to gauge the accuracy of this self-reported data, or to determine if "dinner with the family" denotes all members sitting down to the same table at the same time to the same meal. For example, family members might be helping themselves to food at approximately the same time, but microwaving a burrito to eat in front of the television is different from sitting down to the same table with family members. An observational study like CELF allows for more direct, consistent coding of dinnertime behavior than a survey or questionnaire report.

Shohet et al. (in press) coded and examined videotaped dinners in the 30 CELF families led by heterosexual parents. They found that, over the two weeknights and one weekend night that were filmed, 77 percent of families ate at least one dinner "in unison" (in the same place and at the same time). However, only 17 percent of families ate together in unison on all three days. Over the three days, 63 percent of families had at least one dinner that was "fragmented," with family members eating in different locations and/or at different times (i.e., with meal start times more than 10 minutes apart). In addition, at least one family member, most often the father, missed at least one filmed dinner in fully half of the families. As Shohet and colleagues' results suggest, the families in the CELF sample managed to eat together on a fairly regular basis – but sitting down to dinner together did not appear to be an everyday ritual for most of them. Instead, it appeared that, more often than not, families had to work around diverging schedules or missing family members.

Shohet et al. (in press) also examined meal preparation within the CELF sample. Their analysis of the video data revealed that over 80 percent of family dinners were prepared by only one cook at a time, most often the mother. When both "single-chef" and "multi-chef" dinners were examined, mothers were involved in some capacity in 91 percent of weekday dinners and 81 percent of weekend dinners, while fathers were involved in dinner preparation only about a third of the time. Therefore, it appears that the burden of dinner preparation falls disproportionately on women, at least within the CELF sample, and that other family members do not seem to be sharing in this workload.

Physiological Stress

Not only did CELF's intrepid families endure being videotaped, tracked, and questioned, but they provided saliva samples four times a day for three of the days they participated in the study. Family members' saliva was then analyzed for levels of cortisol, a hormone that has been associated with stress and arousal. Most cortisol research to date has been conducted in laboratory settings – for example, asking participants to give a speech or take a test and measuring how much their cortisol levels increase. Incorporating cortisol sampling into a naturalistic study like CELF is treading new ground, although more and more naturalistic studies are tracking cortisol, since it is a fairly durable and stable hormone that lends itself to repeated sampling over time.

Analyses of the adults' cortisol (Saxbe, Repetti, & Nishina, in press) revealed that, in keeping with other research, cortisol shows a strong diurnal rhythm: cortisol levels typically start out high and decrease sharply over the morning, then taper off over the rest of the day. For the women in the CELF sample, marital satisfaction (as measured by the Marital Adjustment Test) seemed to be linked to this daily pattern. Women who were lower in marital satisfaction showed a "flatter" cortisol slope: their cortisol levels were lower in the morning and did not show as much of a decrease over the course of the day. A flattened slope is a cortisol profile that has been tied to chronic stress, burnout and even mortality risk (Sephton, Sapolsky, Kraemer, & Spiegel, 2000), suggesting that, at least for the women in our sample, the quality of the marital environment may be related to physical health.

Marital satisfaction also appeared to be associated with women's recovery from the workday, when evening cortisol level was examined in conjunction with parents' afternoon cortisol and with their diary ratings of afternoon work events. On workdays that parents rated as being busier, evening cortisol levels tended to be lower than average, suggesting that physiological recovery was exaggerated after higher workload days. For women but not for men, this relationship was moderated by marital satisfaction, such that women with higher marital satisfaction showed more dramatic decreases in cortisol after the close of a busy day.

The relationship between marital satisfaction and women's cortisol patterns is intriguing and bears further study. Both epidemiologists and social scientists have observed that, for men, marriage appears to offer a general health and well-being benefit, but that, for women, the health boost conferred by marriage is more dependent on the quality of the marriage than on the simple fact of being married (Kiecolt-Glaser & Newton, 2001). In other words, while married men tend to live longer than unmarried men, women who are unhappily married do not appear to live any longer than single women. These cortisol findings suggest a possible physiological mechanism for that phenomenon.

It remains unclear why marital satisfaction may be especially meaningful to women's stress hormone fluctuations. Some of the other findings reported in this chapter might provide clues, however. For example, according to the tracking and ESM results analyzed by Graesch et al. (2006), women appear to devote a significant chunk of their weekday evening time to chores, more so than men or children, and report more stress and irritation when in the presence of other family members than do their husbands or children. Women also were involved in the preparation of more than 90 percent of dinners observed by CELF researchers (Shohet et al., in press). If women's marital satisfaction ratings reflect their feelings about the quantity and quality of their time, and the division of domestic labor in their household, it makes sense that women who are overworked at home would show cortisol patterns reflecting both more chronic stress and greater marital dissatisfaction. This hypothesis can be tested by exploring relationships between cortisol patterns and behavioral observations at home, a project that is underway.

Conclusions and Future Directions

As we hope these preliminary conclusions and speculations have illustrated, families' current "weather" is volatile and hard to describe in monolithic terms. However, a few themes seem to underlie a number of the disparate findings discussed here. For example, families report that they enjoy their time together, at least when sampled "in the moment," but finding time to connect appears to be challenging for families, given the relative infrequency of family gatherings in our sample and the preponderance of distracted reunions between family members. Similarly, while families report positive feelings during family dinners, only 17 percent of families in the CELF sample managed to sit down to the evening meal together on all three of the days they were tracked by researchers (Shohet et al., in preparation). Both household chores and high-tech media appear to increase family members' "distractibility," with different distractions affecting different family members. For example, chores appear to absorb more of women's time, while indoor leisure consumes the largest proportion of children's time. However, there is some evidence, mostly anecdotal at this point, that family members are able to connect around entertainment media like television and video games, suggesting that families' desire to be together might influence the pursuit of a potentially isolating activity.

While family time appears to be mostly positive and rewarding, mothers' emotional experience at home seems to be more conflicted, with mothers reporting some feelings of stress and irritation while doing chores and in the presence of other family members. The fact that mothers spent the greatest percentage of their time at home engaged in household labor might help to explain these ambivalent feelings, along with the fact that mothers were involved with the preparation of over 90 percent of family dinners and were often home with children for several hours as principal caregivers before their husbands returned.

This evidence for women's mixed emotional experience at home is echoed by other studies. A telephone survey of Ohio parents (Roxburgh, 2006) found that, while mothers and fathers were about equally likely to express dissatisfaction with the time they had available to spend with their families (only about a fifth of parents reported being completely satisfied with their family time), fathers were more likely to express the desire for *more time* to spend with spouses and children, while mothers were more likely to want to improve the *quality* of family time. Women are also more likely to report "always feeling rushed" than men, and other time diary studies have found a 30-minute "leisure gap" between men and women, such that men tend to enjoy about a half-hour more leisure time than women each day (Mattingly & Sayer, 2006). Many researchers have suggested that women's workload at home exceeds that of men's, not merely in terms of total hours but also the nature of the work done by women. For example, time diary studies have found that when husbands and wives divvy up household tasks, women are more likely to be responsible for chronic, largely unavoidable tasks like meal preparation and childcare, while tasks that are more likely to fall under men's purview, like yard-work and home repairs, often allow for more flexibility in scheduling (Mattingly & Sayer, 2006). A recent Australian study found that, not only do women spend more time engaged in child care than men, but their child care time tends to involve more multitasking, more physical labor, less scheduling flexibility, and more overall responsibility for managing children's activities (Craig, 2006).

As these studies suggest, and as the CELF/ESM evidence supports, mothers' time at home is not consistently relaxing and pleasurable, at least to the same degree as it is for fathers and children. Mothers' feelings about their more taxing "second shift" might help to explain why women's cortisol patterns appeared to be linked with their ratings of marital quality. It is possible that, when household demands are especially burdensome for women, both their marital satisfaction and their stress responding systems are affected.

The research described in this chapter is still at a preliminary stage, as we and other CELF collaborators continue to parse this large dataset. However, it is our hope that the CELF findings presented in this chapter helps to illustrate how a naturalistic, *in situ* study can complement data from other research methodologies. Not only do the CELF data offer us a view of family life "from the ground," but its use of observational rather than self-report data helps to circumvent some of the biases or problems with recollection that can challenge a retrospective survey study. For example, a study of the 500 Families dataset (Lee & Waite, 2005) found large and sometimes significant differences between husbands' and wives' accounts of the time they devoted to housework, depending on whether they estimated this time in terms of hours per week on a question-naire, or responded to ESM prompts that sampled their activities in the moment. By combining information from multiple sources, including close observation, self-report, physical tracking, and even physiological measures like cortisol, researchers can converge on the real experience of life within the contemporary family and take the temperature of work–family realities today.

References

Ahrentzen, S., Levine, D. W., & Michelson, W. (1989). Space, time, and activity in the home: A gender analysis. *Journal of Environmental Psychology*, *9*(2), 89–101.

Arnold, J. E., & Lang, U. A. (2003). The changing landscape of home: Reflecting and shaping middle-class family lives. Center for Everyday Lives of Families (Working Paper).

Bianchi, S. M., Milkie, M. A., Sayer, L. C., & Robinson, J. P. (2000). Is anyone doing the housework? Trends in the gender division of household labor. *Social Forces*, *79*, 191–228.

Bianchi, S. M., & Raley, S. B. (2005). Time allocation in families. In S. M. Bianchi, L. M. Casper, & R. Berkowitz King (Eds.), *Work, family, health, and well-being.* (pp. 21–42). Mahwah, NJ: Lawrence Erlbaum.

Craig, L. (2006). Does father care mean fathers share? A comparison of how mothers and fathers in intact families spend time with children. *Gender & Society*, *20*(2), 259–281.

Crouter, A. C., Tucker, C. J., Head, M. R., & McHale, S. M. (2004). Family time and family members' psychosocial adjustment: A longitudinal study of adolescent siblings and their mothers and fathers. *Journal of Marriage and Family*, *66*, 147–162.

Dempsey, N. P. (2005). Television use and communication within families with adolescents. In B. Schneider, & L. J. Waite (Eds.), *Being together, working apart: Dual-career families and the work-life balance* (pp. 277–296). New York: Cambridge University Press.

Fiese, B. H., Tomcho, T. J., Douglas, M., Josephs, K., Poltrock, S., & Baker, T. (2002). A review of 50 years of research on naturally occurring family routines and rituals: Cause for celebration? *Journal of Family Psychology*, *16*(4), 381–390.

Fulkerson, J. A., Story, M., Mellin, A., Leffert, N., Neumark-Sztainer, D., & French, S. A. (2006). Family dinner meal frequency and adolescent development: Relationships with developmental assets and high-risk behaviors. *Journal of Adolescent Health, 39*, 337–345.

Graesch, A. P. (2006). An ethnoarchaeological study of contemporary U.S. houses and households. Center for Everyday Lives of Families (Working Paper).

Graesch, A. P., Broege, N., Arnold, J. E., Owens, A., & Schneider, B. (2006). Family activities, uses of space, and emotional well being: A collaborative merging of time diary and ethnoarchaeological data. Center for Everyday Lives of Families (Working Paper).

Hochschild, A. R. (1997). *The time bind: When work becomes home and home becomes work.* New York: Metropolitan Books.

Kiecolt-Glaser, J., & Newton, T. (2001). Marriage and health: His and hers. *Psychological Bulletin, 127*(4), 472–503.

Kubey, R., & Csikszentmihalyi, M. (1990). *Television and the quality of life. How viewing shapes everyday experience,* Hillsdale, NJ: Lawrence Erlbaum.

Lee, Y.-S., & Waite, L. J. (2005). Husbands' and wives' time spent on housework: A comparison of measures. *Journal of Marriage and Family, 67*, 328–336.

Mattingly, M. J., & Bianchi, S. M. (2003). Gender differences in the quantity and quality of free time: The U.S. experience. *Social Forces, 81*(3), 999–1030.

Mattingly, M. J., & Sayer, L. C. (2006). Under pressure: Gender differences in the relationship between free time and feeling rushed. *Journal of Marriage and Family, 68*, 205–221.

Ochs, E., Graesch, A., Mittman, A., Bradbury, T., & Repetti, R. L. (2006). Video ethnography and ethnoarchaeological tracking. In M. Pitt-Catsouphes, E. E. Kossek, & S. Sweet (Eds.), *Handbook of work and family: Multi-disciplinary perspectives and approaches* (pp. 387–409). Mahwah, NJ: Erlbaum.

Ochs, E., & Shohet, M. (2006). The cultural structuring of mealtime socialization. In R. Larson, A. Wiley, & K. Branscomb (Eds.), *Family mealtime as a context of development and socialization* (pp. 35–50). San Francisco, CA: Jossey-Bass.

Pigeron, E. (2006). Learning to be connected: A look at technology-mediated social worlds. Center for Everyday Lives of Families (Working Paper).

Roxburgh, S. (2006). "I wish we had more time to spend together . . ." The distribution and predictors of perceived family time pressures among married men and women in the paid labor force. *Journal of Family Issues, 27*(4), 529–553.

Saxbe, D. E., Repetti, R. R., & Nishina, A. (in press). Marital Satisfaction, Recovery from Work, and Diurnal Cortisol in Working Parents. *Health Psychology.*

Schneider, B., & Waite, L. J. (Eds.) (2005). *Being together, working apart: dual-career families and the work-life balance.* New York: Cambridge University Press.

Sephton, S., Sapolsky, R., Kraemer, H., & Spiegel, D. (2000). Diurnal cortisol rhythm as a predictor of breast cancer survival. *Journal of the National Cancer Institute, 92*, 994–1000.

Shohet, M., Ochs, E., Campos, B., & Beck, M. (in press). Coming together at dinner: A study of working families. In B. Schneider (Ed.), *Why workplace flexibility matters: A global perspective.*

Story, L. B., & Repetti, R. L. (2006). Daily occupational stressors and marital behavior. *Journal of Family Psychology, 20*(4), 690–700.

Vandewater, E. A., Bickham, D. S., Lee, J. H., Cummings, H. M., Wartella, E. A., & Rideout, V. J. (2005). When the television is always on: Heavy television exposure and young children's development. *American Behavioral Scientist, 48*(5), 562–577.

Wilson, A., & Boehland, J. (2006). Small is beautiful. *Journal of Industrial Ecology, 9*(1–2), 277–287.

10

Work, Family, and Health: Work–Family Balance as a Protective Factor Against Stresses of Daily Life

Joseph G. Grzywacz, Adam B. Butler, and David M. Almeida

Work–family balance is increasingly viewed as a public health issue. Halpern's (2005) presidential address to the American Psychological Association, for example, contends that "work and family" is the critical issue of our time, and that difficulty balancing work and family is a major threat to the health and well-being of adults and children. Researchers have suggested that the quality of the interrelationship between work and family is a leverage point for adult health because it has the potential to affect health via multiple pathways (Grzywacz & Fuqua, 2000). A recent report by Corporate Voices for Working Families contends that flexibility in the workplace is a corporate imperative because, in part, it contributes to healthier employees by helping them successfully balance work and family responsibilities. These and other realities have contributed to calls by public and private organizations to focus on adults' ability to integrate work and family as a fundamental strategy for building the health of the population (Halpern, 2005; National Institute for Child Health and Human Development, 2004).

Research linking work–family balance, as an explicit construct, to health is less well established than policy debates and public forums suggest. There is little consistency in the meaning and measurement of work–family balance across studies because it remains conceptually under-developed (Greenhaus & Allen, 2006; Grzywacz & Carlson, 2007). Typically, work–family balance is equated with the absence of work–family conflict, but this practice is coming under scrutiny as accumulating evidence suggests that balance is more than the absence of conflict (Frone, 2003; Grzywacz & Bass, 2003; Hammer, Cullen, Neal, Sinclair, & Shafiro, 2005; Kinnunen, Feldt, Geurts, & Pulkkinen, 2006). Further, research tends to focus on the health effects of specific indicators of work–family balance, without considering the potential that balance may exert its health effects by exacerbating (or attenuating) other life circumstances or situations. Finally, even if work–family balance is equivalent to the absence of work–family conflict, the vast majority of published studies have limited ability to make causal inferences because they are based on cross-sectional study designs.

The goal of this chapter is to broaden thinking about the meaning of work–family balance and how it may shape adult health. In this chapter, we posit that work–family balance can be viewed as an enduring circumstance characterizing the mutual interdependence between an individual's work and family lives (Werbel & Walter, 2002). Drawing on previous research examining contextualized models of health, we further posit that balance will have direct health effects and that it will benefit health by buffering individuals from the deleterious effects of daily hassles. We explore these ideas using data from the combined National Survey of Midlife Development in the United States and the National Study of Daily Experiences.

Background

Defining Work–Family Balance

Work–family balance has received scant research attention despite its popularity as a metaphor in the business world (Greenhaus & Allen, 2006; Grzywacz & Carlson, 2007). The vast majority of research invokes the balance concept without clearly defining it, or defines it explicitly or implicitly as the absence of work–family conflict (e.g., Hill, Hawkins, Ferris, & Weitzman, 2001). Likewise, practical attempts to promote "balance" focus primarily on reducing conflicts between work and family (Quick, Henley, & Quick, 2004). Although this definition places the balance concept within a rich nomological network of research, the mere absence of conflict inadequately captures positive aspects of the work–family interface that likely contribute to a balanced work–family arrangement. More specifically, recent theoretical and empirical work has recognized the importance of work–family enrichment or facilitation for completely understanding linkages between work and family (e.g., Aryee, Srinivas, & Tan, 2005; Frone, 2003; Greenhaus & Powell, 2006; Grzywacz & Butler, 2005; Grzywacz &

Marks, 2000; Voydanoff, 2004). (Note, the distinction between "enrichment," "positive spillover," and "facilitation" is not well articulated in the literature. Consistent with Greenhaus and Powell's (2006) recent theorizing, we assume these different labels are tapping a similar concept, one we refer to as "enrichment.")

An alternative conceptualization of balance follows from a literal interpretation of the metaphor, focusing on the equality of roles. In an influential paper, Marks and MacDermid (1996) used the term "evenhanded" to describe balance, emphasizing full engagement across life's roles. Kirchmeyer (2000) similarly emphasized the importance of distributing personal resources across life roles equitably to achieve balance. Others have emphasized that equal satisfaction with different roles epitomizes balance (e.g., Kofodimos, 1993). Although these definitions are true to the balance metaphor, it is dubious whether "equal" investment and satisfaction in work and family is possible or that it produces optimal outcomes (Grzywacz & Carlson, 2007). Indeed, Greenhaus, Collins, and Shaw (2003) found that self-reported quality of life was higher for individuals who devoted more resources to, and were more satisfied with, their family than work. Thus, equality in terms of resource investment or satisfaction in both work and family may not result in beneficial outcomes as implied by the balance metaphor.

A recent essay provides a foundation for an alternative conceptualization of work–family balance that shifts attention toward the interrelationship between the work and family domains. Drawing on examples from biological systems found in nature, Werbel and Walter (2002) suggest that work and family can be viewed as mutualistic, or interdependent, symbionts that are connected by a common element: an individual who routinely spends a portion of his/her daily life within each domain. The contention that work and family are mutualistic is based on the observation that most families need one or more members to be successfully engaged in the workforce in order for the family to carry out basic functions (Kanter, 1977); likewise, most organizations need and benefit from their employees' well-functioning families. For these authors, "work and family" is fundamentally an issue of energy exchange, such that excess energies (or resources) held by one domain are freely shared with domains lacking those energies. From this point of view, work–family balance can be conceptualized as the degree to which both work and family mutually benefit from the interrelationship created by the sharing of an individual member.

Viewing balance in terms of the degree of interdependence or mutual benefit between work and family is consistent with recent theorizing.

Frone (2003), for example, defined work–family balance as a situation where there was little interference between work and family (i.e., low levels of work-to-family and family-to-work conflict) and where the values and activities of each domain benefited the other (i.e., high work-to-family and family-to-work enrichment). Likewise, Barnett (1998) described a balance-like concept in terms of low conflict and high compatibility between work and family roles. Most recently, Voydanoff's (2005a) conceptualization of balance also highlights the exchange of valued resources between work and family to satisfy within-domain and cross-domain demands. Each of these ideas suggest that work–family balance is optimized when the benefits that work and family provide for each other exceed the difficulties that one may create for the other.

We assume that work–family balance, or the degree of mutual benefit between work and family, is a relatively stable attribute. This assumption is based on several strands of thought. First, the basic configuration of an individual's work and family life as well as corresponding responsibilities are not subject to substantial day-to-day or even month-to-month variation. Next, individuals purposefully organize their work and family lives in order to maintain some level of consistency across time (Moen & Wethington, 1992; Morehead, 2001). Clearly unexpected events such as a child's sickness or computer snafus arise, but it is unlikely that such events significantly alter the basic exchanges between work and family. Should events such as these become chronic, individuals will likely modify their strategies for combining work and family to recreate some level of stability or consistency in their daily lives (Kirkcaldy & Martin, 2000).

Work–Family Balance and Health

There is a substantial body of research suggesting that work–family balance contributes to adult health (for a recent review, see Greenhaus, Allen, & Spector, 2006). Poor work–family balance, typically operationalized in terms of high work–family conflict, has been associated with several indicators of physical health including hypertension, comorbid physical conditions, as well as self-reported health and somatic complaints (Adams & Jex, 1999; Frone, Russell, & Cooper, 1997; Grandey & Cropanzano, 1999; Grzywacz, 2000; Kinnunen et al., 2006; Thomas & Ganster, 1995). Likewise, several studies note that poor work–family balance, again operationalized in terms of elevated work–family conflict, is associated with general distress, depressive symptomatology, as well as psychiatric disorders including depression, anxiety disorder and behavior patterns indicative of alcoholism (Frone, 2000; Frone et al., 1997; Grzywacz & Bass, 2003; Hammer et al., 2005; Vinokur, Pierce, & Buck, 1999).

Unfortunately, research linking work–family balance, as an explicit concept, and health is limited. First, there is little prospective research examining the effects of work–family balance on adult health (cf. Frone et al., 1997; Hammer et al., 2005; Kinnunen, Geurts, & Mauno, 2004). The absence of prospective research makes it impossible to determine if poor work–family balance contributes to poorer health, or if poor health undermines adults' ability to balance work and family effectively. Next, previous research does not completely operationalize work–family balance because it focuses almost exclusively on work–family conflict (Eby, Casper, Lockwood, Bordeaux, & Brinley, 2005; Greenhaus et al., 2006) without giving attention to the benefits that work and family provide for each other. Cross-sectional evidence has linked work–family enrichment with sub-clinical and clinical indicators of mental health (Grzywacz, 2000; Grzywacz & Bass, 2003). One study has examined the prospective association of work–family conflict and work–family enrichment on depression (Hammer et al., 2005), but there has been no research examining physical health outcomes. Finally, previous research has relied on narrow conceptual arguments in positing linkages between work–family balance and health. The typical argument is that the absence of work–family balance is a poignant stressor because of the profound meaning ascribed to work- and family-related roles, and that the chronic stress of work–family imbalance undermines health via several pathways. Although compelling, it is becoming increasingly clear that stressors can act on health in complex and multifaceted ways (Taylor, Repetti, & Seeman, 1997) suggesting that a simple "direct effects" model may not adequately capture the health effects of work–family balance.

The Present Study

In this study we posit that work–family balance can benefit physical and mental health in multiple ways. First, we posit that work–family balance will have a direct effect on adults' physical and mental health. This thinking is informed by substantial previous research reporting that indicators of balance like work–family conflict or work–family enrichment are associated with health outcomes. Our contribution to this literature is that we characterize individuals' work–family balance in terms of both work–family conflict and enrichment, and we examine prospective health effects. Second, we posit that work–family balance is a buffer of life stress.

That is, we suggest that a mutually beneficial interrelationship between work and family provides protection from the vicissitudes of daily life and will attenuate the negative health effects of exposure to stressors. The notion that chronic life conditions increase vulnerability to the health consequences of stress is consistent with other lines of research that are not focused on work–family balance per se. Evidence indicates, for example, that enduring socioeconomic hardship contributes to elevated vulnerability to life stressors (Aneshensel, 1992; Grzywacz, Almeida, Neupert, & Ettner, 2004; McLeod & Kessler, 1990). Results from other studies indicate that the health-related implications of daily stressors are elevated for individuals living with chronic hardships such as overcrowding or poor neighborhood quality (Caspi, Bolger, & Eckenrode, 1987; Lepore, Evans, & Palsane, 1991). Collectively, this evidence suggests that individuals in chronic hardship, such as being in a poorly balanced work and family arrangement, may have more intense responses to stressors.

Finally, there is reason to expect that relationships among work–family balance, stress, and health may differ for men and women. Evidence suggests, for example, that exposure and reaction to stressors differs between women and men (Almeida, Wethington, & Kessler, 2002; Turner, Wheaton, & Lloyd, 1995). There is also widespread belief that work and family role domains are strongly gendered (Eby et al., 2005; Larson, Richards, & Perry-Jenkins, 1994). Research focused on gender differences in the effects of alternative conceptualizations of balance has produced inconsistent results (Frone, 2003; Eby et al., 2005); nevertheless, there is evidence suggesting that work–family balance may influence women more strongly than men. Rothbard (2001), for example, found more resource depleting and enriching links between work and family for women than men. Findings such as these as well as summaries of the literature (Eby et al., 2005) suggest that the quality of interdependence between work and family may be more salient to women than men, suggesting that work–family balance will serve as a stronger buffer of life stress for women than men.

In summary, we argue that work–family balance can be conceptualized in terms of the degree of mutual benefit between work and family, and that the absence of work–family balance can affect health directly as well as by exacerbating the deleterious health effects of stressors. Based on our conceptualizations and previous research we hypothesized that:

Hypothesis 1: Individuals for whom work and family are not balanced will have poorer physical and mental health than individuals with work–family balance.

Hypothesis 2: Individuals for whom work and family are not balanced will be more vulnerable to unexpected daily demands than individuals with work–family balance such that the effect of stressors on indicators of physical and mental health will be greater for those without work–family balance.

Hypothesis 3: The buffering effect of work–family balance on the stressor-health association will be stronger for women than men.

Method

Sample

Data for the analyses are from the National Study of Daily Experiences (NSDE). Respondents were 1,031 adults (562 women, 469 men), all of whom had previously participated in the National Survey of Midlife Development in the United States (MIDUS), a nationally representative telephone-mail survey of 3,032 people, aged 25–74 years, carried out in 1995–6 under the auspices of the John D. and Catherine T. MacArthur Foundation Network on Successful Midlife. Respondents in the NSDE were randomly selected from the MIDUS sample and received $20 for their participation in the project. Over the course of eight consecutive evenings, respondents completed short telephone interviews about their daily experiences. Data collection spanned an entire year (March 1996 to April 1997) and consisted of 40 separate "flights" of interviews with each flight representing the eight-day sequence of interviews from approximately 38 respondents. The initiation of interview flights was staggered across the day of the week to control for the possible confounding between day of study and day of week. Of the 1,242 MIDUS respondents contacted, 1,031 agreed to participate, yielding a response rate of 83 percent. Respondents completed an average of 7 of the 8 interviews, resulting in a total of 7,221 daily interviews.

The NSDE subsample and the MIDUS sample from which it was drawn had very similar distributions for age, marital status, and parenting status. The NSDE sample had a slightly greater percentage of women (54.5 percent versus 51.5 percent of the samples, respectively), was better educated (60.8 percent of the MIDUS sample had at least 13 years of education versus 62.3 percent of the NSDE subsample) and had a smaller percentage of minority respondents than the MIDUS sample. Of the NSDE sample, 90.3 percent were Caucasian, 5.9 percent African-American and 3.8 percent all other races, versus 87.8 percent Caucasian, 6.8 percent African-American, and 4.4 percent all other races for the MIDUS sample. Respondents for the present analysis were on average 47 years old. Thirty-eight percent of the households reported having at least one child under 18 years old in the household. The average family income was between $50,000 and $55,000. Men were slightly older than women, had similar levels of education and were more likely to be married at the time of the study (77 percent of the women versus 85 percent of the men).

Measures

Work–Family Balance
Work–family balance was operationalized based on Frone's (2003) contention that work–family balance reflects low levels of work–family conflict and high levels of work–family enrichment. Construction of this variable proceeded in three steps. First, levels of work-to-family conflict, family-to-work conflict, work-to-family enrichment, and family-to-work enrichment were computed using published items (Grzywacz & Marks, 2000). Second, each variable was then dichotomized into high versus low using a median split. Finally, four mutually exclusive categories were created reflecting different characterizations of work–family balance, including: *balanced* (i.e., low work-to-family and family-to-work conflict and high work-to-family and family-to-work enrichment), *imbalanced* (i.e., high work-to-family and family-to-work conflict and low work-to-family and family-to-work enrichment), *blurred* (i.e., high work-to-family or family-to-work conflict and high work-to-family or family-to-work enrichment), and *segmented* (i.e., low work-to-family or family-to-work conflict and low work-to-family or family-to-work enrichment). Although the "balanced" and "imbalanced" labels correspond with Frone's conceptualization, we needed to create labels for other possible combinations. We reasoned that individuals with high levels of conflict and high levels of enrichment had very permeable work and family boundaries; consequently, we labeled this arrangement "blurred". By contrast, we reasoned that those with low conflict and low enrichment had relatively impermeable work and family boundaries so we labeled this arrangement "segmented."

Mental Health
Mental health was operationalized using an inventory of ten emotions expanded from the psychological distress scale designed for the MIDUS survey (Mroczek & Kolarz, 1998) and queried during each telephone

interview. This scale was developed from the following well-known and valid instruments: The Affect Balance Scale (Bradburn, 1969), the University of Michigan's Composite International Diagnostic Interview (Kessler, McGonagle, Zhao, Nelson, Hughes, Eshleman et al., 1994), the Manifest Anxiety Scale (Taylor, 1953), and the Center for Epidemiological Studies Depression Scale (Radloff, 1977). Respondents were asked how much of the time today did they feel: worthless; hopeless; nervous; restless or fidgety; that everything was an effort; and so sad that nothing could cheer you up. Response categories for the index items were 1 = none of the time, 2 = a little of the time, 3 = some of the time, 4 = most of the time, and 5 = all of the time. Scores across the ten items were summed ($\alpha = .89$).

Physical Health
Physical health was operationalized using a shortened version of the physical symptom checklist (Larsen & Kasimatis, 1991). Items that overlapped with the psychological distress scale (e.g., "urge to cry") were omitted. Our 5-item scale assessed five constellations of symptoms: aches/pain (headaches, backaches, and muscle soreness), gastrointestinal symptoms (poor appetite, nausea/upset stomach, constipation/diarrhea), chest pain or dizziness (symptoms often associated with cardiovascular functioning), flu symptoms (upper respiratory symptoms; sore throat, runny nose; fever; chills) and a category for "other" physical symptoms or discomforts. Open-ended responses to the other physical symptoms question were subsequently coded and across the five items were summed ($\alpha = .71$).

Daily Stressors
Daily stressors were assessed through a semi-structured Daily Inventory of Stressful Experiences (DISE, Almeida et al., 2002). The DISE is a semi-structured instrument containing seven "stem" questions for identifying whether stressful events occurred in various life domains, as well as a series of questions for probing affirmative responses. For each daily interview, individuals who responded affirmatively to any of the stem questions received a value of one on an indicator variable of *any stress* and were coded zero otherwise.

Analyses

The method used to examine the associations among work–family balance, stressor exposure, physical symptoms, and psychological distress within individuals over time was based on a multilevel model, also commonly referred to as a hierarchical linear model (HLM, Bryk & Raudenbush, 1992). In this multilevel model, a lag-analysis was used, with prior day physical symptoms predicting current day physical symptoms, and prior psychological distress predicting the level of psychological distress reported on the current day. By controlling for prior-day values for physical symptoms and distress when predicting the current day values, the specification is equivalent to (but more flexible than) a change score model. Stressor exposure was defined as whether the respondent experienced any stressor. Respondents reporting no stressors were the comparison group.

The simple form of an HLM can be conceived of as two separate models, one a within-person model (Level 1) and the other a between-person model (Level 2). A distinctive feature of HLM is that the intercepts and slopes are allowed to vary across persons (Lee & Bryk, 1989), allowing estimates of between-person models of within-person variability. To examine the temporal links between daily psychological distress and stressors, we fit a within-person model essentially equivalent to 1,031 regressions assessing daily covariation of stressors and distress. The unit of observation for each of these regressions is the person-day, so the sample size for each of these regressions is $N = 8$. Using a simple example in which health depends on a single explanatory variable – stressors – the model can be expressed as:

$$\text{Level 1:} \quad \text{HEALTH}_{it} = a_{0i} + a_{1i}\text{STRESSOR} + e_{it}, \qquad (10.1)$$

where HEALTH_{it} is the reported health outcome (i.e., physical symptoms or psychological distress) of Person_i on Day_t, STRESSOR indicates whether Person_i experienced a stressor on Day_t, a_{0i} is the intercept indicating Person_i's average level of health when no stressor was reported, a_{1i} is the slope indicating the association between stressor exposure and health for Person_i, and e_{it} is the random component or error associated with distress of Person_i on Day_t. To estimate average effects for the entire sample, the intercepts and slopes of the Level 1 within-person model become the outcomes for the Level 2 between-person equations as follows.

$$\text{Level 2:} \quad a_{0i} = B_0 + d_i, \qquad (10.2)$$

$$a_{1i} = B_1 + g_i \qquad (10.3)$$

The sample size for each of the Level 2 regressions is N = 1,031. Equation 10.2 shows that Person$_i$'s average health score across the diary days (a_{0i}) is a function of the intercept for the entire sample (B_0) – the grand mean of the sample – and a random component or error (d_i). Likewise, equation 10.3 shows that Person$_i$'s slope between distress and health (a_{1i}) is a function of the grand mean of the entire sample (B_1), and a random component or error (g_i). As discussed earlier in this paragraph, this basic model was extended to include prior day physical symptoms or negative affect as covariates for their respective outcomes to attenuate the possibility of reverse causality, whereby previous days poor health (physical or mental) contributed to both experiencing a stressor and health problems on any given day.

HLM provides the flexibility to allow the intercepts and slopes to vary across persons by stable individual characteristics (e.g., BALANCE). For example, to examine differences in the daily covariation of distress and stressor exposure by levels of work–family balance, one can formulate the following model

$$\text{Level 1:} \quad \text{DISTRESS}_{it} = a_{0i} + a_{1i}\text{STRESSOR} + e_{it} \tag{10.4}$$

$$\text{Level 2:} \quad a_{0i} = B_0 + B_1(\text{BALANCE}) + d_i, \tag{10.5}$$

$$a_{1i} = B_2 + B_3(\text{BALANCE}) + g_i \tag{10.6}$$

Equations 10.5 and 10.6 model BALANCE differences in Level 1 intercepts and slopes. Of particular note is equation 10.6 because it considers the differential vulnerability hypothesis by testing whether the stressor-distress slopes (a_{1i}) vary according to degree of work–family balance.

In these analyses, a model where the slope is constrained to be equal across subjects (for example, a model where the strength of the association between distress and stressor exposure is the same across all participants) is compared to one where the slopes are allowed to vary across individuals (in this example, a model where the association is not the same across individuals with differing socioeconomic status). The models are compared by taking the difference between the obtained model fits [i.e., −2 ln(Likelihood)] and testing its significance with the degrees of freedom equal to the difference in the number of parameters of the two models (df = 2, in this example) (Bryk & Raudenbush, 1992). If the models are not significantly different, the model constraining the slopes to be equal is chosen for reasons of parsimony.

Results

Work–family balance is a relatively uncommon situation in this national sample. Approximately 9 percent of working adults met the critieria for "balanced" indicated by high levels of work–family enrichment and low levels of work–family conflict (Table 10.1). A slightly greater proportion of working adults were classified as having an "imbalanced" work–family arrangement (11 percent) or one characterized by higher levels of conflict than enrichment. The most common work–family arrangement in this sample of working adults was "blurred" or an arrangement characterized by high levels of work–family enrichment and high levels of work–family conflict; however, nearly as common was a "segmented" arrangement characterized by low work–family conflict and low work–family enrichment.

Bivariate and multivariate analyses provide support for the hypothesis that the absence of work–family balance will undermine health. Bivariate correlations suggest that "imbalance" is associated with greater physical symptoms and psychological distress (Table 10.1); however, there are few robust correlations among the other work–family arrangements and the health outcomes. Turning to the multivariate analyses, our models present strong evidence that work–family balance is a protective factor for physical health (see Model 1, Table 10.2). The average number of reported physical symptoms was higher for individuals with an "imbalanced" and "blurred" (trend level) work–family arrangement in contrast to those with a balanced arrangement, controlling for previous day symptoms. For individuals with an "imbalanced" work and family arrangement, the average physical symptom score was .73 units higher; an increase of nearly one-half of a standard deviation. Consistent with the second hypothesis positing that work–family balance acts as a buffer of life stress, Model 2 of Table 10.2 indicates that the effect of stressor exposure on physical symptoms is greater among individuals who have a "segmented" and those who have an "imbalanced" work–family arrangement relative to those with a balanced work–family arrangement. Consistent with our hypothesis that work–family balance is more important to women's than men's health, trend level evidence suggests that being in an imbalanced work–family arrangement exacerbates the effect of stress exposure on physical health for women, but this trend-level effect is attenuated for men (Model 3, Table 10.2).

Turning to the mental health outcome, results of hierarchical linear models provided partial support for our first hypothesis (Model 1, Table 10.3). As hypothesized, individuals in an imbalanced work and family

Table 10.1 Means, standard deviations, and inter-correlation among primary independent variables.

	M	SD	1	2	3	4	5	6	7
Work–family balance									
1. Balanced	0.09	0.28		-0.09*	-0.25***	-0.26***	-0.10*	-0.09	-0.16**
2. Imbalanced	0.11	0.31	-0.12*		-0.26***	-0.27***	-0.08	0.08	0.21***
3. Segmented	0.39	0.49	-0.25***	-0.30***		-0.68***	-0.14**	-0.09	-0.07
4. Blurred	0.41	0.49	-0.25***	-0.30***	-0.64***		0.14**	0.09	0.05
5. Stress exposure†	2.81	1.88	-0.13*	0.16**	-0.18***	0.13**		0.24***	0.24***
6. Psychological distress‡	1.78	2.85	-0.09	0.19***	-0.09	0.01	0.26***		0.44***
7. Physical symptoms‡	1.56	1.56	-0.03	0.17***	-0.07	-0.02	0.21***	0.61***	

Notes: * $p < .05$; ** $p < .01$; *** $p < .001$ (two-tailed); † Stress exposure reflects the average number of days participants reported a stressor; ‡ Psychological distress and physical symptoms reflect the grand mean for all participants across all interview days; Correlations above the diagonal are for women, below are for men.

Table 10.2   Results of hierarchical linear models estimating change in physical symptoms.

	Model 1 Main effects	Model 2 Vulnerability	Model 3 Gendered vulnerability
Gender (women = 1)	−0.22**	−0.22**	0.13
Work–family balance			
Segmented	0.19	0.09	0.22
Imbalanced	0.73***	0.49**	0.82**
Blurred	0.22†	0.19	0.34†
Balanced	*Reference*	*Reference*	*Reference*
Stress exposure	0.35***	0.03	−0.01
Interaction terms			
Segmented*Stress		0.42*	0.57*
Imbalanced*Stress		0.67**	0.60†
Blurred*Stress		0.21	0.34
Men*Stress			0.11
Men*Segmented			−0.28
Men*Imbalanced			−0.62†
Men*Blurred			−0.29
Men*Segmented*Stress			−0.37
Men*Imbalanced*Stress			0.09
Men*Blurred*Stress			−0.34

Notes: † $p < .10$; * $p < .05$; ** $p < .01$ ***; $p < .001$ (two-tailed); All models control for the effects of age, education, income, race/ethnicity, and previous day physical symptoms.

arrangement reported higher levels of psychological distress, controlling for previous day distress. Mean differences in psychological distress for those with a balanced versus imbalanced work–family arrangement were sizeable; approximately one-third of a standard deviation. Evidence in model 2 suggests that living in an imbalanced work and family arrangement exacerbates the effect of stress exposure on mental health. However, once gender interactions are introduced into the model, it becomes clear that gender shapes the buffering potential of work–family balance (see Model 3, Table 10.3). The effect of stress on psychological distress is large and significant for women ($b = 1.14$, $p < .05$), but there is no evidence that the absence of work–family balance exacerbates the mental health effects of stress exposure among women. By contrast, for men, the effect of stressor

Table 10.3 Results of hierarchical linear models estimating change in psychological distress.

	Model 1 Main effects	Model 2 Vulnerability	Model 3 Gendered vulnerability
Gender (women = 1)	−0.05	−0.06	0.08
Work–family balance			
Segmented	0.21	0.21	0.26
Imbalanced	0.85***	1.02**	1.03†
Blurred	0.26	0.46	0.48
Balanced	Reference	Reference	Reference
Stress exposure	0.90***	0.59*	1.14**
Interaction terms			
Segmented*Stress		0.41	−0.02
Imbalanced*Stress		0.89**	−0.35
Blurred*Stress		0.20	−0.15
Men*Stress			−1.30*
Men*Segmented			−0.10
Men*Imbalanced			−0.10
Men*Blurred			−0.04
Men*Segmented*Stress			1.03†
Men*Imbalanced*Stress			2.65***
Men*Blurred*Stress			0.82

Notes: † $p < .10$; * $p < .05$; ** $p < .01$; *** $p < .001$ (two-tailed); All models control for the effects of age, education, income, race/ethnicity, and previous day psychological distress.

exposure on psychological distress among those in a balanced work and family arrangement is lower for men than for women ($b = −1.30, p < .05$). However, for men in an imbalanced work and family arrangement, the effect of stressor exposure on psychological distress is substantial ($b = 2.65, p < .001$).

Discussion

The primary goal of this study was to examine the association between work–family balance and health using a prospective study design. Although leading a balanced work and family life is implicitly believed to contribute to health and overall well-being, this assumption has not previously been subjected to scientific scrutiny. Much of the extant research on associations between work–family interactions and health have been limited to examinations of work–family conflict rather than balance *per se*. Using a definition of balance that included enriching as well as conflicting work–family experiences, we found that individuals in an imbalanced work and family arrangement report poorer daily physical and mental health. Moreover, an imbalanced work and family arrangement accentuates the negative impact of daily stressors on physical and mental health. These findings clearly show that there are negative health consequences associated with an imbalanced work and family life and imply there is a substantial public health benefit to promoting work–family balance in the population (Grzywacz & Fuqua, 2000; Halpern, 2005).

Before discussing the health implications of work–family balance, it is important to again clarify what we believe a balanced work–family life is. Few researchers have tried to measure balance as a construct that is distinct from work–family conflict, often defining balance as low levels of interrole conflict. We believe that the distinction between work–family conflict and work–family balance is important and more than semantic. Although reducing conflict between life roles is likely to benefit one's health (Greenhaus et al., 2006), we believe the concept of balance implies something more than the absence of conflict; more specifically, we define balance as both having a high level of positive interactions between work and family as well as a low level of conflict between the roles. This conceptualization suggests that programmatic attempts to promote balance require a dual approach of reducing conflicts and promoting enrichment. Consequently, in addition to initiatives like workplace flexibility and on-site child care to reduce conflict between work and family, it is important to develop policies and programs focused on building synergies between individuals' work and family lives. Unfortunately, research upon which to build recommendations is lacking, but some evidence suggests that building greater worker autonomy and helping workers advance and make a difference in their organization may contribute to enrichment (Butler, Grzywacz, Bass, & Linney, 2005; Grzywacz & Butler, 2005; Voydanoff, 2005b).

The results of this study provide compelling evidence suggesting that the quality of the interrelationship between work and family affects adult health. Across both outcomes reflecting physical and mental health, we found greater decrements to health during the study period for individuals in an imbalanced (i.e., low enrichment, high conflict) versus a balanced (i.e., high enrichment, low conflict) work–family arrangement. These results are consistent with several cross-sectional studies showing that elevated work–family conflict is associated with poorer health (Frone, 2000; Grandey & Cropanzano, 1999; Grzywacz, 2000; Thomas & Ganster, 1995), and they add to the limited number of prospective studies documenting the health effects of experiences reflecting the interrelationship between work and family (Frone et al., 1997; Hammer et al., 2005; Kinnunen et al., 2004). Further, these results dovetail nicely with those from cross-sectional studies showing that work–family enrichment buffers the relationship between work–family conflict and mental health (Grzywacz & Bass, 2003) and prospective evidence indicating the salience of work–family enrichment on mental health (Hammer et al., 2005).

New to the work–family literature is our finding that a mutually beneficial interrelationship between work and family buffers the effects of life stress. Specifically, we found that when individuals were exposed to stressors, the decrement to health was greater for individuals whose work and family lives were imbalanced than for those who were balanced. Recognizing that the items used to operationalize balance were measured one year prior to the assessment of health symptoms, our results provide strong evidence suggesting that a work and family life characterized by a mutually beneficial interrelationship may enhance individual health by creating a context that helps individuals more effectively adapt to unexpected daily demands. Research is needed to replicate and clarify these findings; nonetheless, they are exciting because they suggest that work–family balance can affect health through multiple channels, thereby making it a salient leverage point for improving the health of the population (Grzywacz & Fuqua, 2000; Halpern, 2005).

Although the division of work and family labor is intricately tied to gender (Eby et al., 2005; Larson et al., 1994), the extant literature provides inconsistent evidence of gender differences in the experience of work–family conflict and enrichment (Byron, 2005; Frone, 2003). Yet, gender may still moderate relationships between work–family experiences and life outcomes. We asked whether work–family imbalance differentially increased vulnerability to daily stressors for women and men. We did not find that imbalance increased women's vulnerability to physical complaints, and contrary to expectation, we found that the effect of stressor exposure on psychological distress was elevated among men with an imbalanced work and family arrangement. This finding is difficult to interpret, but it suggests that imbalance may play a more significant role in men's mental health than women's, perhaps because men are less likely to use available resources (e.g., organizational policies) to improve their work–family arrangement (Pleck, 1993). Although research should continue to explore potential gender differences in the ability of work–family balance to benefit health, we do not want to over-interpret our isolated finding.

Our study has several implications for the conceptualization of work–family balance. First, it is clear that health-related consequences of work–family experiences may be shaped by the interaction between conflict and enrichment. This reinforces the importance of considering enrichment, or the positive side of the balance equation, when examining work–family relationships, and to fully understand the rich interplay between these two primary domains of adult life. Second, it is important for future research to examine the relative stability of work–family balance in daily life. Our work–family balance measures were collected as part of a cross-sectional study, so we examined overall impressions of balance, finding that they were prospectively related to daily health. This implies that relatively stable levels of balance do exist that may affect important life outcomes like health. Yet, prior studies have found significant daily variation in both work–family conflict and enrichment (Butler et al., 2005). It would be valuable to determine if balance is, in fact, a relatively enduring phenomenon or if it is more dynamic in nature. Anticipating that work–family balance does have some enduring features, it will be vital for future research to clearly identify modifiable factors that enable mutually beneficial interrelationships between adults' work and family lives.

In summary, our results indicate that individuals whose work and family lives are mutually beneficial have better physical and mental health. Some of these health effects were direct; however, some of the health advantage resulted from the protection a balanced work and family arrangement provided individuals from the negative effects of daily stress. Although more research is needed to fully understand what work–family balance is and how it ultimately affects individual health, the results of this study support claims that promoting work–family balance in the adult population is a viable strategy for improving population health.

Acknowledgment

The research was partially supported by a grant from the Alfred P. Sloan Foundation (2006-5-22WPF).

References

Adams, G. A., & Jex, S. M. (1999). Relationships between time management, control, work-family conflict, and strain. *Journal of Occupational Health Psychology, 4*, 72–77.

Almeida, D. M., Wethington, E., & Kessler, R. C. (2002). The Daily Inventory of Stressful Events: An interview-based approach for measuring daily stressors. *Assessment, 9*, 41–55.

Aneshensel, C. S. (1992). Social stress: Theory and research. *Annual Review of Sociology, 18*, 15–38.

Aryee, S., Srinivas, E. S., & Tan, H. H. (2005). Rhythms of life: Antecedents and outcomes of work-family balance in employed parents. *Journal of Applied Psychology, 90*, 132–146.

Barnett, R. C. (1998). Toward a review and reconceptualization of the work/family literature. *Genetic, Social & General Psychology Monographs, 124*, 125–182.

Bradburn, N. (1969). *The structure of psychological well-being.* Oxford: Aldine.

Bryk, A. S., & Raudenbush, S. W. (1992). *Hierarchical linear models: Applications and data analysis methods.* Thousand Oaks, CA: Sage Publications Inc.

Butler, A. B., Grzywacz, J. G., Bass, B. L., & Linney, K. D. (2005). Extending the demands-control model: A daily diary study of job characteristics, work-family conflict and work-family facilitation. *Journal of Occupational and Organizational Psychology, 78*, 155–169.

Byron, K. (2005). A meta-analytic review of work-family conflict and its antecedents. *Journal of Vocational Behavior, 67*, 169–198.

Caspi, A., Bolger, N., & Eckenrode, J. (1987). Linking person and context in the daily stress process. *Journal of Personality and Social Psychology, 52*, 184–195.

Eby, L. T., Casper, W. J., Lockwood, A., Bordeaux, C., & Brinley, A. (2005). Work and family research in IO/OB: Content analysis and review of the literature (1980–2002). *Journal of Vocational Behavior, 66*, 124–197.

Frone, M. R. (2000). Work-family conflict and employee psychiatric disorders: The national comorbidity survey. *Journal of Applied Psychology, 85*, 888–895.

Frone, M. R. (2003). Work-family balance. In J. C. Quick & L. E. Tetrick (Eds.), *Handbook of occupational health psychology* (pp. 143–162). Washington, DC: American Psychological Association.

Frone, M. R., Russell, M., & Cooper, M. L. (1997). Relation of work-family conflict to health outcomes: A four-year longitudinal study of employed parents. *Journal of Occupational and Organizational Psychology, 70*, 325–335.

Grandey, A. A., & Cropanzano, R. (1999). The Conservation of Resources model applied to work-family conflict and strain. *Journal of Vocational Behavior, 54*, 350–370.

Greenhaus, J. H., & Allen, T. D. (2006, March). *Work-family balance: Exploration of a concept.* Paper presentation, Families and Work Conference, Provo, UT

Greenhaus, J. H., Allen, T. D., & Spector, P. E. (2006). Health consequences of work-family conflict: The dark side of the work-family interface. In P. L. Perrewe & D. C. Ganster (Eds.), *Research in occupational stress and well-being* (Vol. 5, pp. 61–98). Amsterdam: JAI Press: Elsevier.

Greenhaus, J. H., Collins, K. M., & Shaw, J. D. (2003). The relation between work-family balance and quality of life. *Journal of Vocational Behavior, 63,* 510–531.

Greenhaus, J. H., & Powell, G. N. (2006). When work and family are allies: A theory of work-family enrichment. *Academy of Management Review, 31,* 72–92.

Grzywacz, J. G. (2000). Work-family spillover and health during midlife: Is managing conflict everything? *American Journal of Health Promotion, 14,* 236–243.

Grzywacz, J. G., Almeida, D. M., Neupert, S. D., & Ettner, S. L. (2004). Socioeconomic status and heath: A micro-level analysis of exposure and vulnerability to daily stressors. *Journal of Health and Social Behavior, 45,* 1–16.

Grzywacz, J. G., & Bass, B. L. (2003). Work, family, and mental health: Testing different models of work-family fit. *Journal of Marriage and Family, 65,* 248–262.

Grzywacz, J. G., & Butler, A. B. (2005). The impact of job characteristics on work-to-family facilitation: Testing a theory and distinguishing a construct. *Journal of Occupational Health Psychology, 10,* 97–109.

Grzywacz, J. G., & Carlson, D. S. (2007). Conceptualizing work–family balance: Implications for practice and research. *Advances in Developing Human Resources, 9*(4), 455–471.

Grzywacz, J. G., & Fuqua, J. (2000). The social ecology of health: Leverage points and linkages. *Behavioral Medicine, 26,* 101–115.

Grzywacz, J. G., & Marks, N. F. (2000). Reconceptualizing the work-family interface: An ecological perspective on the correlates of positive and negative spillover between work and family. *Journal of Occupational Health Psychology, 5,* 111–126.

Halpern, D. F. (2005). Psychology at the intersection of work and family: Recommendations for employers, working families, and policymakers. *American Psychologist, 60,* 397–409.

Hammer, L. B., Cullen, J. C., Neal, M. B., Sinclair, R. R., & Shafiro, M. V. (2005). The longitudinal effects of work-family conflict and positive spillover on depressive symptoms among dual-earner couples. *Journal of Occupational Health Psychology, 10,* 138–154.

Hill, E. J., Hawkins, A. J., Ferris, M., & Weitzman, M. (2001). Finding an extra day a week: The positive influence of perceived job flexibility on work and family life balance. *Family Relations, 50,* 49–58.

Kanter, R. M. (1977). *Work and family in the United States: A critical review and agenda for research and policy.* New York: Russell Sage Foundation.

Kessler, R. C., McGonagle, K. A., Zhao, S., Nelson, C. B., Hughes, M., Eshleman, S., et al. (1994). Lifetime and 12-month prevalence of DSM-III-R psychiatric disorders in the United States: Results from the National Comorbidity Survey. *Archives of General Psychiatry, 51,* 8–19.

Kinnunen, U., Feldt, T., Geurts, S., & Pulkkinen, L. (2006). Types of work-family interface: Well-being correlates of negative and positive spillover between work and family. *Scandinavian Journal of Psychology, 47,* 149–162.

Kinnunen, U., Geurts, S., & Mauno, S. (2004). Work-to-family conflict and its relationship with satisfaction and well-being: A one-year longitudinal study on gender differences. *Work and Stress, 18,* 1–22.

Kirchmeyer, C. (2000). Work-life initiatives: Greed or benevolence regarding workers' time? In C. L. Cooper & D. M. Rousseau (Eds.), *Trends in organizational behavior* (Vol. 7, pp. 79–93). West Sussex, UK: John Wiley & Sons.

Kirkcaldy, B. D., & Martin, T. (2000). Job stress and satisfaction among nurses: Individual differences. *Stress Medicine, 16,* 77–89.

Kofodimos, J. R. (1993). *Balancing act.* San Francisco: Jossey-Bass.

Larsen, R. J., & Kasimatis, M. (1991). Day-to-day physical symptoms: Individual differences in the occurrence, duration, and emotional concomitants of minor daily illnesses. *Journal of Personality, 59,* 387–423.

Larson, R. W., Richards, M. H., & Perry-Jenkins, M. (1994). Divergent worlds: The daily emotional experience of mothers and fathers in the domestic and public spheres. *Journal of Personality and Social Psychology, 67,* 1034–1046.

Lee, V. E., & Bryk, A. S. (1989). A multilevel model of the social distribution of high school achievement. *Sociology of Education, 62,* 172–192.

Lepore, S. J., Evans, G. W., & Palsane, M. N. (1991). Social hassles and psychological health in the context of chronic crowding. *Journal of Health and Social Behavior, 32,* 357–367.

McLeod, J. D., & Kessler, R. C. (1990). Socioeconomic status differences in vulnerability to undesirable life events. *Journal of Health and Social Behavior, 31,* 162–172.

Marks, S. R., & MacDermid, S. M. (1996). Multiple roles and the self: A theory of role balance. *Journal of Marriage and the Family, 58,* 417–432.

Moen, P., & Wethington, E. (1992). The concept of family adaptive strategies. *Annual Review of Sociology, 18,* 223–251.

Morehead, A. (2001). Synchronizing time for work and family: Preliminary insights from qualitative research with mothers. *Journal of Sociology, 37,* 355–369.

Mroczek, D. K., & Kolarz, C. M. (1998). The effect of age on positive and negative affect: A developmental perspective on happiness. *Journal of Personality and Social Psychology, 75,* 1333–1349.

National Institute for Child Health and Human Development (2004). *Developing study designs to evaluate the health benefits of workplace policies and practices.* Retrieved August 1, 2005 from http://grants.nih.gov/grants/guide/notice-files/NOT-HD-04-007.html

Pleck, J. H. (1993). Are "family-supportive" employer policies relevant to men? In J. C. Hood (Ed.), *Men, work, and family* (pp. 217–237). Thousand Oaks, CA: Sage.

Quick, J. D., Henley, A. B., & Quick, J. C. (2004). The balancing act – At work and at home. *Organizational Dynamics, 33*, 426–438.

Radloff, L. S. (1977). The CES-D scale: A self-report depression scale for research in the general population. *Applied Psychological Measurement, 1*, 385–401.

Rothbard, N. P. (2001). Enriching or depleting? The dynamics of engagement in work and family roles. *Administrative Science Quarterly, 46*, 655–684.

Taylor, J. A. (1953). A personality scale of manifest anxiety. *Journal of Abnormal and Social Psychology, 48*, 285–290.

Taylor, S. E., Repetti, R. L., & Seeman, T. (1997). Health psychology: What is an unhealthy environment and how does it get under the skin. *Annual Review of Psychology, 48*, 411–447.

Thomas, L. T., & Ganster, D. C. (1995). Impact of family-supportive work variables on work-family conflict and strain: A control perspective. *Journal of Applied Psychology, 80*, 6–15.

Turner, R. J., Wheaton, B., & Lloyd, D. A. (1995). The epidemiology of social stress. *American Sociological Review, 60*, 104–125.

Vinokur, A. D., Pierce, P. F., Buck, C. L. (1999). Work-family conflicts of women in the Air Force: Their influence on mental health and functioning. *Journal of Organizational Behavior, 20*, 865–878.

Voydanoff, P. (2004). The effects of work demands and resources on work-to-family conflict and facilitation. *Journal of Marriage and Family, 66*, 398–412.

Voydanoff, P. (2005a). Toward a conceptualization of perceived work-family fit and balance: A demands and resources approach. *Journal of Marriage and Family, 67*, 822–836.

Voydanoff, P. (2005b). The differential salience of family and community demands and resources for family-to-work conflict and facilitation. *Journal of Family and Economic Issues, 26*, 395–417.

Werbel, J., & Walter, M. H. (2002). Changing views of work and family roles: A symbiotic perspective. *Human Resource Management Review, 12*, 293–298.

Part IV

Politics, Business, and the Legal System: What is the Effect of Work–Family Integration?

Part IV

Introduction

Diane F. Halpern

Why are employers like Google enjoying high profits (at least at the time of this writing) and others, like General Motors, fighting to maintain ever-shrinking profit margins? Of course, there is no simple or single answer and readers can probably guess at a few of the reasons that financial pundits have offered, which include competition from emerging markets in countries in the developing world, most particularly China and India. But there are other answers and other factors that contribute to the success of organizations that the financial analysts will often fail to consider. Some employers have dedicated and loyal workers, an asset that is not captured as a line item on profit and loss statements, but one that can reduce the high cost of employee turnover and boost profits in indirect ways such as having a workforce that does more than what is (minimally) expected from them. There is no single metric to quantify how and how much happy employees add to the bottom line, because they often demonstrate their loyalty in countless small ways, such as offering better service to customers or meeting critical deadlines because they are personally invested in the success of their employer.

The vast literature on organizational development shows that leadership matters, whether it is at the corporate level or among those who enter the political arena at all levels of government. There is the general belief that, on average, women leaders are more attuned to issues that relate to families and to making it easier for employees to care for family members while at work. Of course, this is a generalization and there are many male leaders who care about working families, but it is a belief that is confirmed by the political agendas of Nancy Pelosi, the first woman to assume the role of Speaker of the House of Representatives in the United States and in the agendas of other women leaders around the world. In her chapter, "Politics, Motherhood, and Madame President," Jane Swift, former governor of Massachusetts explains why she believes we need to elect more women to public office so that our national leaders reflect the composition and concerns of our population. Swift speaks from experience as the only person to give birth while governor – and she had twins! The often conflicting demands of motherhood and governor made her acutely aware of the need for better work–family policies and legislation.

The theme that work–family policies are critically important is continued in the chapter written by Donna Klein, executive director of Corporate Voices, an organization that includes some of the largest employers in the US (and globally). These employers have joined together to speak in unison in support of working families and to find cost-effective ways to help their employees meet their family obligations. As Klein explains, a research project on the benefits of flexible work arrangements has led to changes that make it easier for their employees to meet both their work and family obligations. Corporate Voices tackled issues such as affordable child care, elder care, and housing. Many of the employers have a large number of low-skilled and low-wage employees, so they provide programs specific for this sector of the workforce, including classes to improve English-language skills, parenting classes, and assistance with college applications for the children of their employees. These organizations recognize that their employees' family lives are intricately related to their work lives and that it is good business to help employees manage family and work responsibilities.

V. Sue Molina, former director of the Women's Initiative at Deloitte & Touche, one of the "big 5" accounting firms, explains how Deloitte responded to the loss of talented women in accounting. She recognized that for many of the women they employed, family obligations would take them off of the career track for some period of time, but these talented women did not need to become permanently lost talent for Deloitte & Touche. By creating numerous ways that made it easier for employees to take time off and still remain current in their field, Deloitte & Touche was able to create loyal employees who returned to Deloitte & Touche when their family commitments lightened and it was easier to return to work.

Maintaining a fair work place for all employees is not only a good way to protect an employer's investment in their workforce, it is the law. In the final chapter, Joan Williams, a distinguished professor of law at Hastings Law School shows how discrimination against mothers and others who have family care responsibilities is being punished in courts of law with large awards to plaintiffs. She explains how the social psychological construct of stereotyping, including the concept of implicit or automatic stereotyping, is changing how courts think about discrimination. Employers are not free to discriminate against mothers or any employee who asks for or uses

flexible work arrangements and those employers who ignore the importance of family care responsibilities for their employees do so at their own
financial peril.

Taken together, the chapters in the final section of this book provide
a strong case for the return-on-investment for family-friendly employers.
These policies can provide additional profits via more loyal and committed
employees who are less likely to leave their employers, more likely to return
after a family-related leave, and the family-friendly employer can avoid
costly litigation regarding discrimination against employees with family care
responsibilities. Simply put, family-friendly business practices are good
for business. They represent win-win situations in which all stakeholders
enjoy financial and psychological benefits.

11

Politics, Motherhood, and Madame President

Jane Swift

Why are there so few women in politics? What can be done to increase women's participation in public office? Is the United States ready to elect a woman president? My own political career directly relates to these questions. I was pregnant when I campaigned to be governor of Massachusetts. My mother called and said, "Um, how is this all going to work – your pending motherhood and campaign responsibilities?" As I had never been pregnant before, I replied with naiveté, "I just ran a grueling 17-month campaign for Congress. There's only nine months to this election. How tough can it be?" I then proceeded to throw up almost every day for those next nine months and found out just how tough it could be. I delivered my daughter six weeks before my first statewide election, and later I gave birth to twins during my term as governor.

Based on my experiences and similar stories from other women in politics, it is understandable why so few women ever decide to run for elected office. Unfortunately, there are consequences to these decisions that extend beyond the individual lives of the women who hold office. Consider, for example, that when women are elected to public office, they tend to be more concerned with public policies that directly relate to working families and other "traditional" women's issues (Hawkesworth, Casey, Jenkins, & Kleeman, 2001). The fewer women who run for and get elected to political office, the less attention politicians pay to issues directly relevant to women – issues such as child care, family-friendly work policies, and family planning. The challenge for those of us who care about family-related public policies is that we have not made as much progress in electing women to political office as might have been expected by the beginning of the twenty-first century and decades after the women's movement for equality. The focus of this chapter is on how to get more women into the political pipeline with the goal of eventually electing a woman president.

Is the US Ready to Elect a Woman President?

The White House Project (www.TheWhiteHouseProject.org), which is a grass roots initiative designed to support women who are interested and able to run a successful campaign for president, ran a mock election in 2006 among the eight most viable women candidates who could potentially run as Republicans or Democrats for election to the U.S. presidency in 2008. The names of these women are listed in Table 11.1. Interestingly, only one of these eight, Hillary Clinton, is running for the presidential election in 2008.

There are good reasons to focus on the lack of a female President, including the fact that we continue to lag behind many other countries in the world that have had a woman in their highest political office. However, by focusing on the single office of the presidency, we draw attention away from the challenges facing women who are competing for other levels of political office. If we want to achieve parity in politics, then we need a sustained effort to break down the barriers that prevent women's full representation in public office at every level.

As a first step toward breaking the glass ceiling at the highest level of American politics, the pipeline of women in political jobs must increase substantially. For a national-level public office, the pipeline starts in state legislative positions. Although the number of women in state legislative offices has more than doubled since 1979, it has stagnated in the past decade, showing only small increases in the most recent years (Center for American Women and Politics, 2006). Consider, for example, the fact that in 2006, almost 23 percent of legislative seats were held by women, only a slight

Table 11.1   White House Project 8 in 08.

Name and office held	Political party
Senator Hillary Clinton	D-NY
Senator Susan Collins	R-Maine
Atlanta Mayor Shirley Franklin	Democrat
Senator Kay Bailey Hutchinson	R-Texas
Arizona Gov. Janet Napolitano	Democrat
Secretary of State Condoleezza Rice	Republican
Kansas Gov., Kathleen Sebelius	Democrat
Senator Olympia Snowe	R-Maine

increase over the number of legislative seats held by women in 1993, which was approximately 21 percent. The slight change in recent years is in contrast to the more rapid change in the years at the end of the 1970s, when the comparable figure was only 10 percent (Center for American Women and Politics, 2006). The fact that less than a quarter of the critical pipeline seats are currently filled by women explains our woeful participation rate at the next level, which is the United States Congress. Women held 16 percent of the seats in the United States Congress in 2007 (Center for American Women and Politics, 2007). It is interesting that many pro-feminist organizations celebrated the news that women currently hold eight governorships, but 8 out of 50 is not a cause for celebration for anyone who cares about the political representation of women and the election of a woman to the presidency. Simply put, there is too little progress being made in the number of women elected to political office.

To put the current situation in the US in context, the International Parliamentary Union ranks countries according to their success in electing women to federal governing bodies (Inter-Parliamentary Union, 2007). When compared with other countries, the US ranks seventieth, just ahead of Turkmenistan and behind El Salvador, Panama, and Zimbabwe. It is of significant concern that the US is so far behind the rest of the world. The low number of elected women politicians is a likely reason why the US is not more progressive in its work and family policies. Two important questions surface: Why are there so few elected women in political office? and What can Americans do to increase the numbers?

The good news is that when we control for other variables associated with a successful political race, such as being the incumbent, women win as often as men (Center for American Women and Politics). The problem is that women do not run for public office nearly as often as men. Lawless and Fox (2005) explored women's political ambitions by surveying men and women not currently in public office but with similar socioeconomic and educational backgrounds as well as similar qualifications to run for political office. When they were asked if they had ever thought about running for office, 16 percent of the men answered with a definitive "yes" and 39 percent responded that, "It's crossed my mind." By comparison, only 7 percent of women gave an unequivocal "yes" response, and 29 percent responded that the idea had crossed their minds. There cannot be large numbers of women who actually commit to the rigors of a political campaign as long as relatively low percentages are even willing to consider such a commitment.

Interestingly, when the men and women who considered running for office were asked, "What is the first office you would most likely seek," more women (79 percent) than men (69 percent) indicated that they would seek an office at the local level and more than double the percentage of men (15 percent) responded that they would consider running for federal office on their first try for an elected position as compared to women (7 percent). Not a single woman considered running for the United States presidency (having never run for any prior political office), whereas 1 percent of men were willing to consider the highest office as an appropriate place for their first political race (Lawless & Fox, 2005). These data show that women hold markedly different attitudes toward their willingness to run for public office.

Given that women are less likely to see themselves in the role of elected officials, at least beyond the local level, would more women be willing to run for elected office if they were actively recruited? Lawless and Fox (2005) asked the participants in their survey whether an official from a political party or an elected official had ever suggested that they run for public office. They found that 12 percent of the women and 20 percent of the men had been encouraged to run for public office by someone in their political party. Similar disparities were found with the data concerning encouragement from elected officials; 14 percent of the women and 23 percent of the men reported this experience. Thus, even if encouragement and support from one's political party and office holders were an antidote to women's reticence to run for elected office, the strong pattern of male preference is repeated in the degree to which women and men are actively recruited.

The pipeline challenge is further exacerbated by the fact that even when women are invited to run or think about running for public office, a greater proportion decline the invitation. It is more difficult for women to run for public office because they are scrutinized more closely by the media (Braden, 1996). Voters have more negative perceptions of women as political Chief Executive Officers (CEOs), and they believe that women will have more problems integrating the demands of work and family. In fact, any candidates with family care responsibilities will have difficulty meeting the demands of a high level political job and their family's needs, and women more often are the care givers with responsibility for children and other family members who need care. These are interdependent problems because the media shapes the way the general public views political candidates. Unrealistic expectations about the "ideal candidate" and sex role stereotypes contribute to the work–family challenges faced by women candidates.

Differences in Media Coverage

The media portrays women and men political candidates differently. Research focusing on the percentage of coverage for the 2000 Presidential Republican primary candidates on policy issues and on personal attributes examined the amount and type of coverage for four national candidates – George W. Bush, John McCain, Elizabeth Dole, and Steven Forbes (Aday & Devitt, 2001). Elizabeth Dole received less coverage on policy-related issues, including descriptions of her position and record on public policy matters, than the other three male presidential candidates. In fact, she received approximately half the coverage that George W. Bush and John McCain received. In contrast, Elizabeth Dole was more likely to get media attention for her personal attributes, including descriptions of her personality and her attire than the men who were running in that same primary. The relative percentages for each candidate are shown in Table 11.2.

It should be noted that although Elizabeth Dole dropped out of the presidential primary, these data were collected when all four were active candidates. To state the obvious, it is more difficult to convince the public to vote for a candidate when the policies in which people are interested are not covered by the media.

Voter Perceptions of Women as Political CEOs

The perceptions held by voters during a political campaign will influence how they vote, and thus, the ability of women to get elected. Public perceptions of women candidates are qualitatively different from their views of men candidates. For example, women are expected to dress and behave according to implicit standards. "A female candidate who is less 'tailored' – both in the way she carries herself and in her manner of dress – is

Table 11.2 Media coverage: 2000 GOP Presidential Primary.

	% of coverage on policy issues	% of coverage on personal issues
Elizabeth Dole	17.0	35.0
Steve Forbes	22.5	27.0
George Bush	33.0	22.0
John McCain	40.0	16.5

perceived by both male and female voters as less qualified, less of a leader, and less professional" (The Barbara Lee Family Foundation, 2004). Although it would be ideal to have political candidates judged by their position on substantive issues, past experience, ability to run state government, and character, voters instead often judge women candidates on their appearance and personal attributes. Voters make assumptions about women candidates and their families. They worry that a woman candidate with small children could be hindered by torn loyalties, choosing to handle a family emergency when she is needed for a political problem. Voters also assume a male candidate has someone else to care for his family and that a female candidate is the primary caregiver in her family, which is usually true. But this distinction does not apply to all men or women who run for office (The Barbara Lee Family Foundation, 2004).

A study on the "Keys to the Governor's Office" confirmed the perception that women care for others and thus have the dual demands of work and family while men are cared for and therefore have more time and energy for their work (The Barbara Lee Family Foundation, 2001). Some interesting comparisons arise when voters are asked whether they prefer a political candidate who has children. Among voters who prefer candidates with children, there are different preferences for men and women candidates that vary as a function of the age of the children. For example, there was no preference for men (5 percent) or women (5 percent) candidates with children under the age of 12. However, voters were more comfortable with a man who has teenage children (13 percent) as compared to a woman who has teenage children (7 percent); but when they were asked about candidates with adult children, voters preferred women candidates (11 percent) over men candidates (6 percent). Many talented and ambitious women delay their careers to raise their children. It is particularly difficult to get to the highest levels of government and leadership if one does not start until children have reached their own adulthood; at this point in the life span, most professional careers are more than halfway completed.

Work and Family Integration

It is difficult to achieve integration between work and family regardless of one's occupation, but this is especially true for anyone aspiring to a political career. The highly public nature of political jobs and the demands of many of these jobs create unique challenges compared with those that are faced by women in other careers. Moreover, the public sector, as an employer, has not made the same progress that has been slowly evolving in the business sector (i.e., family leave policies). Unless there are policies in the political realm that attract women who are mothers or women who hope to be mothers, then the pipeline challenge for women seeking the highest political offices will persist. The election of a woman to the position of president can be thought of as a matter of mathematics. A large number of women in American society have children, and many, probably a large majority of undergraduate women, want to marry and have children someday. Not surprisingly, if the ranks of the most successful women in politics in 2006 are examined, a large number of them are childless and even greater numbers of them started their careers when their children were already grown. Of the eight successful political women that the White House Project portrayed as potential viable candidates for the Presidency in 2008, half of them never had children (See Table 11.3).

It is imperative to note that I am not questioning women's choice of whether or not to have children; these data merely support the premise that women are deterred from pursuing political jobs by the challenges of motherhood. If a large majority of American women, especially mothers, are not seeking public office, we cannot hope to fill the pipeline, and we will miss important perspectives from women at the highest levels of our democracy.

There are inherent problems for mothers pursuing public office. One of the problems with elected office is that most of the work is done in the evenings and on weekends when the voters are not working. Committing to an elected job necessarily entails running for office, which is almost entirely contingent on being out of the house meeting other people at nights and on weekends. These time demands are a significant barrier to convincing women to enter the political arena.

Table 11.3 White House Project 8 in 08.

Name and office held	Political party	Number of children
Senator Hillary Clinton	D-NY	1
Senator Susan Collins	R-Maine	0
Atlanta Mayor Shirley Franklin	Democrat	3
Senator Kay Bailey Hutchinson	R-Texas	2
Arizona Gov. Janet Napolitano	Democrat	0
Secretary of State Condoleezza Rice	Republican	0
Kansas Gov., Kathleen Sebelius	Democrat	2
Senator Olympia Snowe	R-Maine	0

Second, there are certain inflexible work periods, such as the election season. For example, candidates do not have the option of changing the date of a televised debate if a child gets the flu or has an important sports or school event. The inflexibility of political work leads to constraints and challenges that many women consider when thinking about entering politics and eventually use to justify their decision not to enter this public and demanding field.

Third, there is a great deal of public discomfort with women who have young children and choose demanding work. The perception in our society is that everybody understands that certain people – notably the poor – have to work; however choosing to run for public office is different from "having to work." When voters see a woman with young children choosing what they perceive to be very demanding work, they have negative reactions (Etaugh & Nekolny, 1990). Most people do not like to subject themselves to disapproval from their peers or other important people in their lives. Saying to one's friends, "I'm thinking of running for office" and having the response be, "What's going to happen to your children?" or "Who will take care of your babies?" is a strong signal that one is not going to get psychological and social support from family or friends if the goal of office holding is pursued. Thus there are significant barriers for women, and especially mothers, which prevent them from entering the public arena. However, there are solutions to help women overcome these barriers and increase the number of women in the political pipeline.

Proposals to Improve Work–Family Integration in Public Sector Jobs

Make Public Sector Employment Policies the Best of the Breed

Public sector employment policies for the integration of work and family, especially those that impact the people who work for politicians, must become the standard. Of the eight women in the White House Project discussed earlier in this chapter, six of them, at some point in their early careers, worked in an appointed position as a staff person. Many women who find their way into politics or make a stopover in appointed level politics later run for office. Thus, public sector staff positions must be more family friendly by addressing such issues as flexible work hours, telecommuting, and maternity leave policy. The establishment of national public sector rankings of family friendly employment policies is critical. It is likely that many cities, states, and even federal policies lag behind the private sector and other employers. Because elected officials are responsive to press coverage, the publicity of these results may be the quickest means to drive change in the public sector.

Keep Women Visible and Relevant during Breaks in Careers

We must keep women relevant and engaged during breaks from employment. There is a growing movement by major corporations to acknowledge that there are many highly educated and talented women who have economic freedom and some of these women will take breaks in their careers. Unfortunately, we know it is difficult for women to re-enter the work force after they stop-out. Their skills and their relationships are dated, and Human Resource departments generally do not hold positive views on gaps in one's resume. Yet, in some cases, corporate America has realized that they need these women to re-enter the work force because corporate employers need their skills. Dartmouth and Harvard business schools have designed programs to help women who are ready to re-enter the work force by getting them reconnected and improving and updating their skills. There are 34 corporations that have developed and integrated new best practices in their companies based on the research of Hewlett, Luce, Shiller, and Southwell (2005).

It is imperative that some of these women who re-enter the work force seriously consider and then actually enter politics. The National Women's Political Caucus has developed a model to help women make the important decision to enter politics. Their program identifies potential women candidates for high-level appointments when there has been a change in administration. They maintain a database of talented women who might not otherwise be considered for some of these policy-making agendas. It is realistic to identify women who have either scaled back or are taking breaks in their careers and who may have an interest in running for political office. These women need encouragement to remain politically involved during a change or a slowdown in their careers.

MPA Program for Re-Entering Moms

In order to get more women with a variety of backgrounds to run for public office, the Masters in Public Administration (MPA) programs must help women who already have served or who have an interest in serving in public office. These programs must prepare women for every element of public office. To take on these challenges and address them successfully, women are going to need to think differently and be more focused on solutions rather than on divisions. Women make varied choices based on their own circumstances at different points in their careers. In order to get more women to run for public office it is important to be more accepting and avoid commenting on or assigning some kind of value judgment to the choices that are made.

Conclusions

We know that women in public office bring more attention to work–family issues, such as affordable child care, flexible work schedules, family planning, and other family-friendly public policies. Yet, women are not adequately represented in the public sector; the increase of women in legislative offices in the past few decades has been minimal. There are many challenges for women who want to pursue a career in the public sector. To address these challenges successfully, women have to think differently from their male colleagues and be more focused on solutions to problems related to integrating their own work and family needs. They must avoid value judgments about women's choices and find ways to get voters to do the same. We will not achieve political parity as long as there are negative reactions to the idea of mothers in political office.

The proposed solutions will help women overcome the barriers they face when entering the political pipeline. Women will need to make personal choices based on their own circumstances, which will vary at different times in their lives. Our society needs to be more accepting of women's choices and realize that beliefs and stereotypes about working mothers and work–family integration are creating barriers to the election of more women to public office. Ironically, we need more women in public office to address work–family issues, and yet, it is these same issues that deter women from entering the race for elected positions. The same work–family issues that are critical in business must be addressed in the political realm, if we hope to have women elected to high level offices.

References

Aday, S., & Devitt, J. (2001). Style over substance: Newspaper coverage of Elizabeth Dole's presidential bid. *The Harvard International Journal of Press/Politics, 6*, 52–73.

Braden, M. (1996). *Women politicians and the media.* Lexington, KY: The University Press of Kentucky.

Center for American Women and Politics (2006). *Women in state legislatures 2006.* New Brunswick, NJ: Rutgers, The State University of New Jersey.

Center for American Women in Politics (2007). *Women in the U.S. Congress 2007.* New Brunswick, NJ: Rutgers, The State University of New Jersey.

Center for American Women and Politics (2001). *Women state legislatures: Past, present and future.* Retrieved June 18, 2007, from, http://www.cawp.rutgers.edu/Research/Reports/StLeg2001Report.pdf

Etaugh, C., & Nekolny, K. (1990). Effects of employment status and marital status on perceptions of mothers. *Sex Roles, 23*(5–6), 273–280.

Hawkesworth, M., Casey, K. J., Jenkins, K., & Kleeman, K. E. (2001). *Legislating by and for women: A Comparison of the 103rd and 104th Congresses.* New Brunswick, NJ: Rutgers, The State University of New Jersey: Center for American Women and Politics.

Hewlett, S. A., Luce, C. B., Shiller, P., & Southwell, S. (2005). *The hidden brain drain: Off-ramps and on-ramps in women's careers* (Product No. 9491). Cambridge, MA: Harvard Business School, Center for Work-Life Policy.

Inter-Parliamentary Union (2007, March 31). *Women in national parliaments: World classification.* Retrieved June 4, 2007, from http://www.ipu.org/wmn-e/arc/classif310307.htm

Lawless, J., & Fox, R. (2005). *It takes a candidate: Why women don't run for office.* New York: Cambridge University Press.

The Barbara Lee Family Foundation (2001). *Keys to the governor's office: Unlock the door: The guide for women running for governor* [Brochure]. Brookline, MA: Barbara Lee.

The Barbara Lee Family Foundation (2004). *Cracking the code: Political intelligence for women running for governor* [Brochure]. Cambridge, MA: Barbara Lee.

TheWhiteHouseProject.org (2006, March 10). *Electing a Woman President: A Dry Run.* Retrieved June 18, 2007, from http://www.thewhitehouseproject.org/newsroom/inthenews/2006/ap_031006.php

12

Business Impact of Flexibility: An Imperative for Working Families

Donna Klein

There are many voices in the debate about issues important to working families. Families speak for themselves by voting for or against political candidates perceived as pro- or anti-working class, by joining or failing to join a union, and by working to influence policy makers in their communities and school districts. Official policy groups also speak for working families. Organizations such as the Hoover and Cato Institutes publish white papers and research reports that analyze the impacts on workers and employers of policies that increase the minimum wage or make paid leave mandatory. Politicians speak for working families when they create and vote on legislation that improves lives through universal health care, welfare reform, and labor laws. But, until recently there was one group that was conspicuously silent on the wide range of issues that affect how we live and work – the collective voice of business.

Corporate Voices for Working Families, a non-profit, non-partisan corporate membership organization was founded to end that silence and provide a unified voice for the corporate sector on issues important to working families. A primary goal of Corporate Voices is to expand the understanding of workplace flexibility as a key management tool and to explore the effect of integrating work and life in the business world.

What is Workplace Flexibility?

Workplace flexibility is the ability of a manager and an employee to determine when and where work gets done. In many companies, flexibility will also include the way in which work gets done. It is a twenty-first century response to what was formerly a one-size-fits-all way of working. Companies have increasingly realized that the old industrialized models of working 8.00 or 9.00 a.m. to 5.00 or 6.00 p.m. just do not work in a global economy. Flexibility is one tool and a powerful solution to many of the problems challenging today's workforce grappling to meet the demands of a 24/7 work cycle.

Historically, flexibility was seen as an accommodation, a solution mostly for women, and as a work policy that only benefited employees. It was not thought of as a win-win solution that would benefit both employer and employee. Intuitively, business leaders knew there was a huge advantage for businesses that adopted flexible work policies, but the gains for businesses were not well documented, and they certainly were not well publicized.

The objective of Corporate Voice's flexibility project, *Business Impact of Flexibility: An Imperative for Expansion,* funded by the Alfred P. Sloan Foundation and researched by WFD Consulting, was to understand how organizations measure the effects of flexibility and to clarify the business case for making flexibility a core business concept. If expansion of flexibility practices can be measured by an increase in the number of organizations that offer flexible work arrangements, then flexibility in corporate America is indeed growing.

To examine the hypothesis that flexibility is indeed growing because it is "good for business," Corporate Voices collected data from 29 American companies. And for the first time, we identified a compelling and robust business case for the expansion of flexibility. And this expansion was not done as an accommodation or a policy to only help women build their careers while being able to balance family responsibilities. In addition, flexibility was not a policy designed merely to even the playing field for those with care responsibilities and those without such outside responsibilities. Instead, we found flexibility being used as a key management tool and a core competency. The data across corporations allowed us to examine the concept of flexibility with a very different lens than previously had been used.

Overview of the Research Project

There is a substantial body of data on the effects of flexibility on businesses. Corporations constantly research work-related issues, but most of the research findings are proprietary. A corporation may release its findings from any research project, but the decision about making the research public depends on many factors. A corporation may want media coverage for its findings, or it may want to move some particular social or business agenda that would benefit by making the findings known. But, for the most part, internal data from large corporations are strictly proprietary and likely to remain that way.

Our research goal was to understand how organizations measure and define the business benefits and costs of flexibility. We were pleasantly surprised when we found that corporations are actually using very sophisticated measurement techniques to document the business impact of flexible work policies. The data clearly went way beyond self-reports or anecdotes. Corporations are often criticized for merely asking members of a constituent group whether they "like" some policy and then companies are satisfied with releasing reports of whether employees "like" or "dislike" a policy, as though it were high quality research. In fact, much more sophisticated impact data about the effects of workplace flexibility were and are being collected and used.

Examples of Internal Human Resource Measurement Practices Inside Organizations

Leading-edge corporations are conducting important research on flexibility. Flexibility questions were added to Global People Surveys, which are conducted annually at Ernst & Young. Bristol-Myers Squibb conducts annual work–life surveys that contain questions about flexible work practices. Deloitte measures the impact of flexibility on client satisfaction and on employee satisfaction, thus taking a broad view of the many different groups involved when a company decides to offer flexibility (see Figure 12.1).

In their studies of flexibility, AstraZeneca combined survey data with external research to construct models of financial impact, and PNC evaluated pilot and demonstration projects to see how flexibility affects cycle time in the business world. Cycle time is a measure of the time it takes to go from the start of a transaction to its completion. Depending on the nature of the transaction, cycle time can range from five hours to three weeks. One study from PNC examined bond transactions where cycle time is the length of time between the time when a bond gets "in the door" and when they were able to complete the transaction. Three kinds of business effects were documented: (1) Financial performance and operational outcomes, which are always the hardest to measure; (2) Talent management, which is an assessment of recruitment and retention; and (3) Human capital outcomes, which include engagement, commitment, stress reduction, and burnout measurements. At PNC, the results were startling. Cycle time for

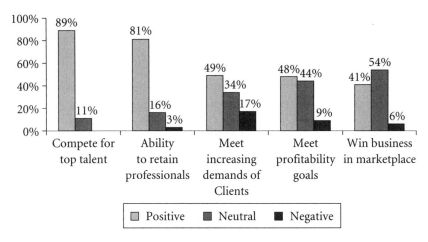

Source: Deloitte flexibility survey: Manager responses

Figure 12.1 Effect of flexible work arrangements on the firm's abilities.

bond transactions were cut in half, Bond Settlements exceptions were reduced 50 to 75 percent, and customer service representatives were able to return new inquiry calls in one day as opposed to two. The company saved money and staff turnover rates decreased dramatically. With these substantial and compelling results as a backdrop, Corporate Voices has been able to elevate the flexibility discussion to investigate flexibility as a key component of business success and global competitiveness within a larger management strategy.

Consider these examples of the effect of flexibility on improved employee retention. Employees at Accenture said that flexibility is the main reason they stayed with this employer. At IBM, flexibility is the second consideration when employees decide whether to move to another job or stay at IBM. Although flexibility is the second reason for all IBM employees in a list of important reasons for working at IBM, it is the number one reason mothers gave in response to questions about their willingness to stay at IBM. As a result, IBM uses flexibility as a recruitment tool to attract the best and the brightest talent. Similar results have been found by other organizations. Ninety-six percent of employees at AstraZeneca said flexibility influences their decision to stay at the company. When Deloitte calculated the savings due to reduced turnover costs, it was an astonishing U.S. $41.5 million!

In a study of recent hires, the Discovery Channel found that 95 percent of their employees reported that the availability of flexible work arrangements was critical to their decision to take the job. Similar hiring

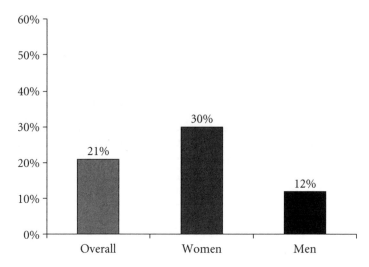

Source: Bristol-Myers Squibb Work–Life Survey

Figure 12.2   Of employees hired in the past 3 years, percentage who were influenced by flexible work arrangements to join the company.

data were reported by Bristol-Myers Squibb who found that 21 percent of new hires said that flexibility was critical in their decision-making. Overall, 30 percent of all women and 12 percent of all men said that flexibility was critical in their decision work for the company. These results are shown in Figure 12.2.

   It is important to continue to document the impact of flexibility at work both on men and women, because in the business world, when an issue is positioned as solely a women's solution, the "proposer" might as well shoot herself in the foot. The only viable position on gender is to advance gender equality as applying to both sexes, which means that every research project needs to report both women's and men's use of and experiences with flexibility.

Human Capital Outcomes

Virtually every company assesses employee satisfaction because satisfaction is traditionally used to predict on-the-job performance. Another commonly used measure to predict job performance is the extent to which employees are engaged in their work and committed to their employer. The Corporate Leadership Council has developed a formula for "discretionary effort," which is defined as going above and beyond the call of duty. Employees high in discretionary effort will routinely outperform their job objectives. A general rule of thumb is that for every 10 percent improvement in commitment scores, employees increase their level of discretionary effort by 6 percent, which increases performance by 2 percent. Thus, it is easy to understand why companies in today's competitive global market are going for increases in discretionary effort. Employees will provide more discretionary effort when they are happy with their employer. According to Hewitt Associates, those companies that have recently experienced double-digit growth have 39 percent more "highly engaged employee base" and 45 percent fewer disengaged employees than peer companies with lower rates of growth.

The Role of Work-Related Stress

Unlike measures of employee satisfaction, engagement, and commitment, the assessment of work-related stress moves in and out of favor in the corporate world. Despite the change in popularity of stress indicators, the report documents that stress is responsible for 19 percent of all absenteeism, 40 percent of all turnover, and 55 percent of the cost of Employee Assistance Programs (EAPs). Stress also accounts for 30 percent of short-term and long-term disability costs, 10 percent of psychotherapeutic drugs, 60 percent of the cost of workplace accidents, and 100 percent of workers compensation and lawsuits due to stress. Given these substantial costs, the corporate world is looking more carefully at stress and its effects on workplace costs. One of the main effects of flexible work options is a reduction in work-related stress. IBM found that higher flexibility scores relates to increased job satisfaction, higher ratings of the company as a whole, a greater sense of accomplishment for the employees themselves, and a higher rating of the workplace as a healthy workplace.

JPMorgan Chase found that access to flexibility, both formal and informal, increases overall satisfaction ratings for their employees. In terms of increased levels of engagement and commitment, AstraZeneca and Deloitte both reported that commitment scores were 28 to 32 percent higher for employees that had access to flexibility. Employees with flexibility are able to work more hours before feeling work–life stress. Measures of this sort are indirectly tapping discretionary effort by showing how an employee will go beyond what is usual or expected at the workplace when they can manage their work and life demands using flexible options. On average, employees with flexibility scored 30 percent lower on stress and burnout indicators.

Ability to Deliver Business Results

Employers care about their bottom line. The single question that drives corporate research on work–life issues is how some variable will affect profits. When data from all 29 companies were compared, it was evident that employees who said they do not have control over their work schedules have significantly lower commitment scores compared to those who said they have the control they need over their work schedules. These data can be used to explain why flexible work options reduce burnout. The differences are seen in a commonly used Burnout Index, where those employees with flexibility report less burnout. These findings are particularly important because they are the first data ever collected on the relationship between flexibility and commitment to one's employer and flexibility and reduced burnout.

In conceptualizing commitment to one's employer, a distinction is usually made between exempt and nonexempt employees. Nonexempt employees are paid hourly and typically earn lower wages than exempt employees. Sometimes nonexempt employees are referred to as "hourly" or "nonprofessional employees." It is conventional wisdom that you cannot give hourly employees as much flexibility in how and when they work as exempt employees. The data reviewed by WFD Consulting for Corporate Voices at three different companies clearly show the opposite – hourly employees are more committed to their employers when they have flexible work options. Both hourly and exempt employees increase their commitment to their employer and report less burnout when they have flexible work arrangements compared with employees who do not. But, the increase in commitment and reduction in burnout is greater for hourly employees than for their coworkers in professional jobs. These conclusions can be seen in Table 12.1, which compares the responses of exempt and nonexempt employees in three different companies. For example, look at the data from Company 3 in Table 12.1. Hourly workers experienced a 63 percent increase in commitment scores when they have flexible work arrangements compared to a 44 percent increase for professional workers. In thinking about these data, keep in mind that even though the employees in the three companies whose data are shown in Table 12.1 were nonexempt, they were not necessarily "low wage earners" by any traditional definition. The employees whose data appear in Table 12.1 earned up to $11 an hour, which according to federal poverty guidelines, is not necessarily low wage.

Table 12.1 Similarities between exempt and nonexempt employees in response to flexibility.

	Company 1 Difference between employees who use flexible work arrangement and those who do not	Company 2 Difference in scores between employees who "have the flex they need" and those who do not	Company 3 Difference in agreement scores for "My manager grants me enough flexibility to meet my personal/family responsibilities"
Commitment scores			
Exempt	+6%	+27%	+44%
Nonexempt	+9%	+23%	+63%
Burnout scores			
Exempt	1.25 times higher for nonflex	4.3 times higher for nonflex	2.67 times higher for nonflex
Nonexempt	1.5 times higher for nonflex	3.5 times higher for nonflex	2.5 times higher for nonflex

Source: Corporate Voices for Working Families, "Business Impacts of Flexibility: An Imperative for Expansion."

(Real) Flexibility Cannot Be Inflexible or Occasional

Our research demonstrates the power of real-time or occasional flexibility. The field of work place flexibility began over a decade ago as an inflexible set of workplace rules that we used to call alternate work arrangements. The term was used to include a compressed work week (e.g., 4 days a week at 10 hours a day), a reduced work week (e.g., less than 35 or 40 hours of work per week) and job sharing. These are all alternative arrangements to the traditional work day, but they were still rigid in that they were not altered to fit short-term or individual needs.

Most companies find it easier to manage work assignments when work schedules are rigid. So originally companies took the concept of flexibility and became very rigid with the way they applied it. The most important finding from our research is that companies who created "as-needed" or occasional flexibility had a halo effect that extended across the company. We also found that flexibility as infrequent as once a month had a dramatic impact on employee morale. We began to think of flexibility as a type of workplace culture. It signifies a respectful arrangement between the management and the employee. At its heart, flexibility is not about creating new schedules or being creative in arranging how people work. It is about mutual respect and the underlying trust between management and their employees. In order for flexibility to really work, management has to trust its employees and the employees need to trust the good intentions of management.

The trust that underlies flexibility pays off financially. GlaxoSmithKline, for example, found that they had greater productivity from their customer service representatives when they were allowed to share jobs. The sales yield for pharmaceutical sales people from AstraZeneca improved when they were given flexible work schedules. First Tennessee Bank also reported an increase in revenue of $106 million when they adopted flexible work options. First Tennessee Bank reported increases in profits in two years after adopting flexibility, and that profit was based on back-of-the-house operations such as processing transaction. For all of these employers, flexibility is the engine that drives the service value chain: increased flexibility leads to increases in employee retention, which drives customer retention, which, in turn enhances profitability. This chain of causal events is well documented across a wide variety of service industries.

Flexibility has afforded PNC the opportunity for more innovation, cross-training, and better use of staff. The more efficient use of staff has allowed PNC to cut their cycle time in half for processing bonds while meeting and even exceeding the service needs of their clients. Nine out of ten managers at Deloitte report that workers on flexible schedules meet or exceed their peers on all nine dimensions of service excellence. The results of our research are clear: we have a solid business case for the positive effects of workplace flexibility across all of the 29 companies that participated in the study. The effects are positive across all industries and all levels of employees. Flexibility is a business imperative. In other words, if a company does not expand its use of flexibility, it is not utilizing a proven management tool that drives global competitiveness.

The conclusion: the broadest impact of flexibility occurs when an organization develops a true culture of flexibility that incorporates a variety of work arrangements, both formal and occasional.

Taking Action

Based on our extensive research and the data across company, industry, and geography, Corporate Voices crafted a statement of support to expand workplace flexibility. The body of evidence was so conclusive that we believe organizations that want to stay competitive and continually improve business results must take action. The statement includes a pledge by executives to engage continually in a dialogue that will elevate flexibility as a key management strategy. The statement was signed by 12 corporate suite executives including 5 CEOs from the participating companies, including Jim Quigley, Deloitte & Touche, Jim Turley, Ernst & Young, and Mark Loughridge, chief financial officer, for IBM. In addition, Corporate Voices took the message to Capitol Hill legislators in Washington, DC, when it convened a Senate briefing on the results soon after the report was released in November 2005.

Based on the research and experience of many firms, these results provide evidence that employers can gain tremendous benefit from providing flexibility in when and how work gets done. For organizations that intend to improve business performance and shareholder value, need to get the best from their employees, and want to compete successfully for talent, flexibility is a critical component to a successful management strategy.

There are many policies that are being discussed both in the halls of America's state and federal legislatures, as well as in those walked by America's CEOs. Many are attempts to level the playing field for all workers and help lower barriers to flexibility. Corporate Voices will continue to conduct research that informs legislators and American business about the bottom-line benefits to workplace flexibility while also representing the business voice to encourage outcomes that improve the lives of America's working families.

The report, *Business Impact of Flexibility: An Imperative for Expansion* is available on-line at; www.corporatevoices.org

Corporate Voices Flexibility Principles

Well implemented flexibility is:

1 A strategic business imperative that enhances company competitive advantage and employee effectiveness:
   - A key element of a multi-faceted business strategy to enhance organizational agility and performance in the global marketplace
   - A tool to unleash employee innovation and creativity in how results are achieved
2 A vehicle to achieve business *and* personal outcomes:
   - A mutual win for the company and the employees, who are the core of business success, it:

  - increases employee commitment and performance in achieving company goals
  - enables greater individual control and ability to achieve personal, as well as professional, objectives.
3 A cultural norm:
   - Flexible work is:
     - invisible, fully integrated into all cultural, management and operational practices and aligned to engender flexible approaches and mindsets
     - universally embraced as the standard operating mode, not a distinct program that must be promoted, managed and enforced
     - included in essential corporate culture communications such as corporate objectives, and mission, vision and values statements
4 Equitably implemented, broadly accessible and utilized:
   - *All* employees can request to work flexibly, regardless of level, gender, role, or life stage through use of a consistently applied, business-oriented process
   - Decisions are based completely on employees' ability to achieve required business outcomes in the context of the team and ongoing business requirements, not to accommodate individuals' personal reasons.
5 Measured solely by results and outcomes:
   - Hours, visibility (face-time), process or location, are not measures of success; business outcomes, employee productivity and engagement are what count
6 Championed by all levels of management, who actively promote a work culture that supports formal – and informal – flexibility:
   - Managers lead by example; clear words and actions are mutually reinforcing; and
   - managers are held accountable for skillfully promoting an environment in which all employees feel supported to request flexibility
7 Embedded in a work culture that is facilitated and reinforced by company infrastructure and systems, where all formal systems align to help create and sustain a flexible work environment:
   - Human resources strategy
     - Performance management and ongoing measurement
     - Linkage to full contribution
     - Human resources tracking systems
     - Flexibility tracking system

- Leadership and management development
  - Leadership profile
  - Manager skill development and required competencies
  - Management training
  - Team development processes
- Succession planning strategy
  - Career development process and supports
- Technology strategy
- Work planning and design mechanisms
- Communication strategy
- Real estate management

8 Compatible with career advancement, which is entirely based on merit and ability to perform the job
- Employees who achieve the skills and business results necessary to perform at a higher level will be recognized for through promotion, when opportunities exist
- Consideration for promotion will exclude employees' flexibility, unless acquisition of requisite skills and experience is diminished as a result of that flexibility
  - Managers will continue to provide as many developmental opportunities to employees who work flexibly as to others without flexibility
- Performance is only one, and not the determining factor to be considered when evaluating employees' flexibility requests
- Management of poor performance is addressed in a timely, constructive and ongoing way, not as newly-introduced reason to refuse a request for flexibility

9 Sustained by proactively fostering trust and respect
- Open communications and partnership exists at all organizational levels
- Personal responsibility and accountability is cultivated
- Managers are trusting and trustworthy
- Employees are trusting and trustworthy
- Co-workers and teammates are trusting and trustworthy

About Corporate Voices for Working Families

Corporate Voices is a nonpartisan, nonprofit corporate member organization with the mission of bringing the private sector into the public dialogue on issues affecting working families. Corporate Voices has over 50 partner companies that collectively employ more than 4 million individuals throughout all 50 states of the US, with annual net revenues of over $800 billion. Over 70 percent of the partner-companies are listed in the Fortune 500 and they are all leaders in developing family support policies for their own workforce.

The idea of creating an organization to represent corporate perspectives was born at a dinner meeting with Congressional representatives over 6 years ago. It was a dinner of like-minded politicians urging corporate leaders to get involved in the domestic policy conversation. Until that time, corporations had officially stayed out of the policy debate. It seemed obvious to the attendees that there was a critical player missing from the political playing fields where policies regarding working families are tossed about and tackled. Most often, the result of these skirmishes reflect the pocketbook advantages of the different teams routing for one outcome or another and those outcomes are not always in the best interest of working families. The need for a corporate presence when issues about working families are being decided was so apparent that the J. Willard and Alice Sheets Marriott Foundation agreed to answer the challenge and provide a grant to start a nonprofit organization that would fill this void. Corporate Voices for Working Families was conceived and remains the first and only organization that represents the private sector view on public policy issues.

And, even in a fiercely political environment, Corporate Voices has remained aggressively nonpartisan enabling the organization to represent fully the views of all member companies. And as a representative of the corporate viewpoint, Corporate Voices has developed expertise, research and policy recommendations related to issues of importance to working families. These issues include supports for low wage working families, early childhood education, after-school programs, youth transitions to adulthood and the world of work, and mature workers. This expertise has allowed Corporate Voices to continually represent American business based on sound policies and practices.

References

All of the references are from: Corporate Voices. *Business Impacts of Flexibility: A Business Imperative.* Retrieved September 20, 2006 from http://corporatevoices.org/

13

Setting the Stage:
Do Women Want it All?

V. Sue Molina

It's hard to believe that until the early 1960s, most newspapers published separate job listings for men and women. Almost exclusively, the higher level jobs (and higher paying jobs) were listed under "Help Wanted – Male." Women need not apply! This led to the enactment of the Equal Pay Act of 1963, which made it illegal to pay women lower wage rates on the basis of their sex. However, there were still varying interpretations of what constituted the same job. In 1970, *Schultz v. Wheaton Glass Company* clarified that jobs need to be "substantially equal" but not necessarily "identical" to fall under the protection of the Equal Pay Act. Furthermore, in 1974, the *Corning Glass Works v. Brennan*, known as the "going market rate" case, held that a company cannot justify paying women lower wages because that is what they traditionally received under the going market rate.

Have We Closed the Gender Wage Gap?

In 1956, women earned just 63.3 percent of the wages men earned. The gap was at its largest in 1966 at 57.6 percent. From 1966 to 2004, the gap closed by about 19 percent over the 38 years, which is an improvement of $^1/_2$ penny per year! (Infoplease, 2004). In 2004, women were earning $76^1/_2$ cents to every dollar earned by men.

There are several reasons why women earn less money than men. When beginning their careers, young women entering the workplace generally start off with wages that are closer to that of comparable young men. For example, in 1997 women under the age of 25 earned 92.1 percent of men's salary, as compared to the 1997 total wage gender gap of 74.2 percent (Infoplease, 2004). Although starting salaries are relatively equal between women and men, the gap widens over time as men advance and women either stay in place or advance at a slower pace. This is especially true for women in traditionally "female" jobs, such as teaching, nursing, social work, and administrative support – where advancement is limited. Women in traditionally female jobs are often referred to as "pink collar workers" or these women are said to live in the "pink ghetto." Pink ghetto jobs offer greater flexibility in work hours than white collar jobs but the downside is that they are lower paying and there are slower, or in some cases no, advancement opportunities.

The percentage of women in an occupation, whether it is a low or high percentage, is not a good indicator of how well women will be paid in relation to men in that occupation. Women comprise a low percentage (44 percent) of college and university professors but a relatively high earnings ratio of 76 percent. On the other hand, physicians have only 32 percent women in their profession and an earning ratio of 52 percent (U.S. Bureau of Labor Statistics, 2005). So if earning power is the major criteria, women would be wise to pick their occupations carefully.

Women in the workforce have increased significantly over the past 50 years. The percentage of women has grown from 30 percent in 1950 to just under 50 percent today (U.S. Bureau of Labor Statistics, 2005). There are more women in the workforce than ever before, and an increasing proportion of these women are mothers. Of all working women today, 71 percent are mothers with children under 18 years of age and 62 percent of working women are mothers with children under the age of 6 (Arnst, 2005).

How Have Women Fared in the Workplace?

Recent studies (e.g., Catalyst, 2002) tracked women's movement into leadership positions in the workforce. They found that women in management, professional, and related occupations make up 50.3 percent of women in the workforce. This reflects the fact that women have comprised a majority in college enrollments since the mid-1980s (Anderson, 2002). However, as the job level increases, the number of women decreases significantly (Catalyst, 2002). For instance, within the Fortune 500 companies, women occupy only 15.7 percent of the corporate officer titles. As we move further up and we break down the corporate officers into line positions and staff positions, there are only 9.9 percent women in line positions and 30 percent women in staff positions. Line positions are significant positions for moving up the corporate ladder, because it is from these positions that corporate positions such as CEO are generally recruited. The low percentage of women in line officer positions is significant, because there are a lot fewer women in line for top level positions of corporate leadership. The percentages continue to drop as we move up the corporate ladder; with only 7.9 percent of the highest titles with the Fortune 500 companies held by women. For top earners, those who make the most money, women consist of 5.2 percent of the top earners.. That is an increase from 1995, where women only constituted 1.2 percent of the top earners. So clearly over the past 10 years progress is being made, albeit slow progress. At the very top of the pyramid are those who are CEOs of the largest 500 corporations in the United States. At that level less than 2 percent of the Fortune 500 CEOs are women.

Women in the public sector have not fared any better. In the senate, there are 14 women senators (out of 100), and there are 67 female representatives (out of 435), which is 15 percent in the U.S. House of Representatives. So have we really made any progress? In both the public sector and corporate America, progress is very slow.

Women are Leaving the Workforce

One of the reasons that more women are not at the top leadership positions is they are leaving the traditional corporate workplace. Why are they leaving and where are they going?

The common assumption when women leave the workplace is that they are going to stay home with children. This was the conclusion of an October 2003 *New York Times* article by Lisa Belkin, "The opt-out revolution" (Belkin, 2003). Belkin interviewed several highly educated, successful women who decided they did not want to do what it takes to get to the "top" of the corporate ladder, that is, work long hours, travel extensively, and not have enough time for family, community service, and friends. The interviewed women all opted to quit and stay home and all but one had children. However, if you listen closely to the women, many also say they were not satisfied with the work environment when they quit. In a recent study of women alumni from a prestigious college, those women who reported a break in their employment or change to part-time employment reported that their workplace was less supportive of their attempts to combine work and family obligations than women who remained continuously employed full time (Quinn, Halpern, & Hartley, under review). Thus it was not that women preferred to be at home fulltime; nonsupportive workplace policies made it difficult for them to maintain both roles simultaneously. But there are other reasons that lead successful women to drop out of the traditional corporate workforce; not all women exit the workforce to stay home with their children.

Many women return to the workforce to start their own businesses or work in other capacities, such as for not-for-profit organizations where the hours are less and there is little or no travel. In the early 1990s, Deloitte & Touche realized that although they were hiring equal numbers of men and women, women were leaving the firm at a higher rate than the men. In a survey of women who left Deloitte & Touche, we found that 70 percent of the interviewed women who left Deloitte & Touch were working full time, 20 percent were working part-time, and the other 10 percent were staying at home with children and indicated that they had intentions of returning to work in the near future.

There has been an increase in the number of women-owned businesses in the US. In 2005, there were 4.7 million self-employed women in the US. This is an increase of 77 percent since 1983 verses a 6 percent increase for men starting their own businesses (U.S. Bureau of Labor Statistics, 2005). According to the Center for Women's Business Research (2006), an organization that tracks women-owned firms, 40 percent, of all privately-held U.S. firms are 50 percent or more owned by women. Between 1997 and 2004, the number of women owned firms increased at nearly twice the rate of all firms (42 percent vs. 23 percent). However, only 3 percent of women-owned businesses have annual revenues greater than $1 million. Approximately 12.8 million people are employed by women owned businesses. Or stated another way, one in 7 employees in the US works in a woman owned business!

Deloitte & Touche was one of the first companies to examine the reasons why women decide to leave the traditional corporate workforce. After many internal focus groups and interviews with women who had left, three primary reasons emerged: (1) the male-dominated environment, (2) perceived obstacles to career advancement, and (3) difficulty in managing work and family commitments.

Male-Dominated Work Environments and Perceived Obstacles

A recent Catalyst research study showed that many corporate workplaces continue to have male-dominated environments that are fueled by male-dominated beliefs. The persistence of male-dominated beliefs in the workplace creates perceived obstacles for the advancement of women. The

Catalyst study, *Women "take care" men "take charge": Stereotyping of U.S. business leaders exposed* (Catalyst, 2005), found that the glass ceiling is firmly in place. Women and men stereotype leaders in the same way except in the area of problem solving. Problem solving is an important competency most commonly associated with effective leadership. The Catalyst study found that women believe that women are better at problem solving than men are, however, men believe that men are superior to women in problem solving effectiveness. In top management positions men still far outnumber women, thus the male held stereotype is the dominant corporate held belief – that is, women are poor problem solvers. The male-held stereotype creates a barrier for women's advancement and to their being leaders in the corporate work environment.

Managing Work and Family Commitments

In many dual-earner families, women still hold the majority of the child-care and household responsibilities. However, fathers are spending more hours performing childcare activities than in the past and therefore, work and family management is important to men as well. In fact, 8 out of 10 of all employees, both men and women, want more workplace flexibility. Greater flexibility, whether it is formal or informal flexibility, is needed in order to manage work and family responsibilities.

The Families and Work Institute found that 67 percent of employees surveyed report high levels of job satisfaction in organizations that afforded them with high levels of workplace flexibility (Galinsky, Bond, & Hill, 2004). Compare this figure to only 23 percent of employees who have high levels of job satisfaction in organizations with low levels of workplace flexibility. High levels of job satisfaction usually equate to higher productivity, better bottom line results, and higher commitment from employees. That is a compelling business reason for greater flexibility (Corporate Voices, 2005).

Flexibility can take many forms. Formal flexible work arrangements include telecommuting, reduced hours while still advancing, reduced hours while not advancing, job sharing, flexible start and stop times, and a combination of any of these arrangements. Informal flexibility is the current hot topic that provides employees the control over when, where, and how they get their jobs done. With flexible work policies, employee evaluations are based on outputs or results rather than inputs.

There are also differences among the workforce generations. A study by the Family and Work Institute (Families and Work Institute (FWI), n.d.),

Generation and gender in the workplace, found that young employees are more likely to be "family-centric," that is, they were more likely to make family a priority over work. Generation X and Y employees are 50 percent and 52 percent family centric, verses Baby Boomers who are 41 percent family centric. Women, in general, are more family centric than men. Young employees believe it is more important for them to have time for family and priorities outside of work. As employees become more family-centric, there is an increased need for family-friendly workplaces and flexible work arrangements to accommodate the changing realities of the workforce.

Deloitte & Touche Initiatives

With a better understanding of why women are leaving the workforce, Deloitte & Touche launched the Initiative for the Retention and Advancement of Women in 1993. The major goals of this initiative were to: (1) increase the number of women in leadership positions; (2) maintain proportionate representation of women at all levels; and (3) provide greater flexibility to manage work and family commitments. Today, the Deloitte & Touche U.S. Chairperson is a women, who was elected by all the partners. Additionally, the number of women at partnership positions has increased since the launch of this initiative. At the start of the initiative, 7 percent of the partners were women, and by 2003 the percentage rose to 16 percent women partners.

The second objective of the Deloitte Touche Initiative was to have pro-portionate representation of women at all levels. This meant that when 50 percent of the people we were hiring were women, in five years we wanted equal percentages of men and women still to be with us. So in our public accounting department, if we started with 100 people, in five years we might only have 70 of those. But of those 70, 35 should be women and 35 should be men. That had not been the case, not even by a long shot. Thus, our goal was to keep that same proportionate representation as women and men advanced up the ladder.

The third goal was to provide greater flexibility for employees to manage their work and family commitments. This goal was accomplished through formalizing flexible work arrangements that leveled the playing field for all women and men who wanted a formal flexible work arrangement. Both men and women were informed of the procedures and guidelines. Deloitte & Touche accomplished this by providing training on requirements and obligations of reduced work arrangements for both the managers and employees on reduced work arrangements.

There are women who decide to drop out of the workforce to stay at home with the intention of returning later. However, dropping out and then coming back to work after several years has proven to be difficult for many women, especially women in technical professions where keeping current about technical matters is essential to the profession. For this reason, Deloitte & Touche recently launched a pilot program, *Personal Pursuits*, which provides assistance to "drop outs," helping them stay current on accounting matters and stay connected with Deloitte & Touche. Participants in the program are provided with continuing education that includes technical training at the national education level as well as local educational training. They remain connected to Deloitte & Touche by receiving invitations to events and functions at the local office. They are also paired with a Deloitte & Touch coach who keeps in touch with them. It is a win-win situation where Deloitte & Touche has the opportunity to win back top talent and the former employee is provided continuing education and connectivity to their profession so that they can return when they are ready. The transition back into the workforces can be made more easily because they have necessary knowledge to be as productive as quickly as possible.

Key Critical Success Factors for Women's Initiatives

Companies need to examine the importance of retaining women. With the changing demographic of the workforce, the success of traditional companies will depend on how they are able to attract, retain, and advance women. Many companies have adopted a Women's Initiative or a Diversity Initiative, or both. From my experience at Deloitte & Touche as the National Partner in Charge of the Women's Initiative, I believe that there are several key critical success factors that must be present in order for any initiative to succeed.

The first critical success factor for any initiative is the full support of the top leaders, especially the CEO. Deloitte & Touche was one of the first companies to adopt a Women's Initiative in 1993, which was formally called the Initiative for the Retention & Advancement of Women. The initiative began when the CEO heard from his 20-something daughters about the difficulties of being a woman in a male-dominated corporate environment. This revelation created the examination of Deloitte & Touche's corporate culture and environment. After many focus group discussions with prior and current partners and employees, Deloitte & Touche launched its

Women's Initiative with the CEO as the champion. He actively promoted the initiative both inside and outside of Deloitte & Touche.

The second critical factor for success is to set and communicate goals. At Deloitte & Touche, goals are set and then communicated both internally and externally through annual reports, news releases, and press conferences. Communication is key once goals are set. Once the goals are broadly communicated, it becomes difficult to retreat from those goals, which creates a sense of urgency and commitment to meeting the goals.

A third critical factor for success is to hold people accountable by tracking results. Because Deloitte & Touche is an accounting firm, a system was developed to track the pipeline of people. There are data on employees by gender, location, level, and job function. Therefore, it is easy to review turnover, retention, and advancement by gender and to hold management accountable for results.

The fourth critical factor for success is to support multiple commitments. The support can be formal flexible work arrangements, such as reduced hours, shared job arrangements, telecommuting, or any combination of the arrangements, and informal flexibility which allows the employee to decide where and when she does her job. Many employers and employees are still struggling with flexibility today, and they will continue to struggle with it in the future. Increasingly we are seeing formal flexibility give way to informal flexibility. With advances in technology and connectivity between employer and employee, it is becoming easier to perform tasks in multiple locations. Men are also increasingly demanding greater informal flexibility, especially given our 24/7 environments and 60 hour work weeks. This is good news for women because the "work–life" issue has traditionally been thought of as a "women's issue." Greater attention will be given by employers when the "work–life" issue becomes an issue for all employees.

The fifth critical factor for success is to promote mentoring for all and engage in proactive succession planning. Women who have strong mentors are generally more successful (Wright & Wright, 1987). So insuring that all women have mentors by using proactive mentoring programs and tracking statistics will help retain and advance women. Deloitte & Touche found that by establishing a formal succession planning process, more women were considered and promoted to leadership positions. Prior to a leadership vacancy, a high potential group of women and men were identified who would receive leadership training and positioning for future leadership roles. By formalizing this process, more women were tapped for leadership positions.

The final critical factor for success is to acknowledge and discuss the different styles that women and men possess. We have already seen that stereotyping of gender styles can have an impact on the advancement of women. Men and women have different behaviors and styles (Eagly & Johannesen-Schmidt, 2001). One style is not the only style, and one style is not necessarily better than another. In fact, diversity of thought and style will make a team solution better than a homogeneous team. It is important to have an open environment where women and men can discuss their different approaches and ways of communicating and accept that either style is appropriate. Companies cannot afford to ignore gender bias or stereotyping. They cannot afford to lose highly talented women because this loss is bad for business and bad for the bottom line. Women are approximately 50 percent of the workforce and leadership talent pool. The opportunity costs of not developing their talent and the costs of turnover – recruiting, training, and unhappy clients – are enormous. A 2000 study by Watson Wyatt Worldwide found that companies with highly committed employees had a 112 percent return to shareholders over 3 years versus a 90 percent return for companies with average employee commitment and 76 percent return for companies with low employee commitment.

Can Women Have It All?

Can a woman have a demanding, successful career as well as have time for family, community, friends, and self? Many women believe that they can have it all – just not all at the same time. Having it all does not mean "work–life balance." It is simply not possible to have a 50/50 split between work and family all the time. Instead there are trade offs at different times that need to be met. There will be periods that work takes priority and other times when family, community, hobbies, and other commitments will take priority.

So, if women can have it all, do they want it all? Usually yes, but they want it all on their terms. The next generation of women will seek success on their terms. They have nothing to prove and do not need to be trail blazers like the baby boomers. If they do not find companies that value them as individuals, then they will seek out or make their own companies or environments where they can succeed. The success of traditional companies depends on understanding what it takes to attract, retain, and advance women. Once they figure it out, they will be very, very successful companies.

References

Anderson, P. M. (2002). *Where the boys no longer are: Recent trends in U.S. college enrollment.* Retrieved October 16, 2006, from http://www.dartmouth.edu/~pmaweb/BEJEAP.pdf

Arnst, C. (2005, March 15). Mommy wars part III. *Business Week Online.* Retrieved October 13, 2006, from http://www.businessweek.com/careers/workingparents/blog/archives/2006/03/mommy_wars_part_2.html

Belkin, L. (2003, October 26). The opt-out revolution. *New York Times.* Retrieved October 13, 2006, from http://www.montana.edu/wrt/opt_out_revolution.pdf

Catalyst (2002). *2002 Catalyst census of women corporate officers and top earners in the Fortune 500.* Retrieved October 13, 2006, from http://www.catalystwomen.org/files/fact/COTE%20Factsheet%202002updated.pdf

Catalyst (2005). *Women "take care," men "take charge": Stereotyping of U.S. business leaders exposed.* Retrieved October 12, 2006, from http://www.catalyst.org/files/full/Women%20Take%20Care%20Men%20Take%20Charge.pdf

Center for Women's Business Research (2006). *Women-owned businesses in the United States 2006.* Retrieved October 13, 2006, from http://www.cfwbr.org/assets/344_2006nationalfactsheet.pdf

Corporate Voices (2005). *Business impacts of flexibility: A business imperative.* Retrieved September 20, 2006 from http://corporatevoices.org

Eagly, A. H., & Johannesen-Schmidt, M. C. (2001). The leadership styles of women and men. *Journal of Social Issues, 57,* 781–797.

Families and Work Institute (FWI). (n.d.) *Generation and gender in the workplace.* Retrieved October 18, 2006, from http://familiesandwork.org/eproducts/genandgender.pdf

Galinsky, E., Bond, J. T., & Hill, E. J. (2004). *When work works: A status report on workplace flexibility.* New York: Families and Work Institute.

Infoplease (2004). *Women's earnings as a percentage of men's, 1951–2004.* Retrieved October 13, 2006, from http://www.infoplease.com/ipa/A0193820.html

Quinn, A., Halpern, D. F., & Hartley, A. A. (under review) The opt-out "revolution": Pull to motherhood or escape from the workplace?

U.S. Bureau of Labor Statistics (2005, May). *Women in the labor force: A databook.* Retrieved October 13, 2006, from http://www.bls.gov/cps/wlf-databook-2005.pdf

Wright, C. A., & Wright, S. D. (1987). The role of mentors in the career development of young professionals. *Family Relations, 36,* 204–208.

14

What Psychologists Need to Know About Family Responsibilities Discrimination

Joan C. Williams

When social psychologists study gender, typically they compare men to women in general. This comparison remains useful, but to have this as the *only* way to study gender is an outdated approach. Economists have documented that, at age 30, women earn over 90 percent of the wages of men; in sharp contrast, mothers average only 60 percent of the wages of fathers (Waldfogel, 1998). This statistic comes from one of a growing number of studies of what economists typically call the "family gap" or the "motherhood penalty."

Psychologists need to build on this literature and to show that mothers' economic vulnerability does not merely reflect the kinds of hard choices all adults have to make: the motherhood penalty also reflects bias and stereotyping. A groundbreaking 2004 issue of the *Journal of Social Issues*, as well as subsequent studies, have documented that motherhood is a key trigger for gender stereotyping (Biernat, Crosby, & Williams, 2004; Correll, Benard, & Paik, 2007).

This chapter first will describe the rapidly growing literature on maternal wall bias. Then it will document the sharp increase in litigation surrounding the maternal wall or, to use the more formal name, family responsibilities discrimination ("FRD"). The discussion then turns to the key role that stereotyping literature is playing in court, discussing how U.S. courts have begun to see maternal wall cases as stereotyping cases. The chapter's final section discusses the need for future research on the stereotypes and biases triggered by workers' family responsibilities.

Studies of the maternal wall stand to make a difference both in psychology and in the reality of workers' lives.

The Motherhood Penalty

New work by economists documents the central role of motherhood in creating economic vulnerability for women. The "family gap" between the wages of mothers and others accounts for an increasing proportion of the "wage gap" between men and women (Budig & England, 2001; Han & Waldfogel, 2001; Joshi, Paci, & Waldfogel, 1999; Waldfogel, 1997). In fact, while the wage gap between men and women has been narrowing, the gap between working women without children and working women with children has actually increased (Waldfogel, 1998). By 1991, "the pay gap between mothers and non-mothers had become larger than the gap between women and men" (Waldfogel, 1998, p. 148). The family gap persists "even after one controls for differences in education, overall work experience, and full-time and part-time work experience" (Waldfogel, 1998, p. 149). It is greatest for single mothers: While the earnings of married mothers relative to average male earnings rose 20 percent between 1980 and 1991, those of previously married mothers rose only 8 percent, and those of never married mothers rose only 3 percent (Waldfogel, 1998).

One potential explanation for the growing family gap is the lost job experience and seniority suffered by mothers who temporarily leave the workforce to care for children; but this explains only part of the family gap, according to an empirical study by Budig and England. They found that no more than one-third of the wage penalty suffered by mothers is attributable to motherhood's interruption of women's employment, including "breaks, more part-time work, and fewer years of experience and seniority" (Budig & England, 2001, pp. 219–20). The motherhood penalty, then, needs to be explained either by the effects of motherhood on productivity or by employer discrimination (Budig & England, 2001).

When the motherhood penalty is calculated over time, the results are staggering. During their prime earning years, women's earnings are only 38 percent of men's earnings (Rose & Hartmann, 2004). The motherhood penalty also makes women more likely to be forced into bankruptcy. Warren and Tyagi (2003) found that "mothers are 35 percent more likely than childless homeowners to lose their homes, [and] three times more likely than men without children to go bankrupt" (p. 13). However, "if a woman remains childless, she reduces her chances of going bankrupt by 65 percent" (Crittenden, 2003, p. 20).

Conventional economic explanations for the gender gap, including the motherhood penalty, focus on the different occupational and lifestyle "choices" made by "rational actors." In a well-known article, economist Solomon Polachek argued that, due to motherhood, women anticipate working fewer years and with more interruptions than men, and therefore "self-select" into occupations requiring lower levels of skill and less educational investment, thereby maximizing their earning potential over time (1981). Nobel prize-winning economist Gary Becker argued that families choose conventional breadwinner/housewife roles because they are economically efficient, allowing the family to gain the advantages that stem from specialization (1981). Even when mothers are employed, Becker argued, their performance does not match men's because of their choices, such as refusing to "work odd hours or take jobs requiring much travel" (1985, p. 843).

Economists are tapping a vernacular understanding that mothers' disadvantaged workplace position reflects their own choice to "opt out" (Williams, Manvell, & Bornstein, 2006). Mothers' decisions to cut back or drop out of the workforce *do* reflect choices. But we often forget, in this context, that choice is not inconsistent with discrimination. Take the example of gays in the military under the "Don't ask, don't tell" policy. Gay soldiers have a choice: They can remain closeted and keep their jobs, or they can live openly and get fired. But this choice occurs within a context of discrimination on the basis of sexual orientation. To quote Bookman, "What exactly are 'voluntary' part-time workers choosing? Are they choosing to work without health insurance or pensions?" (1995, p. 801). Mothers may well choose to spend time with their children, but they do not choose the economic vulnerability that currently accompanies that choice.

The Maternal Wall at Work

The maternal wall at work stems from the clash between the norm of the ideal, or valued, worker, and the schema of the good mother. Good jobs typically are designed around an "ideal worker" who starts to work in early adulthood and works, full time and full force, for 40 years straight (Williams, 2000). This workplace ideal is framed around men's bodies and life patterns: no man needs time off for childbirth, and American women still do (conservatively) two-thirds of the child care (Casper & Bianchi, 2002). Social psychologists have confirmed that good jobs typically are gendered masculine (Glick, Wilk, & Perreault, 1995; Williams, 2000).

When good jobs are designed around men and masculinity, stereotypes and bias arise in everyday workplace interactions. This is particularly true because the available 24/7 ideal-worker norm conflicts with the conventional schema of a "good mother." Biernat and Kobrynowicz have documented that the apparent parallel standards of the "good father" and the "good mother" are in fact "shifting standards" that embed gender schemas (1997). Their study found that men who described themselves as "very good fathers" actually spent about the same amount of time away from their children as did women who described themselves as only "all right" mothers (Kobrynowicz & Biernat, 1997, p. 587). The "very good mother" was more likely than the "very good father" to be described as "willing to always be there and to do anything for the children" (Kobrynowicz & Biernat, 1997, p. 592). Obviously, no one can both "always be there" for her children and be available 24/7 for her employer. The implicit gendering of good jobs clashes with our intensive ideals of motherhood, thereby creating the maternal wall at work.

Motherhood is associated with negative competence assumptions that are so strong that maternal wall bias often is not subtle at all. In an age of "subtle stereotyping" and "implicit bias," the bias triggered by motherhood often is neither subtle nor implicit – it is 1970s style discrimination in the new millennium (Selmi, 2005). While maternal wall bias includes old-fashioned hostile prescriptive stereotyping, it also includes benevolent stereotyping and more subtle patterns of cognitive bias. These patterns are detailed below.

Ironically, maternal wall bias affects men as well as women, by policing men into breadwinner roles and women out of them. Men who seek to play an active role in family care may well encounter hostile prescriptive stereotyping that clearly sends the message that caregiving is a suitable role only for women.

Prescriptive Stereotyping

Most employers today know that it is illegal gender discrimination to make such statements as "women don't belong in this kind of job" or "women don't belong in the workforce." Yet employers continue to make similar statements about mothers. Some employers still do not recognize that a statement that "mothers belong at home with their children," or that "this is no job for a mother" is not simply "tough love" – it is gender stereotyping.

Hostile Prescriptive Stereotyping
Hostile prescriptive stereotyping occurs when individuals are punished for not conforming to gender role prescriptions. In some cases, the hostility

could not be more explicit. In *Bailey v. Scott-Gallaher*, for example, a mother called to find out when she was to return from maternity leave, only to be told by the company president that she was fired because "she was no longer dependable" and "[her] place was at home with her child" (1997, p. 505).

The clash between the ideal-worker norm and the norm of the always-available mother creates role incongruity that can undercut employed mothers. Given the stereotype that mothers should always be available to their children, some employers assume that mothers will not also be effective workers. For example, in *Trezza v. Hartford, Inc.*, the general counsel of the legal department in which the plaintiff worked told her that "working mothers cannot be both good mothers and good workers, stating, 'I don't see how you can do either job well'" (1998, p. 2). In another case, a female civil engineer in Pennsylvania was awarded $3 million in a jury verdict (later overturned) because she was passed over for promotions after the birth of her son (Belser, 1999, p. B1). She testified that the president of the company asked her, "Do you want to have babies or do you want a career here?" (Belser, 1999, p. B1). Insisting that a mother choose between having children and having a career reflects the self-fulfilling prophecy that women, but not men, need to choose between career and family.

Men also face hostile prescriptive stereotyping when employers expect them to take on the breadwinner role, providing for their families by totally devoting themselves to work. Two anecdotes that young fathers shared with the Center for WorkLife Law (which I direct) are illustrative. An attorney who believed he was entitled to eight weeks of unpaid family and medical leave when his baby was born instead took only his accrued vacation days in short spurts because he had heard that any leave he took, whether paid or not, would be frowned upon by the law firm's partners. A few weeks after the baby was born, when criticized by a partner, the attorney said that he was often up at night with the colicky new baby. The partner responded by saying "[Your wife] is on maternity leave" – the unspoken assumption being that she should take care of such things. Another young man, an academic, told a mentor that he was afraid even to *ask* for parental leave because he believed that, even if he did not take the leave, the disapproval sparked by his request would end his chances for tenure.

Of course, the young academic may have been mistaken. But social science research indicates that, when compared to mothers, fathers who took a parental leave were recommended for fewer rewards and were viewed as less committed (Allen & Russell, 1999; Dickson, 2003). Fathers who had even a short work absence due to a family conflict were recommended for fewer rewards and had lower performance ratings (Butler & Skattebo, 2004;

Dickson, 2003). Not surprisingly, the desire to avoid this type of bias in the workplace likely plays a key role in men's decisions not to request leaves or flexible work schedules (Colbeck & Drago, 2005). (Men typically talk in terms of disapproval, which implies that coworkers believe that these men should be behaving as breadwinners who leave caregiving responsibilities to their wives.)

Benevolent Stereotyping
Though often well-intentioned, benevolent stereotyping also can lead to significant workplace harms. A classic example of benevolent stereotyping occurred in the case *Trezza v. The Hartford, Inc.*, in which an employer failed to consider the plaintiff, a mother, for a promotion based on the assumption that she would not want the position, which required travel, because she had a family (1998). Although the employer may have had good intentions, he should have asked the mother whether she wanted the job, and let her decide. (The parties ultimately settled for an undisclosed amount.)

The problem with benevolent stereotyping emerges clearly when we consider a situation in which a husband and wife both worked for the same law firm. After they had a baby, the mother was sent home promptly at 5.30 p.m. – she had a baby to take care of. The father, in sharp contrast, was kept working even later than ever – he had a family to support (Williams & Segal, 2003). Note how benevolent stereotyping by the employer pushes families into conventional gender roles, even if the families had a different vision of family life. The simple way to avoid this is for the employer to *ask* mothers, and fathers, whether they want to work long hours or travel or move for a promotion, thereby avoiding stereotype-driven assumptions.

Descriptive Stereotyping

Descriptive stereotypes embed untested, stereotype-driven assumptions about what a mother wants or how she will behave. Perhaps the most prevalent and harmful are the negative competence assumptions associated with motherhood. More subtle forms of descriptive stereotyping include the attribution and leniency biases that affect perceptions of workplace performance when evaluating mothers.

Negative Competence Assumptions
A number of studies have demonstrated how negative competence assumptions affect mothers. For example, while research participants rated

"businesswomen" as high in competence, alongside businessmen, they rated "housewives" as very low in competence, alongside stigmatized groups such as the elderly, blind, "retarded," and "disabled" (to quote the terms tested by the researchers) (Eckes, 2002, p. 110; Fiske, Cuddy, Glick, & Xu, 2002, pp. 881, 887).

Correll and colleagues (2007) found "consistent, significant evidence for the motherhood penalty over a broad range of measures" (p. 1332). For example, they "found that evaluators rated mothers as less competent and committed to paid work than nonmothers, and consequently, discriminated against mothers when making hiring and salary decisions"; however, "fathers experienced no such discrimination" (Correll et al., 2007, p. 1332). An earlier study found that maternal wall bias can be triggered by pregnancy: performance reviews of female managers "plummeted" after pregnancy, in part because pregnancy triggers the stereotype of women as irrational and overly emotional (Halpert, Wilson, & Hickman, 1993, p. 655).

Whether the stereotype is that a mother is "irrational," "less competent," or "uncommitted," a mother's ability to succeed in the workplace is undermined by the stereotypical assumptions made by her coworkers and superiors at work. She then is forced to compensate for the bias by meeting a higher performance standard and, failing to do so, faces sanctions based on these descriptive stereotypes.

Leniency and Attribution Bias
Other forms of descriptive bias also affect mothers, particularly when mothers request or move to part-time or flexible schedules in traditionally masculine jobs. Consider the following quote from a lawyer:

> Before I went part-time, people sort of gave me the benefit of the doubt. They assumed that I was giving them as fast a turn-around as was humanly possible. After I went part-time, this stopped, and they assumed that I wasn't doing things fast enough because of my part-time schedule. As a result, before I went part-time, I was getting top of the scale performance review. Now I'm not, though as far as I can tell the quality of my work has not changed. (Williams & Segal, 2003, p. 97)

This mother encountered two types of cognitive bias. The first is leniency bias; after she went part-time and her motherhood became salient, her coworkers no longer gave her the benefit of the doubt. Leniency bias describes the situation where objective rules are applied rigidly to out-groups (here, part-time mothers) but leniently to in-groups (other full-time workers).

Thus mothers (or part-timers) may be forced to continually prove themselves, while others are given the benefit of the doubt. According to another
study: "[T]he rule appears to be, when judgments are uncertain, give an
in-group member the benefit of the doubt. Coldly objective judgments seem
to be reserved for members of the out-groups" (Brewer, 1996, p. 65).

   This mother also encountered attribution bias (Williams, 2003). After
she went part-time, people assumed that she was home with her children
in situations in which they assumed that other lawyers were working. They
attributed her absence to non-work causes, driven by the stereotype that
mothers are not serious about work.

The Sharp Rise in Litigation Challenging Family Responsibilities Discrimination

Lawsuits filed by workers alleging discrimination due to family caregiving
responsibilities have risen in number from a total of eight during the 1970s
to 358 between 2000 and 2005 (Still, 2006). The rise has been most acute
during the past decade, which saw 481 cases, as compared to 97 cases in
the decade before (Still, 2006). This nearly 400 percent increase in the
number of such lawsuits filed in the past ten years is all the more dramatic,
given that employment discrimination cases in general decreased 23 percent between 2000 and 2005 (Still, 2006).

   Women file 92 percent of family responsibility discrimination cases;
perhaps surprisingly, only 38 percent of the plaintiffs who file these cases
are professionals (Still, 2006). This finding may possibly be explained by
two factors: (1) women in non-professional positions may have fewer
employment options, making the typical solution to work–family conflict
– finding a new job or "opting out" – less possible and necessitating a
legal fight for their jobs; and (2) non-professionals are more likely to work
in unionized environments, making them more aware of their legal rights
(Still, 2006).

   Lawsuits involving family responsibilities discrimination (FRD) hold
substantial potential for liability (Still, 2006; Williams & Calvert, 2006).
While employment discrimination cases in general are difficult to win, with
typical win rates around 20 percent (and as low as 1.6 percent according
to one recent study of race and gender cases), plaintiffs in family responsibility discrimination cases have a greater than 50 percent win rate
(Still, 2006). At least 75 FRD cases involved liability in excess of $100,000
(C. Calvert, personal communication, September 26, 2006). To date, the

largest individual recovery in an FRD case is $11.65 million; the largest class recovery is $49 million (C. Calvert, personal communication, September 7, 2006; McAcree, 2002; "Verizon paying $49 million," 2006).

The Central Role of Stereotyping in the Development of FRD Case Law

Stereotyping evidence has played a central role in the recent surge of FRD cases. The U.S. Supreme Court may have sparked this trend with its decision in a 2003 Family and Medical Leave Act case, *Nevada Department of Human Resources v. Hibbs*. In *Hibbs*, the Supreme Court explicitly recognized the impact of gender stereotypes in the work–family context. Writing for the majority, Chief Justice Rehnquist noted that "[t]he fault line between work and family [is] precisely where sex-based generalization has been and remains strongest" (*Nevada Dept. of Human Resources v. Hibbs*, 2003, p. 738). He also commented on the way both men and women are affected by stereotypes in this context: "Stereotypes about women's domestic responsibilities are reinforced by parallel stereotypes presuming a lack of domestic responsibilities for men. These mutually reinforcing stereotypes created a self-fulfilling cycle of discrimination" (*Nevada Dept. of Human Resources v. Hibbs*, 2003, p. 736). Although Justice Rehnquist was a notoriously conservative judge, he appeared to view the values surrounding family caregiving as "family values" (Williams, 2004).

The precedent established in *Hibbs* quickly led to an even more important decision in *Back v. Hastings on Hudson Union Free School District* (2004). In this case, the Second Circuit held that an employment action based on stereotypes about motherhood is a form of gender discrimination prohibited by the Equal Protection Clause of the Fourteenth Amendment to the Constitution. Elana Back was a school psychologist who had received outstanding performance reviews until she became a mother. She was denied tenure by supervisors who allegedly made comments to her such as it was "not possible for [her] to be a good mother and have this job," and that they "did not know how she could perform her job with little ones" (*Back v. Hastings on Hudson*, p. 115). The court ruled that making stereotypical assumptions about a mother's commitment to her job is sex discrimination, even if the mother does not have evidence that similarly situated fathers were treated differently. In previous cases, mothers facing discrimination often had been required to point to a "comparator" – a similarly situated male employee who was treated differently. The *Back* decision found that a comparator was unnecessary: gender stereotyping evidence could stand alone as proof of gender discrimination.

Significantly, the court recognized the link between bias against mothers and gender discrimination despite the lack of expert testimony at trial and without citing any specific study documenting maternal wall stereotyping. The court stated, "It takes no special training to discern stereotyping in the view that a woman cannot 'be a good mother' and have a job that requires long hours, or in the statement that a mother who received tenure 'would not show the same level of commitment . . . because [she] had little ones at home'" (*Back v. Hastings on Hudson*, 2004, p. 120). This finding by the court in *Back*, like those of courts in other FRD cases (for example, the 2006 case of *Sivieri v. Commonwealth of Massachusetts*, discussed below), shows how the use and recognition of stereotyping evidence have changed over time since the famous 1989 U.S. Supreme Court decision in *Price Waterhouse v. Hopkins*. In *Price Waterhouse*, the Court heard stereotyping evidence through testimony from an expert (Susan Fiske). In recent FRD cases, however, courts have taken a commonsense approach, willing to accept stereotyping theories without expert testimony. This approach makes the stereotyping theory accessible to a much broader range of plaintiffs: after all, expert testimony is expensive, and, if courts were to require it, far fewer plaintiffs could afford to base their cases on a stereotyping theory.

State courts as well as federal courts have relied on a stereotyping theory in maternal wall cases. In *Sivieri v. Commonwealth of Massachusetts*, a Massachusetts court recognized the pervasiveness of the negative competence assumption associated with motherhood. The plaintiff, a paralegal with an excellent performance record, noticed that employees in her workplace had made negative comments about children and working mothers. After she herself took maternity leave, she was rejected for promotions, harshly criticized, and subjected to comments from supervisors about mothers of small children (*Sivieri v. Commonwealth of Massachusetts*, 2006). In response to the defendant's motion for summary judgment, the court wrote, "It would blink reality to deny that a considerable part of our society believes that mothers are principally responsible for the care of young children and are therefore less effective as employees" (*Sivieri v. Commonwealth of Massachusetts*, 2006, p. 23).

In another opinion written by a conservative judge, Richard Posner, the Seventh Circuit recognized that the subtler forms of cognitive bias can also lead to discrimination in the 2004 case *Lust v. Sealy*. Lust, an area sales manager, was an ambitious, successful salesperson who was denied a promotion to a management position based on her supervisor's assumption that, because she had children, she would not want to move – despite the fact that she had never told him that and had, in fact, repeatedly expressed her desire to be promoted. The jury awarded significant damages. The Seventh Circuit affirmed, but reduced the punitive damages award, in an opinion that highlighted the subtle bias and noted that, while subtle, it was reasonable for the trial court to regard it as bias (*Lust v. Sealy*, 2004).

In short, stereotyping evidence has played an important role in cases involving family responsibilities discrimination. It was an FRD case in which the Second Circuit held that a plaintiff who can show evidence of gender stereotyping need not provide evidence of a comparator (a similarly situated man treated differently) (*Back v. Hastings on Hudson*, 2004). Courts in FRD cases also have taken a path that makes it easier for a broad range of plaintiffs to rely on stereotyping evidence, by refusing to insist that plaintiffs, in order to rely on a stereotyping theory, engage the services of an expensive expert witness and fight motions (also expensive) to defend the credentials of the chosen expert.

The Need for Further Research

Several different types of studies could play an important role in helping employers avoid family responsibilities discrimination. These include: (1) studies that deconstruct the dichotomy between conscious and unconscious motivations; (2) further studies that document how cognitive bias can be controlled; and (3) further studies that explore the links between theoretical approaches to gender bias and work schedules.

Studies That Deconstruct the Conscious/Unconscious Dichotomy

It was natural, decades ago, to frame the study of cognitive bias as an updating and redefinition of the Freudian "unconscious." That terminology has outlived its usefulness. The portrayal of cognitive bias as "unconscious" carries significant risks when the social psychology of stereotyping enters the practical arena of litigation and gender bias training designed to avoid litigation by changing behavior. If psychologists continue to characterize cognitive bias as "unconscious," then the obvious question from an employer's standpoint is why he or she should be held responsible, or liable, for behavior of which he or she was completely unaware.

The employer's argument is developed in an article by law professor Amy Wax entitled "Discrimination as accident" (1999). In it, Wax analogizes cognitive bias to an unavoidable industrial accident and argues against the imposition of liability. "If the process of stereotyping is unconscious, an individual will be unaware that stereotypical expectancies are at work in [his or her] social judgments" (Wax, 1999, p. 1137). Because stereotyping is inevitable and impossible to avoid, imposing liability "will do little to advance the cause of fair and accurate compensation for victims" (Wax, 1999). Not only will imposition of liability fail to help victims, Wax argues, it will be expensive, imposing steep costs on employers that they have no way of avoiding. The obvious conclusion, Wax concludes, is that imposing high costs that accomplish nothing makes no sense. Given that "liability for unconscious discrimination will not deter unconscious discrimination," such discrimination should not be actionable in the courts (Wax, 1999, p. 1175).

Employers interpret Title VII, the major federal employment statute, to require "intentional" discrimination; thus the argument that "unconscious" bias is not intentional is entirely predictable. The dichotomy between "conscious" and "unconscious" acts gives social psychology a distinctly pro-employer spin once it leaves psychology and enters the public sphere.

If the description of cognitive bias as "unconscious" were accurate, this argument would not be so sobering. But this description is misleading. The on-off "conscious versus unconscious" formulation needs to be replaced by the image of consciousness as a continuum, in which people exercise considerable control over when and whether they do the work necessary to bring something into their consciousness.

What people choose to bring to consciousness is often a function of social position and social power. "The powerless direct their attention up the hierarchy"; they need to do so, because the powerful have power over them (Oakes, 2004, pp. 104–105). In sharp contrast, the powerful have far less motivation to direct attention towards the less powerful. "They tend, therefore, to categorize and to form highly stereotypical impressions" of the powerless (Oakes, 2004, pp. 104–105, citing Fiske & Depret, 1996).

In short, the less powerful know more about the more powerful than vice versa. For example, American Blacks know more about Whites than Whites know about Blacks, as W. E. B. DuBois pointed out long ago with his observation that African Americans have a "double-consciousness," in which their outlook acknowledges that Black and White communities in the United States look at ordinary social interactions differently (DuBois, 2006, p. 3). No one, to my knowledge, has ever claimed that Whites look at situations through a lens of Black culture and expectations. A similar dynamic holds for gender: men who completely lack the ability to see things from women's viewpoint are criticized as "clueless."

Should cluelessness be a defense? No: That vernacular phrase acknowledges that the decision to remain "clueless," in many social contexts, is a choice tied to social power position. A lab study by Ridgeway and her colleagues has documented that low power individuals are motivated to pay careful attention to higher power individuals because they lack control over the relationship (Ridgeway & Smith-Lovin, 1999). The same study found that higher power individuals do not need to pay as much attention to less powerful people. As a result, higher power people can rely on stereotypes to guide their interactions (Ridgeway & Smith-Lovin, 1999).

More empirical studies would be welcome, to help defang the "cluelessness" defense – for example, the argument by a male employer that he was unaware that he was engaging in implicit bias against a female employee, or by a White employer that she was unaware that she was holding a Black employee to a higher standard than a White employee (an example of leniency bias). The cluelessness defense entrenches existing patterns of privilege and discourages the necessary examination of bias that can prevent workplace discrimination. Law professor Michael Selmi comments on the oddness of this defense: "After all . . . the person who speeds 'uncontrollably' ('I did not know I was going 80 mph') is not told that slowing down is beyond her control, she is told to look at the speedometer" (Selmi, 1999, p. 1238).

Describing cognitive bias as unconscious is both inaccurate and dangerous. It excuses the conduct that results from bias, by using an expression of social privilege (cluelessness) to excuse the continued exercise of social privilege (discrimination). Psychologists can help defang the cluelessness defense by shifting away from the old-fashioned term "unconscious," towards terminology that reflects that decisions about what to bring into consciousness are sensitive to both social context and social status. The alternative terminology I have proposed is "unexamined bias" (Williams, 2003, p. 439). Note that the implicit association test (IAT) works well only in conditions where decisions are made in a split second. In the real world of employment, we expect such split-second decisions to be double-checked with self-imposed quality controls. If individuals or institutions choose not to implement such controls, they are not blamelessly "unconscious" of the motivations and the consequences of their actions. They simply failed to take the necessary care, and the result was a decision that was not thought through. We as a society have the power to insist that individuals and institutions should be more measured and more thoughtful – particularly now that the mass of publicity surrounding the IAT (namely Malcolm Gladwell's book, *Blink*) has publicized the troubling effects of uncorrected snap decisions.

Controlling subtle stereotyping is particularly important in view of studies that show that "subtle" implicit biases have very real impacts in the workplace. Valian found that "success is largely the accumulation of advantage, exploiting small gains to get bigger ones" (Valian, 1999a, p. 1049; Valian, 1999b, pp. 142–4). One of Valian's experiments set up a model that built in a tiny bias in favor of promoting men; after a while, 65 percent of top level employees were male (Valian, 1999a).

Studies that Document How Cognitive Bias Can Be Controlled

A key advantage of the term "unexamined bias" is that it sends the message that "subtle" cognitive biases can be controlled. A growing literature on the "malleability" of cognitive bias shows how one may increase one's own awareness of personal bias through self-reflection and evaluation – and how one can control the expression of bias through suitable workplace procedures. Blair surveyed the existing literature and found that whereas "just a few years ago, there were only a handful of studies on the malleability of automatic stereotypes and prejudice . . . the situation today is quite different, with nearly 50 investigations of their flexibility and responsiveness to a wide range of strategic, social, and contextual influences" (Blair, 2002, p. 244). In fact, Blair finds that there is "now bountiful evidence that automatic attitudes – like self-reported attitudes – are sensitive to personal, social and situational pressures" (Blair, 2002, p. 256). In sum, stereotypes may be automatic, but when actors are under social pressure to control them, they tend to do so (Hunt, Borgida, Kelly, & Burgess, 2005).

This analysis provides important insight into workplace behavior and "corporate culture." Law professor Susan Sturm refers to cognitive bias as "subtle" in her influential article contrasting "first generation discrimination" (which she associates with the open aversive racism at Texaco and Mitsubishi) with "second generation discrimination," which "is difficult to trace directly to intentional, discrete actions of particular actors" (2001, pp. 458, 468). Second generation discrimination, she argues, is "shaped by organizational culture" and is "a byproduct of ongoing interactions shaped by the structures of day-to-day decision-making and workplace relationships" (Sturm, 2001, pp. 469–70). The malleability studies hold the potential to provide decision-makers with guidance on how to change corporate culture so as to decrease or eliminate unwanted bias.

Studies that Explore the Link between Gender and Work Schedule

For 25 years, work–life experts have documented what is commonly called "the business case" for family-friendly workplace policies: economic analyses showing that it makes business sense for employers to abandon the old ideal-worker model, in favor of a model more suitable to a workforce in which 70 percent of all households have all adults in the labor force (Kornbluh, 2003; Williams, 2003, pp. 85–6). Insisting on the old ideal-worker model today creates what experts have called "workplace–workforce mismatch" (Christensen, 2005, p. ix).

Culminating 25 years of documentation of the business case for family-friendly policies, a recent influential study by Corporate Voices for Working Families reported that "the business case to expand workplace flexibility is substantial and compelling" (Corporate Voices for Working Families, 2005, p. 4). Large companies in competitive industries, such as Deloitte, Accenture, and IBM, all have found that flexible work scheduling allows them to retain more of their employees and reduce turnover related costs (Corporate Voices for Working Families, 2005). Deloitte estimated that it saved $41.5 million in 2003 alone (Corporate Voices for Working Families, 2005). Companies also have found that flexible work scheduling makes recruiting new talent easier, increases employee satisfaction, improves productivity and decreases stress-related costs (Corporate Voices for Working Families, 2005). In short, flexible workplaces help enhance a company's competitiveness and its bottom line.

Considering the well-documented business case for workplace flexibility, it is surprising that more companies are not implementing flexible work scheduling. A recent training event I attended offers an explanatory clue. The training was on stereotyping and implicit bias, to members of the high-hours legal profession. Feedback from the audience was that the presentation failed to capture the subtlety with which implicit biases play out in legal workplaces today. The strong message was that much, if not most, of the gender stereotyping in the legal profession surrounds issues of part-time work.

Sociologists have long documented the powerful stigma associated with reduced-hours schedules. Epstein and her coauthors reported a powerful stigma against part-time lawyers and concluded that these lawyers were viewed as "time deviants" who "flouted" the amount of hours traditionally required by attorney work (Epstein, Seron, Oglensky, & Saute, 1999, p. 4). Mothers who worked part-time were seen by their peers as neither good lawyers nor good mothers (Epstein et al., 1999). Another study documented that people who take advantage of flexible work schedules, overwhelmingly mothers, are told that the flexibility policies "are only for employees who are not serious about career advancement" (Glass, 2004, p. 367). The Project for Attorney Retention, which I co-founded in 2000, has also found robust evidence of stigma associated with part-time schedules in law firms, as did an earlier study of part-time lawyers in Boston (Williams & Calvert, 2001; Employment Issues Committee of The Women's Bar Association of Massachusetts, 2000).

One obvious question is whether the stigma associated with part-time work is a variant of maternal wall bias. Given that women are stereotyped by subtype, and that the "mother" subtype carries with it the implicit time norm of the "always available" mother, one might suspect that, even if a woman evades bias after she has children, bias may arise when she shifts to a part-time or flexible schedule and her gender becomes salient.

Only a few studies explore stereotypes and biases triggered by part-time work. One study found that college women viewed parents who worked part-time as less professionally competent than full-time workers (Etaugh & Folger, 1998). Another found that employed women did not agree: they did *not* view parents who had reduced their hours as less competent than full-time workers (Etaugh & Moss, 2001). A third study, with a sample composed largely of college students, differentiated between part-time men and part-time women. That study found that women part-timers were viewed as less communal than female homemakers, but less agentic than women who work full-time. In other words, part-timers got the worst of both worlds (Eagly & Steffen, 1986). Male part-timers fared even worse. They were·seen as even lower in agency than male homemakers (Eagly & Steffen, 1986). Other studies show that women who work part-time are, on average, less contented than women who work full time (Barnett & Rivers, 2004).

To summarize, although women who work part-time do not see themselves as less competent than other workers, others do; the negative stereotypes triggered by men who work part-time are even more negative. No wonder so few men choose flexible schedules and so many women working part-time are miserable.

More studies are needed of the biases triggered by women's part-time work; more studies also are needed of the schema of the "ideal worker." The resumé study by Correll et al. discussed earlier, documented that motherhood is associated with a lack of job commitment (2007). More study is needed to document that the schema of the ideal worker conflates long hours with both commitment and talent. This conflation involves a logical confusion – for example, the term "go getter" confuses job commitment and promotion potential with work schedule. A worker may well be very talented and very committed and yet still need work–life balance. Sociologists have documented this conflation, which no doubt plays a role in generating the stigma associated with part-time and flexible work. Hochschild quotes one manager who states explicitly that companies often promote people based on schedule rather than on talent:

> Time has a way of sorting people out at this company. A lot of people that don't make it to the top work long hours. But all the people that do make it work long hours . . . The members of the Management Committee of this company aren't the smartest people in this company, we're the hardest working. We work like dogs. (Williams, 2000, p. 74, citing Hochschild, 1997, pp. 56–7)

Sociologists' work suggests that not only occupational categories, but also work schedules, are gendered. Turning to Hochschild again, quoting a blue-collar worker: "Here in the plant, we have a macho thing about hours. Guys say, 'I'm an eighty-hour man!' as if describing their hairy chests" (Williams, 2000, p. 59, citing Hochschild, 1997, p. 128). Do work schedules serve as a way to signal masculinity? The only relevant study I am aware of found that fathers who work part time may well find themselves worse off than mothers who work part time: Male part-timers are perceived as losers, "even lower in agency than the male homemaker" (Eagly & Steffen, 1986, p. 259; Etaugh & Folger, 1998, p. 221). The assumption apparently is that a man who is working part-time is unable to get a full-time job – an assumption clearly driven by the default schema that men are, to the best of their abilities, breadwinners. Through this lens, men who work part-time are seen as defective breadwinners. It would be intriguing to see not only more studies on men and part-time work, but more studies on men and long hours.

A final fruitful area for further study is to follow up on the studies of Glick and his colleagues of the gendering of occupations (Glick, 1991; Glick, et al., 1995). This line of research also will help us understand the extent to which work roles are an arena in which men enact masculinity. Such studies are important to help gain insight into the very powerful negative messages that men often receive when they request reduced schedules – or even ask for parental leave. It may be that such men are not only "time deviants," but they are seen as ineffectual, given that being a "person to be reckoned with," if one is a man, is intertwined with a competent enactment of hegemonic masculinity.

Conclusion

Social psychologists already have played an important role in documenting the existence of family responsibilities discrimination. Their work has
been taken very seriously by the courts, who are increasingly likely to accept
stereotyping evidence as proof of discrimination. Yet much more remains
to be done. Social psychologists need to abandon the outdated terminology of the "unconscious," substituting instead more updated terminology
(based on the malleability studies) that send the message that cognitive
bias is, instead, "unexamined." In addition, studies of the intertwining of
gender and work schedule could be extraordinarily helpful in unraveling
the sources of the stigma associated with part-time work and in assessing
whether, and how, the long-hours culture so prevalent in good jobs in the
United States is intertwined with the public performance of masculinity.

Acknowledgments

Grateful thanks to James Hurst, Matthew Melamed, and Claire-Therese Luceno for
their expert research assistance and to Stephanie Bornstein for her proofreading help.

References

Allen, T. D., & Russell, J. E. A. (1999). Parental leave of absence: Some not so fam-
    ily friendly implications. *Journal of Applied Social Psychology, 29*, 166–191.
Back v. Hastings on Hudson Union Free School District, 365 F.3d 107 (2d Cir. 2004).
Bailey v. Scott-Gallaher, Inc., 480 S.E.2d 502 (Va. 1997).
Barnett, R., & Rivers, C. (2004). *Same difference: How gender myths are hurting our
    relationships, our children, and our jobs*. New York: Basic Books.
Becker, G. S. (1981). *A treatise on the family*. Cambridge, MA: Harvard University
    Press.
Becker, G. S. (1985). Human capital, effort, and the sexual division of labor. *Journal
    of Labor Economics, 3*(1), S33–S58.
Belser, A. (1999, April 30). Mommy track wins. *Pittsburgh Post-Gazette*. Retrieved
    October 30, 2006, from http://www.post-gazette.com/regionstate/
    19990430lawsuit2.asp
Biernat, M., Crosby, F. J., & Williams, J. C. (Eds.) (2004). The maternal wall: Research
    and policy perspectives on discrimination against mothers [Special Issue]. *Journal
    of Social Issues, 60*(4).

Biernat, M. & Kobrynowicz, D. (1997). Gender- and race-based standards of competence: Lower minimum standards but higher ability standards for devalued groups. *Journal of Personality and Social Psychology, 72*(3), 554–557.

Blair, I. V. (2002). The malleability of automatic stereotypes and prejudice. *Personality & Social Psychology Review, 6*, 242–261.

Bookman, A. (1995). Flexibility at what price? The costs of part-time work for women workers. *Washington and Lee Law Review, 52*, 799–814.

Brewer, M. B. (1996). In-group favoritism: The subtle side of intergroup discrimination. In D. M. Messick & A. E. Tenbrunsel (Eds.), *Codes of conduct: Behavioral research into business ethics* (pp. 160–171). New York: Russell Sage Foundation.

Budig, M., & England, P. (2001). The wage penalty for motherhood. *American Sociological Review, 66*, 204–225.

Butler, A. B., & Skattebo, A. L. (2004). What is acceptable for women may not be for men: The effect of family conflicts with work on job performance ratings. *Journal of Occupational and Organizational Psychology, 77*, 553–564.

Casper, L. M., & Bianchi, S. M. (2002). *Continuity and change in the American family*. Thousand Oaks, CA: Sage Publications, Inc.

Christensen, K. E. (2005). Foreword. In S. Bianchi, L. M. Casper, & R. B. King (Eds.), *Work, family, health, and well-being* (pp. ix–xi). Mahwah, NJ: Lawrence Erlbaum Associates.

Colbeck, C. L., & Drago, R. (2005, November & December). Accept, avoid, resist: Faculty members' responses to bias against caregiving . . . and how departments can help. *Change*. Retrieved October 30, 2006, from http://www.carnegiefoundation.org/change/sub.asp?key=98&subkey=829

Corporate Voices for Working Families (2005, November). *Business impacts of flexibility: An imperative for expansion*. Washington, DC: Corporate Voices for Working Families.

Correll, S. J., Benard, S., & Paik, I. (2007). Getting a job: Is there a motherhood penalty? *American Journal of Sociology, 112*(5), 1297–1338.

Crittenden, A. (2003, August 31). Mothers most vulnerable. *The American Prospect*. Retrieved October 30, 2006, from http://www.prospect.org/cs/articles?article=mothers_most_vulnerable

Dickson, C. E. (2003). *The impact of family supportive policies and practices on perceived family discrimination*. Unpublished dissertation, California School of Organizational Studies, Alliant International University.

DuBois, W. E. B. (2006). *The souls of Black folk*. West Valley City, UT: Waking Lion Press. (Original work published 1903).

Eagly, A. H., & Steffen, V. J. (1986). Gender stereotypes, occupational roles, and beliefs about part-time employees. *Psychology of Women Quarterly, 10*(3), 252–262.

Eckes, T. (2002). Paternalistic and envious gender stereotypes: Testing predictions from the stereotype content model. *Sex Roles, 47*(3/4), 99–114.

Employment Issues Committee of The Woman's Bar Association of Massachusetts (2000). *More than part-time: The effect of reduced-hours arrangements on the retention, recruitment, and success of women attorneys in law firms.* Boston, MA: Employment Issues Committee of The Woman's Bar Association of Massachusetts.

Epstein, C. F., Seron, C., Oglensky, B., & Saute, R. (1999). *The part-time paradox: Time norms, professional life, family and gender.* New York: Routledge.

Etaugh, C., & Folger, D. (1998). Perceptions of parents whose work and parenting behaviors deviate from role expectations. *Sex Roles, 39*(3/4), 215–223.

Etaugh, C., & Moss, C. (2001). Attitudes of employed women toward parents who choose full-time or part-time employment following their child's birth. *Sex Roles, 44*(9/10), 611–619.

Fiske, S. T., & Depret, E. (1996). Control, interdependence and power: Understanding social cognition in its social context. *European Review of Social Psychology, 6,* 31–61.

Fiske, S. T., Cuddy, A. J. C., Glick, P., & Xu, J. (2002). A model of (often mixed) stereotype content: Competence and warmth respectively follow from perceived status and competition. *Journal of Personality and Social Psychology, 82*(6), 878–902.

Gladwell, M. (2005). *Blink.* New York: Little, Brown & Company.

Glass, J. (2004). Blessing or curse? Work-family policies and mother's wage growth over time. *Work and Occupations, 31*(3), 367–394.

Glick, P. (1991). Trait-based and sex-based discrimination in occupational prestige, occupational salary, and hiring. *Sex Roles, 25*(5/6), 351–378.

Glick, P., Wilk, K., & Perreault, M. (1995). Images of occupations: Components of gender and status in occupational stereotypes. *Sex Roles, 32* (9/10), 565–581.

Halpert, J. A., Wilson, M. L., & Hickman, J. L. (1993). Pregnancy as a source of bias in performance appraisals. *Journal of Organizational Behavior, 14,* 649–663.

Han, W., & Waldfogel, J. (2001). Child care costs and women's employment: A comparison of single and married mothers with pre-school-age children. *Social Science Quarterly, 82*(3), 552–568.

Hochschild, A. (1997). *The time bind: When work becomes home and home becomes work.* New York: Metropolitan Books, Henry Holt & Co.

Hunt, J. S., Borgida, E., Kelly, K. M., & Burgess, D. (2005). The scientific status of research on gender stereotyping. In D. L. Faigman, D. H. Kaye, M. J. Saks, & J. Sanders (Eds.), *Modern scientific evidence: Vol. 2. The law and science of expert testimony* (pp. 580–620). Eagan, MN: Thomson West.

Joshi, H., Paci, P., & Waldfogel, J. (1999). The wages of motherhood: Better or worse? *Cambridge Journal of Economics, 23*(5), 543–564.

Kobrynowicz, D., & Biernat, M. (1997). Decoding subjective evaluations: How stereotypes provide shifting standards. *Journal of Experimental Social Psychology, 33*(6), 579–601.

Kornbluh, K. (2003). The parent trap. *The Atlantic Monthly, 291*(1), 111–114.

Lust v. Sealy, Inc., 277 F. Supp. 2d 973 (W. D. Wis. 2003), *aff'd* 383 F.3d 580 (7th Cir. 2004).

McAcree, D. (November 11, 2002). Family leave suit draws record $11.65m award. *The National Law Journal.*

Nevada Dept. of Human Resources v. Hibbs, 538 U.S. 721 (2003).

Oakes, P. (2004). The root of all evil in intergroup relations? Unearthing the categorization process. In M. B. Brewer & M. Hewstone (Eds.), *Social cognition* (pp. 102–119). Malden, MA: Blackwell Publishing Ltd.

Polachek, S. W. (1981). Occupational self-selection: A human capital approach to sex differences in occupational structure. *Review of Economics and Statistics, 63*(1), 60–69.

Price Waterhouse v. Hopkins, 490 U.S. 228 (1989).

Ridgeway, C. & Smith-Lovin, L. (1999). The gender system and interaction. *Annual Review of Sociology, 25,* 191–216.

Rose, S. J., & Hartmann, H. I. (2004). *Still a man's labor market: The long-term earnings gap.* Institute for Women's Policy Research Paper No. C355. Washington, DC: Institute for Women's Policy Research.

Selmi, M. (1999). Response to Professor Was: "Discrimination as accident": Old whine, new bottle. *Indiana Law Journal, 74*: 1233–1251.

Selmi, M. (2005). Sex discrimination in the nineties, seventies style: Case studies in the preservation of male workplace norms. *Employee Rights & Employment Policy Journal, 9*(1), 1–50.

Sivieri v. Commonwealth of Massachusetts, 21 Mass.L.Rptsr. 97 (2006).

Still, M. (2006). *Litigating the maternal wall: U.S. lawsuits charging discrimination against workers with family responsibilities.* San Francisco, CA: Center for WorkLife Law, University of California, Hastings College of the Law.

Sturm, S. (2001). Second generation employment discrimination: A structural approach. *Columbia Law Review, 101*(3), 458–568.

Title VII of the Civil Rights Act of 1964, 42 U.S.C.S. §§2000e–2000e-17 (Lexis 2006).

Trezza v. Hartford, Inc., No. 98 Civ. 2205, 1998 WL 912101 (S.D.N.Y. Dec. 30, 1998).

Valian, V. (1999a). The cognitive bases of gender bias. *Brooklyn Law Review, 65*(4), 1037–1061.

Valian, V. (1999b). *Why so slow? The advancement of women.* Cambridge, MA: The MIT Press.

Verizon paying $49 million in settlement of sex bias case: Discrimination against pregnant women claimed. (2006, June 6). *Seattle Post-Intelligencer.* Retrieved October 20, 2006, from http://seattlepi.nwsource.com/business/272846_verizonbias06.html

Waldfogel, J. (1997). The effect of children on women's wages. *American Sociological Review, 62*(2), 209–217.

Waldfogel, J. (1998). Understanding the "family gap" in pay for women with children. *The Journal of Economic Perspectives, 12*(1), 137–156.

Warren, E., & Tyagi, A. (2003). *The two-income trap.* New York: Basic Books.

Wax, A. L. (1999). Discrimination as accident. *Indiana Law Journal, 74*(4), 1129–1231.

Williams, J. (2000). *Unbending gender: Why family and work conflict and what to do about it.* New York: Oxford University Press.

Williams, J. (2003). The social psychology of stereotyping: Using social science to litigate gender discrimination cases and defang the "cluelessness" defense. *Employee Rights and Employment Policy Journal, 7*(2), 401–458.

Williams, J. (2004). *Hibbs* as a federalism case; *Hibbs* as a maternal wall case. *University of Cincinnati Law Review, 73*(2), 365–398.

Williams, J., & Calvert, C. T. (2001). *Balanced hours: Effective part-time policies for Washington law firms. Final report* (2nd ed.). Project for Attorney Retention, Program on Gender, Work & Family, American University, Washington College of Law. Retrieved October 30, 2006, from http://www.pardc.org/Publications/BalancedHours2nd.pdf

Williams, J., & Calvert, C. T. (2006). *WorkLife Law's guide to family responsibilities discrimination.* Center for WorkLife Law, University of California, Hastings College of the Law.

Williams, J. C., Manvell, J., & Bornstein, S. (2006). *Opt out or pushed out: How the press covers work–family conflict.* Center for WorkLife Law, University of California, Hastings College of the Law. Retrieved October 30, 2006, from http://www.uchastings.edu/site_files/WLL/OptOutPushedOut.pdf

Williams, J., & Segal, N. (2003). Beyond the maternal wall: Relief for family caregivers who are discriminated against on the job. *Harvard Women's Law Journal, 26*, 77–162.

15

Issues and Trends in Work–Family Integration

Bettina J. Casad

Research in the work–family domain has advanced in the past 30 years to reflect the complexity of issues that face families in the twenty-first century. This volume has addressed many of these issues, including effects of maternal employment on mothers and children, myths of maternal employment, diversity in families, implications for employment practices, and public policy. This chapter highlights the major themes and findings from the chapters in this volume, offers a critique of the current research, and suggests implications of these findings for policy and research.

Maternal Employment

Maternal employment is here to stay. Several researchers noted the historical norm of maternal employment (Tan, this volume) and the increasing trend of mothers in the paid workforce (Molina, this volume; Saxbe & Repetti, this volume; Tan, this volume). Dual-earner families constitute 78 percent of employees in the US (Bond, Thompson, Galinsky, & Prottas, 2003). Over half of mothers with children under the age of one work outside the home (Erel, Oberman, & Yirmiya, 2000). Less than 3 percent of American families have the traditional family type of a stay-at-home mother and a breadwinning father (Gilbert & Rader, 2001).

Despite the pervasiveness of maternal employment, a predominately negative portrayal of employed mothers and myths regarding maternal employment's harmful effects persist (Gottfried & Gottfried, this volume; LeMaster, Marcus-Newhall, Casad, & Silverman, 2004; Tan, this volume). The evidence that maternal employment is bad for children is weak and limited (Gottfried & Gottfried, this volume; Tan, this volume), and several benefits to maternal employment for mothers and children have been documented.

Benefits of Maternal Employment for Mothers

There are many positive aspects of work–family integration that are often ignored in the work–family conflict research domain (Gottfried & Gottfried, this volume; Grzywacz, Butler, & Almeida, this volume). The overwhelming focus on work–family *conflict* has dominated the literature, although there is a trend to examine positive aspects of work–family issues, focusing on *integration, interaction, enhancement, balance,* and *positive spillover* (Gottfried & Gottfried, this volume; Grzywacz et al., this volume; Halpern & Murphy, 2005). Several benefits of maternal employment include improved psychological well-being, higher self-esteem, stronger sense of personal identity, greater personal satisfaction, and financial decision-making power (Galinsky, 2005; Gottfried & Gottfried, this volume; LeMaster et al., 2004; Marcus-Newhall, Casad, LeMaster, Peraza, & Silverman, this volume; Tan, this volume). Maternal employment and more specifically, work–family balance can be a protective factor against daily mental health decrements, depression, anxiety, and physical ailments (Grzywacz et al., this volume; LeMaster et al., 2004; Tan, this volume). Indeed, families without work–family balance are more likely to experience negative mental and physical health outcomes (Grzywacz et al., this volume).

Benefits of Maternal Employment for Children and Families

Benefits of maternal employment for children include better academic performance, higher cognitive performance, infrequent behavioral problems, and higher quality maternal attention to children's needs (Tan, this volume). The Fullerton Longitudinal Study followed a national cohort of 130 children of single and dual-earner families, with the first assessment taking place at infancy and the final follow-up at age 24 (Gottfried & Gottfried, this volume). First, results found no support for the claim that maternal employment is detrimental to children's cognitive, emotional, academic, or social development (Gottfried & Gottfried, this volume). A major predictor of children's outcomes was mothers' attitudes toward their dual roles of parenting and employment. Specifically, mothers' positive attitudes toward balancing work and family are related to: (1) children's educational outcomes including higher academic achievement, more positive attitudes and interest in school, greater intrinsic motivation for school learning, fewer behavioral problems, greater independence and self-help skills, and greater educational stimulation; (2) family outcomes including greater family cohesion, less family conflict, and greater maternal involvement with children; and (3) children's adulthood outcomes such as having more egalitarian gender roles and greater satisfaction with their own employment (Gottfried & Gottfried, this volume).

A major benefit of maternal employment for children and families is the increased role of fathers in caretaking (Gottfried & Gottfried, this volume). Fathers in dual earner families are more involved with child care than their fathers were, although they are still less involved than mothers (Halpern, 2004; Gottfried & Gottfried, this volume). In one study, 30 percent of men surveyed reported that they take equal or greater responsibility for child care and household tasks in married dual-earner families (Halpern, 2004). Research documenting increased paternal involvement in childcare has shown positive effects on children, including improved social adjustment, higher IQ, higher academic achievement, and improved performance on several other affective and cognitive outcomes (Gottfried & Gottfried, this volume). The increased involvement of fathers in caretaking provides new role models and more egalitarian models of work–family balance for children of dual-earner couples.

Challenges of Maternal Employment for Mothers, Children, and Families

It is not maternal employment per se that poses challenges for families and children; rather it is work–family imbalance (Grzywacz et al., this volume). Work–family imbalance is associated with negative effects on mental and physical health (Grzywacz et al., this volume). Despite the fact that the majority of families in the US have two breadwinners, mothers still take on the majority of household chores (Gilbert, 1993; Hochshild, 1989; Pleck, 1992; Saxbe & Repetti, this volume). Through daily diary studies using the experience sampling method and intensive daily naturalistic observations, researchers have found that mothers were most likely to report negative affect, stress, and irritation while doing household chores in the weekday evenings after returning from work (Saxbe & Repetti, this volume). Mothers were most likely to spend their time in the kitchen preparing a meal. In contrast, fathers reported more positive affect in the evening, as they were most likely to be engaging in leisure time alone or with a child (Saxbe & Repetti, this volume). However, time spent with the entire family, such as sharing a meal, was associated with positive affect for mothers and fathers, and was linked to decreased stress hormones among women in happy marriages (Saxbe & Repetti, this volume). Thus, increasing shared time at home is one way that families can achieve more balance. One way for mothers to reduce their stress and negative affect, boost positive affect, and reduce stress hormones, is to get fathers and children to share in household chores, which was not a common trend in one naturalistic observational study of families' daily lives (Saxbe & Repetti, this volume). A balanced division of household labor is an underutilized protective factor for family imbalance, and a way that families can make shared time during weekday evenings more routine. Indeed, children who have regular routines of spending time with their families during the weeknights, particularly having a shared meal, have shown less anxiety and improved academic performance compared to children without such a family routine (Saxbe & Repetti, this volume).

Despite the increase of mothers in the workforce, the amount of time mothers spend with children is stable and up from 20 years ago, regardless of increases in work hours. But how? Mothers reallocate their priorities by decreasing personal time, decreasing housework, decreasing volunteer work, decreasing free time pursuits, and having fewer children (Gottfried, 2005). Thus, in order to have positive, enriching experiences in both the work and family domains, forgoing some personal time and free time pursuits may be a necessity. Indeed, the societal norm for good mothering tends to be unrealistic, termed by feminist scholars as "*intensive mothering.*" Women today are expected to be not just good mothers, but exceptional mothers (Arendell, 2000). In her book for the popular press, *Perfect Madness,* Judith Warner (2005) calls this the Mommy Mystique and suggests that the lives of today's mothers are characterized by anxiety, perfectionism, and exhaustion caused by the current cultural demands placed on mothers. Indeed, research has found that employed mothers report having less personal time and having to adhere to strict schedules to maintain work–family balance (Halpern & Murphy, 2005; Hochschild, 1989, 1997; Kossek & Ozeki, 1998; LeMaster, Casad, & Marcus-Newhall, 2007).

A major challenge to maternal employment, and therefore for dual-earner families, is finding high quality, flexible and affordable daycare. Women consistently point to daycare as a source of strain in their quest to balance work and family (Elman & Gilbert, 1984; LeMaster et al., 2004, 2007; Scarr, Phillips, & McCartney, 1989). If mothers are dissatisfied with their childcare arrangements, such as if they are low quality, not affordable, or have inflexible hours of operation, employment can be a stressor (Galinsky, 2005). Public perceptions and parents themselves portray daycare as a bad influence on children's development (Galinsky, 2005; Tan, this volume). As Galinksy (2005) notes, out-of-home childcare does not replace parental care, rather it is a support for employed parents. Positive experiences with childcare are related to improved work–family balance (Galinsky, 2005). There are several benefits for children with high quality daycare such as fewer behavioral problems, improved cognitive abilities, improved language skills, better school preparedness, and social and emotional development (Tan, this volume). However, it should be noted that a minority of children in daycare for extended periods of time have shown cognitive and behavioral problems (Tan, this volume).

Diversity Considerations in the Work–Family Interface

The work–family balance literature has been limited in scope, primarily including samples of predominately middle class, middle aged, European American, and heterosexual couples. Three chapters in this volume sought to help remedy this gap in the literature by examining work–family balance issues among families with lower socioeconomic status (SES) (Marcus-Newhall et al., this volume), ethnic minorities (Marcus-Newhall et al., this volume), older adults (Cleveland, this volume), and gay, lesbian, and bisexual couples (Badgett, this volume).

Low Socioeconomic Status and Ethnic Minority Populations

It has been widely documented that families with lower SES are afflicted with many more mental and physical health problems than families of higher SES (see Tan, this volume). Families with lower SES are more likely to have a dual-earner couple, and thus are an important population to include in research on work–family balance given the additional burdens they face struggling to meet their families' economic needs. It also has been documented that some racial and/or ethnic differences exist in the experience of work–family balance (Gottfried & Gottfried, this volume; LeMaster et al., 2004: Marcus-Newhall et al., this volume). Marcus-Newhall and colleagues (this volume) examined the role of SES, race, and other cultural factors in mothers' experience with balancing work and family responsibilities. Among the dual-earner couples in the sample, one third of the families had an annual household income of $34,000 or less, one third between $35,000 and $55,000, and the final third making more than $55,000. Additionally half the sample of employed mothers from dual-earner couples were Latina and half were Euro-American. Results indicated that lower SES Euro-American mothers with more traditional sex role attitudes reported more work stress than lower SES Latina mothers. This raises the important issue of the role of choice in employment (see Tan, this volume). If mothers do not prefer fulltime employment, but must do so for economic reasons, then work stress is more likely (Casad, Marcus-Newhall, & LeMaster, 2007). Further Marcus-Newhall and colleagues found that religiosity served as a buffer for life stress, particularly among lower SES Latina mothers. In sum, the inclusion of cultural factors that play a role in families' abilities to cope with the challenges of work–family balance are important to furthering our understanding of cultural differences and similarities among mothers of varying SES and racial groups.

Older Adults in the Workforce

Adults have longer life expectancies today than previous generations, which affects the dynamics of the workplace. Many adults are employed through their 60s and 70s and continue to enjoy the personal identity derived from employment. However, age stereotypes can affect older employees' self-perceptions and opportunities available to them at work (Cleveland, this volume). A common stereotype of older adults is that they are warm and likeable, but incompetent (Fiske, Cuddy, Glick, & Xu, 2002) and that they are forgetful, less creative, slow, and less physically able (Cleveland, this volume). These stereotypes can affect opportunities available to older adults in the workplace. For example, older adults may be less likely to get challenging job assignments and may be overlooked for training and development opportunities (Cleveland, this volume). Ironically, older adults are less likely to have voluntary absenteeism and turnover than younger adults, and further they report high levels of job satisfaction (Cleveland, this volume), which is a predictor of employee productivity (Klein, this volume).

In addition to potential discrimination in career development and advancement opportunities, older adults may face discrimination in using family-friendly work policies (Cleveland, this volume). Research suggests that older adults often shift their focus from work to family, and thus are interested in obtaining balance between work and family (Cleveland, this volume). However, employers and coworkers may perceive family-friendly work policies as a benefit for younger parents who are expecting a new child or who have young children at home, particularly mothers (Anderson, Morgan, & Wilson, 2002; Williams, this volume). Although older adults may have grown children, the grandparent role often becomes an important one and taking family leave to be with young grandchildren may be very important (Cleveland, this volume). Employers need to consider how the aging workforce impacts their employee development and family-friendly policies and take care not to discriminate on the basis of age.

Another important area in which age affects the workplace is in the increasing demands eldercare poses for today's working adults (Cleveland, this volume). A result of longer life expectancies is that many middle aged adults are providing care for their aging parents. Many of these middle aged adults also simultaneously may be caring for young children, termed the "sandwich generation" (Cleveland, this volume). Providing eldercare can lead to greater work–family conflict among care providers, as well as increased stress, lost work time, lost advancement opportunities, and mental and physical health ailments (Cleveland, this volume). As with childcare responsibilities, research suggests women have a disproportionate level of responsibility for eldercare (Cleveland, this volume). Since family-friendly work policies are either perceived to be or are actually designed for parents to care for young children, employees with eldercare responsibilities may be at a disadvantage. Employers need to consider the shifting demographic of the American workforce and the greater demands placed on work–family balance by crafting family-friendly work policies that include flexibility and leave for eldercare.

Gay and Lesbian Workers

The majority of research in the work–family domain has focused on heterosexual married couples and how they balance their work and family responsibilities. An often overlooked population of workers, specifically gay men, lesbians, and bisexual people, also desire work–family balance (Badgett, this volume). Interestingly, even though gay and lesbian couples are more likely to have dual-earner families than heterosexuals (Badgett, this volume), they have been largely ignored in the work–family interaction discussion. Yet gay and lesbian employees and their families face the same struggles, if not worse, with work–life balance as their heterosexual counterparts. Contrary to stereotypes that gay men and lesbians do not have families, as traditionally conceptualized as the nuclear family (Saxbe & Repetti, this volume), a fifth of gay male couples and a third of lesbian couples have children (U.S. Bureau of the Census, 2003). Further, an even greater number of single gay men and lesbians are raising children (Badgett, this volume).

One may convincingly argue that gay and lesbian employees and their families face *greater* difficulty with balancing work and family demands than heterosexual married couples because they often are denied the family-friendly work policies and benefits provided to heterosexual married couples (Badgett, this volume). Gay and lesbian workers face the additional burden of employment discrimination in the form of denied promotion and training opportunities due to their sexual orientation, as only a minority of states in the US have formal policies against this form of discrimination (Badgett, this volume). In order to even attempt to use the family-friendly work policies available to heterosexual married employees, gay and lesbian employees have to be "out" with their sexual orientation, which puts them at risk for discrimination and even being fired (Badgett, this volume).

Businesses should make changes to include gay and lesbian employees in their antidiscrimination and family-friendly policies, as it affects the bottom line (Badgett, this volume). The most productive employees are those who are satisfied with their jobs and have a connection with their employer (Klein, this volume). Employees who are forced to keep their sexual orientation and family situation hidden face additional risk for mental and physical health problems (Badgett, this volume). Further, having antidiscrimination policies that extend family benefits to gay and lesbian workers will make companies more desirable to a greater market of highly qualified employees (Badgett, this volume; Burud & Tumolo, 2004).

Implications for Businesses

An overwhelming amount of research on work–family balance points to the need for employers to develop and implement policies that will assist employees with achieving enriching experiences in both their work and family lives. However, a widely held myth and obstacle that will likely prevent organizations from responding to this need is that businesses cannot afford family-friendly policies. However, Donna Klein, President of Corporate Voices for Working Families states that businesses cannot afford *not to* provide family-friendly policies. "Flexibility is not just a program that benefits the individual; it is a proven management strategy and critical tool in the fight for a competitive advantage in the global marketplace" (Corporate Voices for Working Families (CVWF), 2005).

Research conducted by CVWF defined workplace flexibility as an agreement between management and the employee on *when* and *where* work gets done (Klein, this volume). The model of a Monday through Friday, 9 to 5 work schedule with 100 percent "face-time" in the office is an outdated model (Klein, this volume). Flexible work schedules include combinations

of one or more of the following formal or informal strategies: job sharing, telecommuting, condensed work week, flexible start and stop times,
flexplace, or where the work gets done, mid-afternoon hours, hours around
school schedules, reduced hours in an advancement track, reduced hours
in a non-advancing track, and occasional early release/time off as needed
(CVWF, 2005). Results from a multi-method independent study of 28 organizations indicated workplace flexibility positively affected employee performance *and* improved the organization's financial performance (CVWF,
2005; Klein, this volume). The positive effects of flexibility on employee
performance included increased employee commitment, increased employee
satisfaction, reduced employee stress, increased job engagement, increased
retention rates, decreased employee turnover, and decreased burnout rates
(CVWF, 2005). These benefits from flextime were found for both salaried
and hourly employees and across a wide range of industries (CVWF,
2005). The positive effects of flexibility on the organizations' performance
included improved financial performance, increased productivity, decreased
cycle time, increased customer retention, decreased response time, millions
of dollars saved in prevented turnover, improved innovation and quality,
and increased share holder value/stock prices.

Having flexible work schedules is not just an employee benefit, reward,
or accommodation for employed parents or top employees, it is a business
strategy to attract and retain superior employees and increase market
competitiveness (Klein, this volume). In fact, job flexibility is consistently
among the top three reasons why new employees take a job offer, as well
as a top reason an employee will leave a job (Klein, this volume). Thus the
trend in business is the recognition that family-friendly policies are good
for the bottom line and the development of creative flexible work arrangements. Businesses that do not adapt to this new trend will be left behind
in the marketplace and will have difficulty recruiting the nation's top talent (Burud & Tumolo, 2004; CVWF, 2005; Klein, this volume).

Law

Employees who are not employed by an organization with family-friendly
policies can take comfort in knowing that discrimination against employees
with family obligations is a new battleground in the courts. Employer
discrimination against parents is a violation of Title VII of the Civil Rights
Act and Equal Protection Clause (Williams, this volume). More employees
are suing their employers because they lost their jobs, were passed over for
promotion, or were treated unfairly based on their responsibilities to care

for children or others (Williams, this volume). A significant number of the cases have been successful, resulting in large damage awards or settlements.

According to research conducted by Williams (this volume), cases against employers regarding family responsibilities discrimination (FRD) has risen from eight in the 1970s to 358 between 2000 and 2005. In the 1990s, there were 97 cases, versus 481 in 2000s . . . a 400 percent increase. This is compared to general employment discrimination cases that decreased by 23 percent between 2000 and 2005. Employees have a case for FRD when employers or supervisors assume that an employee will not be able to do certain jobs because of care giving responsibilities or make it difficult for employees to combine their work and family obligations (Williams, this volume).

Williams (this volume) describes several cases in which discrimination against parents is blatant, mirroring 1950s style sexism. However, discrimination resulting from hostile, benevolent, prescriptive stereotypes, and deep-rooted cognitive biases is often more subtle. One major source of discrimination against caretakers is the unrealistic standard against which employees are judged (Williams, this volume). The "ideal worker" norm suggests that employees should be available to their employer 24/7, just as the "ideal mother" norm suggests mothers should be available to their children 24/7 (Williams, this volume). There is an obvious mismatch between these idealized and unrealistic norms. However, employer's expectations often reflect the ideal worker norm, and employees with family care giving responsibilities are most likely to violate the norm.

Just as there is a business case for employers to pay attention to and address the needs of families through non-discriminatory family-friendly policies, so too is there a law case to which employers should pay attention. Taking stock of recent legislation on FRD and examining one's own polices is another strategy employers can take to protect their bottom line and keep their employees satisfied and productive. The trend in this domain is a shift in perceiving family-friendly work policies not as a "benefit," but rather an entitlement and employers need to get on board or face the legislative consequences.

Implications for Public Policy

The Family Medical Leave Act (FMLA) was established in 1992 to provide employees 12 weeks of unpaid leave to care for a child or family member. The policy protects employees from being fired, but does not provide any compensation (Halpern, Tan, & Carsten, this volume). The first state to provide paid family leave is California. California instituted the California Paid Family Leave Insurance Program (CPFL) in July 2004, which provides six weeks of partially paid leave for an employee to care for a new child or ill family member (Halpern et al., this volume). Since CPFL is relatively new, the impact on California caregivers is unknown.

Halpern and colleagues (this volume) conducted a survey of Los Angeles County residents to determine how their care giving responsibilities relate to their well-being and whether they have knowledge of CPFL. Results showed that the majority of caregivers reported financial strain from taking time off of work, and half reported having no paid time off (Halpern et al., this volume). Caregivers reported decreased well-being from the demands of their employment and caretaking roles, especially those who faced the threat of losing their jobs (Halpern et al., this volume). Although many respondents reported positive attitudes toward CPFL, more than half said they could not afford to take six weeks off for only 55 percent of their salary (Halpern et al., this volume). Thus, CPFL could be beneficial to caregivers who suffer financial, mental, and physical hardships, but the compensation is not sufficient to meet their needs. Additional research should be conducted to evaluate the effectiveness of the CPFL, as only 1 percent of the respondents in Halpern and colleagues' (this volume) study were able to use CPFL. A revision of this policy should be made to meet better the needs of caregivers. There is a risk that the under use of CPFL will signal to policy makers that the policy is not needed, when in actuality it is very much needed, but is an ineffective policy that needs to be revised.

Another issue with public policies designed to help employees balance their work and family demands is the consequences of using such policies. For example, research shows that fathers who take advantage of paternity leave offered by their employers face negative performance ratings, stigma from their coworkers, and fewer rewards (Dickson, 2003). Drago and colleagues have examined this issue among faculty in institutions of higher education (Drago, Colbeck, Hollenshead, & Sullivan, this volume). Their research shows that faculty will minimize or hide their family responsibilities to avoid the possible stigma and negative effects on their career success (Drago et al., this volume).

To examine the relationship between this "bias avoidance" and the availability of work–family polices, Drago and colleagues (this volume) surveyed a stratified random sample of faculty and administrators at several U.S. colleges and universities. Results indicated that women faculty were more likely to engage in bias avoidance behaviors, such as lying about the reason for being late when it was due to childcare issues, indicating the presence of gender inequalities in academe. Further, there was some evidence for a relationship between the number of family-friendly policies and bias avoidance, such that more policies predicted less avoidance behaviors. The evidence was stronger for a relationship between a greater number of policies and a reduction of bias avoidance around *specific* behaviors relevant to the policy. For example, having a policy that offers a reduced teaching load would be related to the specific bias avoidance behavior of not asking for a reduced teaching load to meet family responsibilities. These findings suggest that increasing the number and scope of policies will likely reduce bias avoidance behaviors, but that alone is not sufficient. This research has implications for how effective policies will be if employees minimize or hide their care giving responsibilities rather than use existing policies.

Implications for Communities

An unexamined aspect in the work–family balance research domain is the role of community in improving families' health and well-being. Barnett and Gareis (this volume) argue that corporations cannot meet the needs of families alone and the community should be examined as another resource to assist with work–family balance. For example, there is a disparity in most communities between adults' work schedules and the schedules of most local commerce. School schedules still reflect the agricultural workday, releasing children at two or three in the afternoon, and full-day kindergarten classes are rare (Barnett & Gareis, this volume). Many public services, such as local businesses, home repairs and deliveries, and health and medical services operate on a Monday through Friday 9 to 5 schedule, putting a strain on working adults' access to community resources (Barnett & Gareis, this volume).

To examine the role of the community in achieving work–family integration, Barnett and Gareis (this volume) conducted a survey with working families on their perceptions of community resource fit. The researchers divided community resources into two categories, work and school, to assess the compatibility of work and school schedules. Results indicated that among married mothers, greater work resource fit was related to decreased distress, decreased work-to-family and family-to-work conflict, and higher job-role quality. Further, school resource fit was related to decreased job disruptions and higher marital-role quality. For married fathers, high work and school resource fit was related to higher job-role quality.

This preliminary research suggests a new area ripe for further examination. The role of community in helping working families balance their competing demands seems substantial. Researchers should continue to explore the link between community and work–life balance. With enough research evidence, a case can be made to institute public policies and community changes to bring community resources more in line with the lifestyles of today's dual-earner families.

Research Strengths in this Volume

This volume of research has its strengths in the diversity of topics and methodologies used to examine issues in the work–family domain. A variety of methodological approaches, including longitudinal (Gottfried & Gottfried, this volume), randomized national samples (Drago et al., this volume), case analyses (Klein, this volume; Williams, this volume), experience sampling (Grzywacz et al., this volume), and ethnographic observations (Saxbe & Repetti, this volume), provide rich data that advance our knowledge of current issues and trends in the work–family interface. Many of the researchers noted deficits in the literature including a dearth of research on the physical and mental health effects of work–family imbalance, older adults, and diverse populations, and this volume attempts to address these gaps in the literature.

Weaknesses and Areas for Improvement

Although this volume presents research that takes a multi-method approach, the research presented herein is still afflicted by some of the common gaps in the literature. For example, where are the fathers? The majority of the research presented in this volume, with the exception of Gottfried and Gottfried and Saxbe and Repetti, focused largely on mothers and their role in the work–family interface. Since the most common family type is the dual-earner couple, an inclusion of fathers and their role in work–family balance is critical.

Another problem with some of the present research, reflecting a problem in the existing work–family literature, is the over-reliance on data from middle to upper-middle class heterosexual Caucasians. The role of SES and cultural factors is critical (Badgett, this volume; Cleveland, this volume; Gottfried & Gottfried, this volume; Marcus-Newhall et al., this volume;

90   *Casad*

Tan, this volume) and a diversification of the populations in this research domain is needed.

A related issue to the lack of diverse samples is the question of how applicable the workplace flexibility, work-place policy initiatives, and FRD discussed by Klein, Molina, and Williams are to lower wage earners. Jobs with a flexible work schedule in family-friendly organizations are likely to require advanced education and higher skills, and these types of occupations are the ones with the most employee control (Tan, this volume). Low income families are the least likely to benefit from family-leave policies, such as CPFL and FMLA, because they cannot afford to take time off with reduced or no pay. Also, low income families are least likely to have the resources to hire a lawyer to sue their employer for FRD. Although Klein (this volume) noted that low wage earners, such as housekeepers employed by large hotel chains are likely to have informal work–family policies, informal policies are not sufficient for these low wage earners to achieve work–family balance. Too much of the power and decision-making is left to the employer. Family-friendly work policies need to be formalized and available to all wage earners regardless of the prestige of their organization or occupation. This is where federal and state mandated family leave policies are most needed to supplement the policies available to low wage earners employed by smaller organizations.

Implications for Future Research

Several implications for future research have been noted throughout this chapter. However, there are broader issues raised by the authors in this volume that suggest future research agendas should reframe their approach to work–family integration issues. Research should not focus on maternal employment per se, but the focus should be on the antecedents and consequences of work–family balance and imbalance among dual-earner couples. A more context-oriented approach should examine the role of the home, family, and community environment in achieving work–family balance (Gottfried & Gottfried, this volume; Saxbe & Repetti, this volume), and diverse methodologies should be explored to capture the richness of families' daily lives (e.g., Saxbe & Repetti, this volume). Existing research has largely focused on work–family conflict, and not addressed the role of work–family enrichment (Grzywacz et al., this volume). Families are adaptive and resilient, and a positive approach will more likely capture this than the traditional negative stress model approach (Gottfried, 2005).

Research should broaden its scope from individual factors to macro-level influences, including the community, public policy, workplace issues, and the law. Finally, this is not a women's issue, rather this is a family and public policy issue and a multifaceted approach incorporating psychology, economics, health, public policy, organizational behavior and development, and law will reap the best research outcomes.

References

Anderson, D. M., Morgan, B. L., & Wilson, J. B. (2002). Perceptions of family-friendly policies: University versus corporate employees. *Journal of Family and Economic Issues, 23,* 73–92.

Arendell, T. (2000). Conceiving and investigating motherhood: The decade's scholarship. *Journal of Marriage and the Family, 62,* 1192–1207.

Bond, J. T., Thompson, C., Galinsky, E., & Prottas, D. (2003). *Highlights of the 2002 national study of the changing workforce* (No. 3). New York: Families and Work Institute.

Burud, S., & Tumolo, M. (2004). *Leveraging the new human capital: Adaptive strategies results achieved, and stories of transformation.* Mountain View, CA: Davies-Black Publishing.

Casad, B. J., Marcus-Newhall, A., & LeMaster, J. (2007). *Psychological well-being of younger mothers: The role of age, employment status, choice, and ethnicity.* Manuscript submitted for publication.

Corporate Voices for Working Families (2005, November). Business impacts of flexibility: An imperative for expansion. Retrieved April 25, 2007 from the Corporate Voices for Working Families website: http://www.corporatevoices.org/issues/publications.shtml

Dickson, C. E. (2003). *The impact of family supportive policies and practices on perceived family discrimination.* Unpublished dissertation, California School of Organizational Studies, Alliant International University.

Elman, M., & Gilbert, L. (1984). Coping strategies for role conflict in married professional women with children. *Family Relations, 33,* 317–327.

Erel, O., Oberman, Y., & Yirmiya, N. (2000). Maternal versus nonmaternal care and seven domains of children's development. *Psychological Bulletin, 126,* 727–747.

Fiske, S. T., Cuddy, A. J. C., Glick, P., & Xu, J. (2002). A model of (often mixed) stereotype content: Competence and warmth respectively follow from perceived status and competition. *Journal of Personality and Social Psychology, 82,* 878–902.

Galinsky, E. (2005). Children's perspectives of employed mothers and fathers: Closing the gap between public debates and research findings. In D. F. Halpern &

S. E. Murphy (Eds.), *Changing the metaphor: Work-family balance to work-family integration* (pp. 219–236). Mahwah, NJ: Erlbaum.

Gilbert, L. A. (1993). *Two careers/one family.* Newbury Park, CA: Sage.

Gilbert, L. A., & Rader, J. (2001). Current perspectives on women's adult roles: Work, family, and life. In R. K. Unger (Ed.), *Handbook of the psychology of women and gender* (pp. 156–182). New York: Wiley.

Gottfried, A. E. (2005). Maternal and dual-earner employment and children's development: redefining the research agenda. In D. F. Halpern & S. E. Murphy (Eds.), *Changing the metaphor: Work-family balance to work-family integration* (pp. 197–217). Mahwah, NJ: Erlbaum.

Halpern, D. F. (2004). Public policy, work, and families: The report of the APA presidential initiative on work and families. Washington, DC: American Psychological Association.

Halpern, D. F., & Murphy, S. E. (2005). From balance to interaction: Why the metaphor is important. In D. F. Halpern & S. E. Murphy (Eds.), *Changing the metaphor: Work-family balance to work-family integration* (pp. 3–9). Mahwah, NJ: Erlbaum.

Hochshild, A. R. (1989). *The second shift: Working parents and the revolution at home.* New York: Basic Books.

Hochshild, A. R. (1997). *The time bind: When work becomes home and home becomes work.* New York: Metropolitan Books.

Kossek, E. E., & Ozeki, C. (1998). Work-family conflict, policies, and the job-life satisfaction relationship: A review and directions for organizational behavior-human resources. *Journal of Applied Psychology, 83,* 139–149.

LeMaster, J., Casad, B. J., & Marcus-Newhall, A. (2007). *In their own words: Experiences and attitudes of employed and stay-at-home young mothers.* Manuscript submitted for publication.

LeMaster, J., Marcus-Newhall, A., Casad, B. J., & Silverman, N. (2004). Life experiences of working and stay-at-home mothers. In J. L. Chin (Ed.), *The psychology of prejudice and discrimination: Gender and sexual orientation* (Vol. 3, pp. 61–91). Westport, CT: Greenwood Press.

Pleck, J. (1992). Work-family policies in the United States. In H. Kahne & J. Giele (Eds.), *Women's lives and women's work: Parallels and contrasts in modernizing and industrial countries.* Boulder, CO: Westview.

Scarr, S., Phillips, D., & McCartney, K. (1989). Working mothers and their families. *American Psychologist, 44,* 1402–1409.

U.S. Bureau of the Census (2003, February). *Married-couple and unmarried-partner households: 2000.* Retrieved September 29, 2006, from http://www.census.gov/prod/2003pubs/censr-5.pdf

Warner, J. (2005). *Perfect madness: Motherhood in an age of anxiety.* New York: Riverhead Books.

Index

DATE DUE

OhioLINK NOV 21 REC'D OhioLINK			
MAY 0 8 REC'D MAY 1 5 2010			
MAY 1 7 2010 MAY 1 5 REC'D			
GAYLORD			PRINTED IN U.S.A.

BOWLING GREEN STATE UNIVERSITY LIBRARY
DISCARDED

HD 4904.25 .C449 2008

The changing realities of
work and family